Posttraumatic Growth:
Positive Changes
in the Aftermath of Crisis

The LEA Series in
Personality and Clinical Psychology
Irving B. Weiner, Editor

Posttraumatic Growth: Positive Changes in the Aftermath of Crisis

Edited by

Richard G. Tedeschi
University of North Carolina at Charlotte
Crystal L. Park
Miami University
Lawrence G. Calhoun
University of North Carolina at Charlotte

LAWRENCE ERLBAUM ASSOCIATES, PUBLISHERS
1998   Mahwah, New Jersey   London

Lawrence Erlbaum Associates, Inc., Publishers
10 Industrial Avenue
Mahwah, New Jersey 07430

Cover design by Kathryn Houghtaling Lacey

Library of Congress Cataloging-in-Publication Data

Tedeschi, Richard G.
    Posttraumatic growth : positive changes in the aftermath
of crisis / Richard G. Tedeschi, Crystal L. Park, Lawrence
G. Calhoun.
        p. cm.
    Includes bibliographical references and index.
    ISBN 0-8058-2319-0 (alk. paper)
    1. Suffering. 2. Life change events—Psychological aspects. 3.
Adjustment (Psychology) 4. Self-actualization (Psychology) I.
Park, Crystal L. II. Calhoun, Lawrence G. III. Title.
    BF789.S8T425   1997
    155.9'3—dc21   97-26304
                                                              CIP

Books published by Lawrence Erlbaum Associates are printed on
acid-free paper, and their bindings are chosen for strength and
durability.

Printed in the United States of America
10 9 8 7 6 5 4 3 2 1

Contents

Preface

We have been working to develop information about and interest in the phenomenon of posttraumatic growth (PTG) for several years—in the case of Rich Tedeschi and Lawrence Calhoun, since the early 1980s, and in the case of Crystal Park, since the early 1990s, when she studied religion, coping, and stress-related growth as a graduate student with Lawrence Cohen at the University of Delaware. We have found PTG compelling for various reasons. In our clinical experiences and interviews with research participants, reports of the transformative power of trauma have had a naturally inspiring quality. The paucity of research, together with the ancient themes reflected in the stories of life-changing responses, have suggested that we are looking at a fundamental human experience from a fresh perspective. That these reports are seldom discussed in the research or clinical literature seems to have left traumatologists to conclude that only the most negative outcomes are worthy of our attention. If it is noticed at all, the experience of growth in the aftermath of crisis has been viewed primarily as defensive or illusory. Closer examination of PTG indicates that more than that is going on in many persons who describe this experience. It has been exciting for us to document the phenomenon, devise ways to measure it, and develop theory to explain it. In doing so, we hope we are laying the groundwork for ways to encourage positive change among trauma survivors.

Our goal has been to stimulate both researchers studying trauma, stress, and coping, and clinicians involved in crisis intervention to consider PTG as well as posttraumatic psychological disorders as worthy of attention. We have gathered together a small group of people who have been working on PTG and closely related phenomena, and have asked them to focus on issues of definition and measurement and on the role of individual, situational, and social characteristics in its facilitation. We have also given the contributors an opportunity to suggest theoretical foundations for research and to answer some of the fundamental questions about PTG that remain unexplored. We hope the reader will forgive occasional redundancy that may result because we have asked the contributors to approach the evidence for PTG from various perspectives.

We expect that students of various traumas, including bereavement, physical illness and disability, crime, natural disasters, combat, and social upheaval will find useful descriptions of many aspects of the experiences of people they study in the book. We also expect that those interested in the personal transformations of addicts, religious conversions, and other life-changing experiences will find much of interest. Our ultimate hope is to illuminate the wisdom-producing, transformative experiences of people in very difficult circumstances. To the extent we are able to do so, we may help integrate various insights and findings concerning PTG and provide an impetus to understanding the potential for human development and the processes by which important life changes occur.

We are indebted to our contributors who took on their tasks with enthusiasm, and who provide fascinating examples of PTG, offer theoretical perspectives, and suggest research questions and strategies. We also acknowledge the clients, research participants, and other trauma survivors who have described their experiences so that we might have some insight into how they managed their transformation. We are grateful as well to have worked with Susan Milmoe, our editor at LEA, and Irving Weiner, the editor for the Personality and Clinical Psychology Series of which this book is a part. We are glad that they saw the promise of this project, and have been so supportive, pleasant, and professional through the entire process.

—*Richard G. Tedeschi*
—*Crystal L. Park*
—*Lawrence G. Calhoun*

1

Posttraumatic Growth: Conceptual Issues

Richard G. Tedeschi
University of North Carolina at Charlotte
Crystal L. Park
Miami University
Lawrence G. Calhoun
University of North Carolina at Charlotte

Given the universality of suffering and devastation for individuals and groups of people, how can we account for phenomena such as individual renewal and the rebirth of nations? Historically, in psychology and psychiatry, we have focused almost exclusively on the course of disease and on the maladaptive behavior observed in those who have experienced traumatic events such as losses, abusive childhoods, and other frightening experiences. Most depressive and anxiety disorders, and many personality disorders have been attributed in great part to experiences of fear, discouragement, and damage in the face of adversity.

An influential but relatively small amount of literature that describes how these negative outcomes might be prevented, and how some persons cope successfully with negative events, has existed outside this mainstream disease-oriented framework (e.g., Basic Behavioral Science Task Force of the National Advisory Mental Health Council, 1996). Although there is still much to be learned about recoveries from trauma, we seek to explore the experiences of people who not only bounce back from trauma, but use it as a springboard to further individual development or growth, and the development of more humane social behaviors and social organization.

Posttraumatic growth (PTG) is both a process and an outcome. We see it as developing out of a cognitive process that is initiated to cope with traumatic events that extract an extreme cognitive and emotional toll. These events that initiate PTG have the quality of "seismic events" (Calhoun, 1996) on a psychological level. Consider that earthquakes produce a significant threat to existing structures, and leave little but the poorly functioning rubble of a community in their wake. The remains of old structures must be removed so that new, stronger structures can be built. But a period of confusion and mourning precedes this rebuilding, and there may be worry that it is no use, the task is too great, and aftershocks or future disasters will wipe out all constructive efforts. But eventually, weaknesses of the previous ways of constructing the community are discerned, and changes proposed. New emergency plans may be established based on the experience of surviving an earthquake. And, in the wake of the disaster, the community may reflect later on not only what has been lost, but also the care that members of the community showed, the superior nature of what has been rebuilt, and what has been learned.

Psychologically, similar processes are taking place in many individuals coping with traumas. These traumas call into question the basic assumptions about one's future and how to move toward that future, and therefore produce massive anxiety and psychic pain that is difficult to manage. Inherent in these traumatic experiences are losses such as the loss of loved ones, of cherished roles or capabilities, or of fundamental, accepted ways of understanding life. In the face of these losses and the confusion they cause, some people rebuild a way of life that they experience as superior to their old one in important ways. For them, the devastation of loss provides an opportunity to build a new, superior life structure almost from scratch. They establish new psychological constructs that incorporate the possibility of such traumas, and better ways to cope with them. They appreciate their newly found strength and the strength of their neighbors and their community. And because of their efforts, individuals may value both what they now have, and the process of creating it although the process involved loss and distress. Groups and societies may go through a similar transformation, producing new norms for behavior and better ways to care for individuals within the group.

There has been no single term for the phenomenon of interest here that has been used consistently in the literature. So PTG has been variously referred to as "positive psychological changes" (Yalom & Lieberman, 1991), "perceived benefits" or "construing benefits" (Calhoun & Tedeschi, 1991; McMillen, Zuravin & Rideout, 1995; Tennen, Affleck, Urrows, Higgins, & Mendola, 1992), "stress-related growth" (Park, Cohen & Murch, 1996), and "thriving" (O'Leary & Ickovics, 1995). Taylor has described similar outcomes in people experiencing trauma as "positive illusions" (Taylor & Brown, 1988). Janoff-Bulman (1992) does not provide any specific term for the changes of interest here, but provides a useful theory to explain how the changes occur through the shattering and rebuilding of assumptive worlds. There has been some attention paid to the coping mechanism variously called "positive reinterpretation" (Scheier, Weintraub, & Carver, 1986) and "drawing strength from adversity" (McCrae, 1984) as well.

We are suggesting that the term *posttraumatic growth* is the best descriptor for this phenomenon because this term makes clear that persons experiencing this phenomenon have developed beyond their previous level of adaptation, psychological functioning, or life awareness, that is, they have grown. Second, we are interested in how this growth happens in the aftermath of events that are undesirable in the extreme. "Thriving" could apply to healthy living in any circumstance, and "stress-related growth" may not make clear that the events that are of interest are highly stressful. "Perceived benefits" or "positive illusions" imply that the benefits may not be real or valid. We also want to emphasize that PTG seems to have more impact on people's lives, and involves such fundamental changes or insights about living that it does not appear to be merely another coping mechanism. Therefore, we are treating PTG as a significant beneficial change in cognitive and emotional life that may have behavioral implications as well. The significance of these changes can be so great, that this growth may be truly transformative (Tedeschi & Calhoun, 1995). Furthermore, it may be useful to see posttraumatic growth as the antithesis of posttraumatic stress disorder, emphasizing that growth outcomes are reported even in the aftermath of the most traumatic circumstances, and even though distress coexists with this growth.

This chapter provides a chronological sketch of the development of the concept of PTG and some of the most important research efforts in this area. Related concepts are compared and contrasted with PTG and the concept of PTG is clarified.

BEGINNINGS

The phenomenon we term posttraumatic growth has been recognized for centuries. Religion and literature have described and explained the role of human suffering in bringing people closer to wisdom, truth, and God. The literature of tragedy presents life lessons on morality and human frailty (Krook, 1969; Raphael, 1960). Cultural traditions have incorporated the idea of possibilities for positive change in the aftermath of trauma in the central stories of life. In Egyptian mythology, the phoenix flew over the Arabian Desert for years, fell to the ground, was consumed by flames, and rose again from its own ashes. After the Flood, there emerged a rainbow and a new hope for humanity. After Christ's crucifixion, there was forgiveness of sin for all people who believed that he was the Son of God. The understanding of suffering plays a central role in eastern traditions such as Buddhism and Hinduism as well. Tedeschi and Calhoun (1995) explored the relationship between perspectives on suffering in literary and religious traditions and PTG. We find important precursors to the concept of PTG in other literature that deals with existential issues as well.

Existential Philosophy and Psychology

Existential psychologists have long recognized opportunities for growth in trauma and suffering, and have described trauma as a time when meaning may be created and courage may be found. These views are extensions of the ideas of Kierkegaard (1983) and Nietzsche (1955) who described the usefulness of suffering for personal development. The "courage to be" (Tillich, 1952) or "being mode" (Fromm, 1976) is the result of the stripping away of the inauthentic in the crucible of trauma, in coming face-to-face with nonbeing (May, 1960). One of the ways people are compelled to create more meaningful lives is by the recognition that they sell themselves short, play it safe, and suffer ontological guilt as a result (May, 1983). Traumatic events can reveal the uselessness of attempting to create security, and the possibility that life might be lived to its fullest.

Some descriptive reports of PTG can be found in the literature of existential and humanistic psychology. Jaffe (1985) and Kessler (1987) highlighted many of the issues that are found throughout this book in their descriptions of the bereaved and other trauma survivors, discussing transformations of identity, spirituality, interpersonal relating, and meaning structures. An early attempt to empirically document the effects of trauma on existential issues was made by Ebersole (1970). He asked 36 students to describe the effects of "peak" and "nadir" experiences on their lives, and reported that about one third of them stated that the nadir experiences had long term benefits for them.

People sometimes need some assistance in finding courage in the face of suffering, to allow for the development of meaningful living and an authentic self. Frankl (1961) developed logotherapy on the proposition that people find meaning in life through creativity, love, and suffering, and suggested how this process of finding meaning could be encouraged.

Crisis Intervention and Prevention

Gerald Caplan (1961, 1964) developed a preventive, or early response crisis intervention approach to community mental health that was at variance with the long-term explorative approaches to therapy that had reigned to that time. Caplan saw crises as crucial periods that required definitive intervention, in order to prevent further deterioration. Caplan recognized that crises are essentially situational, and that they usher in a period of psychological disequilibrium. He proposed that most people manage these crisis situations in 4 to 6 weeks, during which changes are wrought that may remain stable within their lives for years afterwards. Such changes may be adaptive or maladaptive, but there is an opportunity for significant learning and psychological growth during this period.

Within the literature that focused on crisis intervention and prevention, there is also some seminal work by Finkel (1974, 1975; Finkel & Jacobsen, 1977) on the concept of "strens" or life events that are "health-promoting" or "growth-potentiating" experiences. Finkel (1974) found that while these strens were positive events in many instances, some research participants mentioned that events that were traumatic were also considered to be strens. It is interesting to note that one participant anticipated the concept of posttraumatic growth by stating "In fact, I cannot see how a stren experience if it is to have an influence on your life, can be devoid of trauma (Finkel, 1974). Events that had elements of both stren and trauma comprised 36% of those reported in Finkel's initial study, prompting him to look into the process by which traumas were "converted" into strens. Finkel (1975) found that about two thirds of his college student participants reported such conversions, that they happened more frequently as they grew up, and that pure, unconverted trauma experiences declined with age. These conversions tended to happen between 2 weeks and 4 months after the event, and were essentially cognitive in nature. In a later study with adults (Finkel & Jacobsen, 1977), two thirds of the sample reported the trauma–stren conversion, although only 15% of total experiences reported fell into this category. Finkel and Jacobsen also distinguished "converters," persons reporting at least one trauma–stren conversion experience from non-converters. For converters, conversion experiences tended to become more frequent in their 20s, and by the mid-30s, they became more frequent than either unconverted traumas or pure strens. In contrast, non-converters continued to report high percentages of unconverted trauma up to age 45, the limit for that study. After beginning his work by attempting to distinguish events that were traumatic from those that were strengthening, Finkel seemed to arrive at the conclusion that certain persons had the ability to convert trauma into growth through some cognitive restructuring mechanism. In a followup to Finkel's work several years later, Ebersole and Flores (1989) asked college students the degree to which their most painful life experiences affected them positively or negatively and if the events changed the meaning of their lives. Ebersole and Flores found that 42% of their students described the impact of their most negative events as positive, and 87% of this group cited a change in meaning of their lives.

THE EVOLUTION OF THE CONCEPT OF POSTTRAUMATIC GROWTH

Until the 1980s, researchers almost never set out specifically to investigate PTG or to understand the processes involved in its emergence. Most of the studies that acknowledged PTG were focused on coping with particular traumatic events, and PTG was mentioned as a coping strategy or was described parenthetically among many characteristics of primarily unfortunate outcomes. Of the few exceptions that spoke directly to the issue of experiencing growth in the aftermath of life crises were Hamera and Shontz (1978), in a study of the effects of life threatening illness, and Taylor (1977), in a discussion of the effects of natural disasters.

Beginning in the mid-1980s, there was an increasing tendency among researchers to give top billing to the findings of PTG in populations as diverse as the bereaved (Calhoun & Tedeschi, 1989–1990; Edmonds & Hooker, 1992; Hogan, Morse, & Tason, 1996; Lehman et al., 1993; Miles & Crandall, 1983; Nerken, 1993; Schwab, 1990), persons suffering from chronic illnesses and disabilities (Tedeschi & Calhoun, 1988; Tennen, Affleck, Urrows, Higgins, & Mendola, 1992), HIV infection (Schwartzberg, 1993), cancer (Collins, Taylor, & Skokan, 1990; Curbow, Somerfield, Baker, Wingard, & Legro, 1993), and heart attacks (Laerum, Johnsen, Smith & Larsen, 1987), parents coping with the medical problems of their children (Abbott & Meredith, 1986; Affleck, Tennen, & Gershman, 1985), survivors of transportation accidents (Joseph, Williams, & Yule, 1993) and house fires (Thompson, 1985), and rape and sexual abuse survivors (Burt & Katz, 1987; Draucker, 1992; Silver, Boon & Stones, 1983; McMillan, Zuravin, & Rideout, 1995; Veronen & Kilpatrick, 1983). Focused attempts to measure PTG and explore the relationship of this construct to other variables have developed in the 1990s (Frazier, Byrne, & Klein, 1995; Joseph, Williams, & Yule, 1993; Park, Cohen & Murch, 1996; Tedeschi & Calhoun, 1996;

Tedeschi, Calhoun, & Page, 1992). Theoretical developments are occurring as well, as attempts are made to account for these more frequently measured outcomes of trauma (Hogan, Morse, & Tason, 1996; Holahan & Moos, 1990; Kast, 1990; Nerken, 1993; Schaefer & Moos, 1992; Tedeschi & Calhoun, 1995; Calhoun & Tedeschi, Chapter 9, this volume). These theoretical developments will be reviewed by O'Leary, Alday, and Ickovics later in this volume.

RELATED AREAS OF THEORY AND RESEARCH

Clearly there are other areas of study that recognize the tendency of some persons to cope successfully and to manage trauma relatively unscathed: the literature on *resilience*, especially in high-risk children; the research on the personality constructs of *hardiness* and *sense of coherence*, focused most often on resistance to disease; and the approaches of *stress inoculation* and *toughening*, processes that can help develop this resistance.

Resilience

Resilient children appear to have an ability to manage life successfully despite difficult family circumstances including poverty, parents with poor education, alcoholism, or mental illness, and marital discord. A longitudinal study by Werner (1989) showed that the majority of children growing up in such environments suffered learning or behavior problems, but about one third developed into well-adjusted adults. Rutter (1987) and Garmezy (1985) considered the characteristics that are associated with such resilience, emphasizing the importance of cognitive abilities that allow for more effective social skills, which in turn produce a larger repertoire of coping strategies to deal with subsequent life difficulties. Success in coping may then lead to greater sense of self-efficacy and self-esteem. Although the concept of resilience has most often been applied to children, it also has applications to adults. Harvey (1996) made a distinction between "recovery" from trauma, and "resiliency." She said that recovery occurs when there is a change from a poor to a desired outcome in any domain of the self affected by trauma. In contrast, resiliency is evident when certain domains of self are not affected by trauma and can be used to cope with trauma-induced difficulties in another domain. For example, a person may use intact spiritual values to cope with difficulties in trusting other people because of victimization. Tedeschi and Calhoun (1995) and Aldwin and Sutton (chap. 3, this volume) provide additional consideration of the links between resilience and PTG.

Sense of Coherence

In some initial studies of women holocaust survivors, Antonovsky (1987) observed substantial individual differences in the ability to tolerate stressful situations, and saw that some people actually seemed to thrive under objectively stressful circumstances. He coined the term "sense of coherence" to refer to a constellation of personality traits that seemed to enable people to deal well with stress. Sense of coherence is concerned with the factors that promote well-being and health, in contrast to psychology and psychiatry's traditional focus on pathogenesis and illness. Sense of coherence is an internal resource that consists of the following three interrelated components: comprehensibility, the extent to which individuals perceive the situations that confront them as predictable; manageability, the extent to which people perceive their resources to be adequate to meet situational demands; and meaningfulness, the extent to which people feel that life is emotionally meaningful and that everyday difficulties are more challenges than hindrances.

Few studies show changes in sense of coherence over time. Instead, most studies focus on relationships between people's levels of sense of coherence, which is considered a stable individual difference variable, and various outcomes of stressful experiences. Sense of coherence has often been found to relate to better physical and mental adjustment (see Schaubroeck & Ganster, 1991, for a review).

Hardiness

In many ways quite similar to the constructs of sense of coherence and of resilience, hardiness is a concept developed by Kobasa (1979) to describe a constellation of personality traits that enables people to resist stress. Hardiness is defined as the tendency to struggle adaptively with life's adversities by perceiving potentially stressful events in less threatening terms (Florian, Mikulincer & Taubman, 1995; Kobasa, 1982). Hardiness is composed of three interrelated elements: a sense of commitment to personal life roles, a sense of control over some aspects of life's problems, and the assumption of a challenge orientation when confronted with problems.

Few studies assess changes in hardiness over time. Instead, most research focuses on relationships between individuals' levels of hardiness and various outcomes of stressful encounters. Hardiness has been shown to be related to better physical and mental health (see Orr & Westman, 1990, for a review). However, there is a fair amount of inconsistency in the literature, with hardiness being considered less a unitary personality dimension and more as three relatively independent aspects of personality, with some aspects (e.g., control) being more consistently related to better adjustment than others (e.g., challenge) (Hull, Van Treuren, & Virnelli, 1987; Wiebe & Williams, 1992). There is evidence that hardiness operates through more adaptive appraisals (i.e., challenge) and coping (i.e., less emotion-focused coping; Florian et al., 1995).

Stress Inoculation

Stress inoculation is an approach to therapy developed by Meichenbaum (1985) that is a psychological analog to biological immunization. The general principle of stress inoculation therapy is that people learn to deal with stress by successfully dealing with stress. Individuals are given opportunities to deal with relatively mild stressors in positive ways, so that they gradually develop a tolerance for more difficult stressors. It is organized around three phases: a conceptual phase, in which clients are asked to participate in the collection of data relevant to understanding the stressors acting on them; a skills training and rehearsal phase, in which clients are taught a variety of coping skills and the proper use of these coping responses; and an application and rehearsal phase, in which clients apply their acquired skills to progressively more difficult situations. In this way, clients' current levels of coping skills are matched against appropriately difficult situations. Stress inoculation therapy has been used effectively to treat clients dealing with a variety of problems, including psychosomatic disorders, work site stress, pain, and chronic illness (Pierce, 1995).

Toughening

Related to stress inoculation is the concept of toughening (Dienstbier, 1992). This is a psychobiological concept that describes how persons with reduced pituitary–adrenal–cortisol response to stress are able to function more capably, and appraise situations in terms of challenge rather than threat. Such appraisals lead to physiological arousal that is experienced as energy without tension, allowing more adaptive functioning. Dienstbier argues that this toughening can be accomplished through a well-designed psychological training regimen. Aldwin and Sutton describe the relationship between toughening and PTG later in this volume.

Although these areas of study focus on positive outcomes in the face of negative life circumstances or events, they do not consider directly the tendency for some persons to report that in the aftermath of trauma their lives were transformed. However, it is likely that many of the persons described as hardy, resilient, toughened, etc. experience posttraumatic growth. Tennen and Affleck (chap. 4, this volume) and Calhoun & Tedeschi (chap. 9, this volume) consider the relationship between individual difference variables and PTG.

TYPES OF GROWTH OUTCOMES

There are several ways that posttraumatic growth manifests itself, and these manifestations may not appear together in the same person. Types of growth outcomes are described as including changes in perception of self, changes in interpersonal relationships, and change in philosophy of life (Tedeschi & Calhoun, 1995). It is important to consider societal manifestations of growth as well, since it appears that traumatic events experienced by individuals and groups can promote profound social change as discussed by Bloom (chap. 8, this volume). We will review the evidence for individual growth outcomes here, recognizing that the vast majority of studies reporting such outcomes were not primarily designed to find them. The methodologies are weak, but the reports of these growth outcomes by researchers also become more striking given they were unanticipated in so many cases.

Perception of Self

Survivor Versus Victim.   Labels that people apply to themselves appear to affect how they will cope with trauma, and trauma in turn may change persons' identities (Epstein, 1990). Perhaps one of the most important steps to PTG is the change in perception of self as a "victim" of trauma to a "survivor" of trauma. In recognition of the importance of labeling, most workers in the field of psychotraumatology encourage this less negative label. The label of survivor subtly introduces people affected by trauma to the idea that they have a special status and strength. However, there is evidence that a unidimensional view of self is not adequate to account for how people respond to life transitions. For example, Showers and Ryff (1996) reported that women who had a differentiated, complex view of the self tended to weather life change more effectively. Tennen and Affleck further consider this issue of cognitive and self-complexity in chapter 4 of this volume.

Self-Reliance.   One of the most common reports of PTG involves the sense that survivors have that "if I survived this, I can handle anything" (Aldwin, Levenson, & Spiro, 1994). Only another trauma may put this to the test, but survivors often have a sense of how they are stronger, and what coping strategies they might rely upon in the case of another difficulty. There is not much literature available to make a case that persons experiencing subsequent trauma would be less vulnerable to it given their PTG arising from previous events, but the idea of trauma as inoculation may be applicable here.

Many reports of a sense of increased self-reliance or self-efficacy come from the literature on spousal bereavement. Several studies have noted that women who lose their husbands later in life, and usually do not remarry, add their husbands' duties to their traditional role of wife. As a result, widows learn to do things that they had never approached before, have a stronger self-image (Lopata, 1973; Shucter, 1986; Thomas, Digiulio, & Sheehan, 1991), report more self-efficacy than when they were married (Calhoun & Tedeschi, 1989-1990; Gilbar & Dagan, 1995; Lund, Caserta, & Dimond, 1993), and express more self-efficacy than long-term married women (Arbuckle & de Vries, 1995). Similar findings of development of more positive views of self have been reported among children (Schlesinger, 1982) and adults (Wallerstein, 1986) experiencing divorce, combat experiences (Aldwin, Levenson, & Spiro, 1994; Elder & Clipp, 1989; Sledge, Boydstun, & Rabe, 1980), and life-threatening medical problems (Andreasen & Norris, 1972; Collins, Taylor, & Skokan, 1990; Curbow, Somerfield, Baker, Wingard, & Legro, 1993).

Vulnerability.   Paradoxically, some persons who report PTG, even those who recognize their strength, often describe a heightened awareness of their vulnerability, mortality, and the preciousness and fragility of life. How is this a growth outcome? A sense of vulnerability that exists alongside positive changes in views of self may prompt positive changes in interpersonal relationships, appreciation for life, and priorities for spending one's time, all discussed later. A sense of strengthening as a result of PTG does not seem to make people see themselves as not needing social support, and combined with a recognition of one's vulnerability, a sense of strength may produce assertiveness in seeking useful support and rejecting that which is less helpful.

Interpersonal Relationships

Self-Disclosure and Emotional Expressiveness. The ability to express feelings and disclose important personal information is shown to be related in positive ways to various indices of mental and physical health (see Pennebaker, 1995, and Park & Stiles, in press, for reviews). Do some individuals who experience traumatic events learn to disclose more about their feelings, or to express themselves more openly? While research has not addressed this issue directly, the limited information appears to indicate that they do. For example, reports of people who have experienced traumatic events indicate that their experiences with social support provided them the opportunity, and perhaps the need, to reveal themselves in ways that were never before necessary. Does increased openness typically ensue? Does such openness remain when the crisis subsides? Although we cannot answer these questions with confidence, people frequently report becoming closer to their spouses and having stronger marriages as a result of traumatic events such as heart attacks (Laerum, Johnsen, Smith, & Larsen, 1987; Michela, 1987), bereavement (Feeley & Gottlieb, 1988; Ponzetti, 1992), and hostage-taking (Sank, 1979).

It should be noted that openness and expressiveness may not always be seen as a more positive way of relating. Some researchers, especially in the area of rape and incest, have described positive developments in interpersonal relationships as a result of trauma in terms of increased caution (Frazier & Burnett, 1994; McMillan et al., 1995; Veronen & Kilpatrick, 1983). It may be that better recognition of who can be safely trusted, and the ability to be emotionally intimate with trusted others, is what may be learned in the aftermath of trauma. Victimization by a trusted person probably presents a more complicated path to growth in the area of interpersonal relationships than other sorts of traumas, such as illnesses or disasters.

Compassion and Giving to Others. Interpersonal relationships may be strengthened by the needs for support among those who are hurting, and also through a reciprocal process in which vulnerability creates empathy, compassion, and greater altruism. Although we are not aware of research directly addressing this issue, it appears that when people recognize their own vulnerability, they may be better able to feel compassion and that some trauma may be a kind of empathy training. Out of this compassion and the experiences of intimacy in the aftermath of trauma may come a need to help others. The gift of trauma is an understanding of events that no one but a survivor can have on the affective level. There often develops a strong motive to share this gift of knowledge with others who experience similar circumstances. This is likely to occur after enough time has passed since the traumatic event for there to be a recognition of enduring strength, and the realization that as a survivor, there is something to be offered. Providing help to others in difficult circumstances can also allow additional healing and the recognition of one's strength through a downward social comparison with those who are still struggling. The recognition of the universality of suffering is one of the foundations on which mutual support programs are based (Holmes, Heckel, & Gordon, 1991; Yalom, 1985).

Philosophy of Life

A variety of cognitive changes regarding fundamental questions about life such as why it is important, what one can expect of it, what contribution one can make, and whether an individual life is important and meaningful, are often affected by trauma. These changes can be grouped into four general categories, which are not mutually exclusive, as follows: changed life priorities, existential changes, spiritual changes, and religious changes (Cook & Wimberley, 1983; Tedeschi & Calhoun, 1995; Yalom & Lieberman, 1991). We have included these issues under the rubric "philosophy of life." However, PTG in this area is not merely an academic exercise in philosophy. These questions become crucial to survival when trauma occurs.

Priorities and Appreciation of Life.   Some traumas that put a person's life in danger can set in motion a sense that one has been spared, and that this gift of a second chance should be treated with care. Several reports of persons who have been taken hostage have demonstrated such changes (Sank, 1979; Simon & Blum, 1987; Strentz, 1979), and they occur in other life traumas as well. Changes in life priorities often involve a greater appreciation for life in general and for the "smaller things" in life (Klass, 1986–1987; Taylor, Lichtman, & Wood, 1984; Tedeschi & Calhoun, 1996). Individuals may report, for example, that the occurrence of a major stressor has made them realize that it is important to spend more time on their intimate relationships, to appreciate each day and its small pleasures more, and to take life easier. Individuals report these changes as highly positive alterations of their sense of what is important. Persons for whom trauma has produced a greater sense of their vulnerability, and therefore an appreciation for life, are often loathe to waste their time on the inconsequential.

Existential Themes and Sense of Meaning. Many traumatic events raise the most fundamental assumptions about life that survivors of trauma previously may have considered only in a superficial fashion. These existential changes can be regarded as growth, but they are not always identified as pleasant by the individual who experiences them, because they are issues of the meaning and purpose of life and the inevitability of personal death (Yalom & Lieberman, 1991). Persons experiencing the loss of a loved one, facing their own terminal illness, or dealing with other crises, may be compelled to more honestly face and experience the fundamental existential questions in ways not possible for persons who are not faced with trauma. Facing existential questions, of course, is not the same thing as resolving them satisfactorily.

Spiritual Development. Some persons are able to use their existing spiritual life or metaphysical beliefs to understand and cope with a trauma (Pargament, 1990; Weisner, Betzer, & Stolze, 1991), perhaps because such beliefs can accommodate so many experiences (Overcash, Calhoun, Cann, & Tedeschi, 1996). Others experience further spiritual development. Spirituality in this context refers to a greater sense of somehow being connected to something transcendent, in ways that were not possible before the struggle with trauma (Calhoun, Tedeschi, & Lincourt, 1992). There can be a greater sense of the presence of God, an increased sense of commitment to one's chosen religious tradition, or a clearer understanding of one's religious beliefs. Furthermore, many persons who must contend with the aftermath of trauma report that they have undergone a religious conversion (Pargament, 1996). Although some persons will understand their spiritual changes within the context of a specific religious belief system, others report a greater awareness of spiritual elements in their lives without using traditional religious language (Kessler, 1987). For others, trauma may set in motion a "spiritual emergency" where important metaphysical beliefs are threatened (Fahlberg, Wolfer, & Fahlberg, 1992). Over time, some of these persons may engage in a spiritual quest—"an open-ended, responsive dialogue with existential questions raised by the contradictions and tragedies of life" (Batson, Schoenrade, & Ventis, 1993, p. 169).

Wisdom. Wisdom is a concept found in many cultures, although the contents of what is considered "wise" varies from place to place and time to time (Assman, 1994). In most cultures, however, wisdom refers to knowledge and skills acquired in the process of aging, and includes characteristics such as a deepened knowledge of self and others, extraordinary understanding of ordinary experience, and exceptional skills of balance, judgment, and communication (Kramer, 1990). An increased understanding about basic issues of living, learned in a powerful fashion through suffering, may be a route to wisdom, although this is certainly not inevitable. Studies of trauma yield some evidence that wisdom may grow out of trauma, but because measures of wisdom have not been employed in trauma research, this evidence is indirect (e.g., Collins, Taylor, & Skokan, 1990; Elder & Clipp, 1989; Lehman et al., 1993). People who have learned about the issues mentioned above—appreciation of life and what priorities are important, how to relate to others successfully, and how to cope with difficulties, and a sense of the spiritual—are often seen as wise.

Researchers in the area of wisdom have recently emphasized both the intellectual and the emotional aspects of this quality, and how they are used in making life decisions. In studying wisdom, it is important to note that Western culture tends to consider wisdom an individual difference variable, and that wisdom is not considered an automatic concomitant of aging or experience (Birren & Fisher, 1990; O'Connor & Wolfe, 1991). Rather, some individuals, through their experiences, become wise.

Certainly the elderly, given the likelihood that they have experienced multiple losses, have an opportunity to experience PTG. Lerner and Gignac (1992) point out that gerontologists increasingly recognize that old age does not necessarily bring about depression, and that even the aged who cope well are not distorting or denying the painful realities of their lives. They imply that the wisdom of the aged is "growth" that has gone beyond successful coping with losses and pain. Instead, life experience, including the painful aspects, has been used among certain elderly persons to create an identity that brings contentment in later life through a "recentering" process of self-discovery and affirmation. The process involves an ability to step back from the immediacy of events and take a broader perspective. In this way, even the most traumatic events can take on various meanings, and evoke less emotional distress. Similarly, Neugarten (1977) described how people who have lived through physical and psychological pain have come to recognize that they are enriched by these events, can see life in its complexity, and see themselves as repositories for eternal truths. Furthermore, there is evidence that wisdom is not reserved for the elderly, and that some much younger persons can operate from a similar perspective on life that wise elders do (Baltes, Staudinger, Maercker, & Smith, 1995). Clearly, there are close relationships between posttraumatic growth, or at least certain aspects of it, and wisdom. The development of wisdom appears to have more to do with life experiences and the ways people cope with and learn from those experiences than age per se.

THE PLAN FOR THIS BOOK

In this introductory chapter, we have attempted to outline the field of PTG in the most general fashion. We suggest a definition of the term and tried to distinguish it from other terms that have been applied to these growth experiences. We show that PTG is related to a variety of other concepts found in the literature on trauma, coping, and development. We mention some of the historical antecedents of the psychological study of PTG. And we give examples of the studies that describe the experiences of growth among various people who have encountered different traumas. These descriptions of PTG raise many questions: Is this growth real? Can it be seen clearly in behavior that others note? How does it happen? How long does such growth take? How many people experience it? Does it last? Are certain kinds of growth associated with certain events or characteristics of those reporting it? Responses to these and other issues in posttraumatic growth will be found in later chapters.

In chapter 2, Lawrence Cohen, Tanya Hettler, and Natalia Payne address some of the issues of valid assessment of PTG. The focus of the chapter is on two recently published instruments: the Stress-Related Growth Scale (Park, Cohen, & Murch, 1996) and the Posttraumatic Growth Inventory (Tedeschi & Calhoun, 1996). The authors also suggest research strategies in posttraumatic growth.

Chapter 3, written by Carolyn Aldwin and Karen Sutton, provides a developmental perspective on PTG. Aldwin and Sutton review a series of studies that indicate that early stressful experiences can have positive developmental affects. The evidence for PTG among children and adults is considered, and a deviation–amplification model that accounts for these findings is suggested.

In chapter 4, Howard Tennen and Glenn Affleck review the relationship between several personality variables and reports of PTG, especially optimism/pessimism, cognitive complexity and self-complexity, hope, and the Big Five personality dimensions. They suggest a more process-oriented approach to studying the relationship between personality and PTG at the level of personal concerns and narratives. They discuss different routes to PTG, some gradual and others abrupt, some effortful and others outside awareness.

Jeanne Schaefer and Rudolph Moos in chapter 5 consider the characteristics of traumatic events and other environmental and contextual factors that are linked to posttraumatic growth.

In chapter 6, Virginia O'Leary, Sloan Alday, and Jeanette Ickovics review theoretical approaches to PTG. Some of these approaches represent general theories of change that the authors consider in relation to PTG, while other models reviewed have been focused specifically on growth after trauma.

Crystal Park considers, in chapter 7, the implications of PTG in the life of the individual. She looks at the relationships between PTG and mental and physical health, and responses to subsequent trauma. She also discusses the evidence concerning the degree to which PTG endures.

Chapter 8 provides an opportunity to consider how individual and group experiences with trauma encourage social change. Sandra Bloom provides examples from many historical events, demonstrating how trauma can be transformed on the social level through education, mutual help, rescuing, witnessing, political action, humor, and art.

Finally, in chapter 9, two of the editors, Lawrence Calhoun and Richard Tedeschi, attempt to integrate all that has gone before in their discussion of conceptual issues in PTG. They present a comprehensive model of the phenomenon and suggest some research directions. The potential for clinical applications is also addressed.

REFERENCES

Abbott, D. A., & Meredith, W. H. (1986). Strengths of parents with retarded children. *Family Relations, 35*, 371–375.

Affleck, G., Tennen, H., & Gershman, K. (1985). Cognitive adaptations to high-risk infants: The search for mastery, meaning, and protection from future harm. *American Journal of Mental Deficiency, 89*, 653–656.

Aldwin, C. M., Levenson, M. R., & Spiro, A. (1994). Vulnerability and resilience to combat exposure: Can stress have life-long effects? *Psychology and Aging, 9*, 34–44.

Andreasen, N. L., & Norris, A. S. (1972). Long-term adjustment and adaptation mechanisms in severely burned adults. *Journal of Nervous & Mental Disease, 154*, 352–362.

Antonovsky, A. (1987). *Unraveling the mystery of health: How people manage stress and stay well.* San Francisco: Jossey-Bass.

Arbuckle, N., & de Vries, B. (1995). The long-term effects of later life spousal and parental bereavement on personal functioning. *The Gerontologist, 35*, 637–647.

Assman, A. (1994). Wholesome knowledge: Concepts of wisdom in a historical and cross-cultural perspective. In D. L. Featherman, R. M. Lerner, & M. Perlmutter (Eds.), *Life-span development and behavior* (Vol. 12, pp. 187–224). Hillsdale, NJ: Lawrence Erlbaum Associates.

Baltes, P. B., Staudinger, U. M., Maercker, A., & Smith, J. (1995). People nominated as wise: A comparative study of wisdom-related knowledge. *Psychology and Aging, 10,* 155–166.

Basic Behavioral Science Task Force of the National Advisory Mental Health Council. (1996). Basic behavioral science research for mental health: Vulnerability and resilience. *American Psychologist, 51,* 22–28.

Batson, C. D., Schoenrade, P., & Ventis, W. L. (1993). *Religion and the individual: A social-psychological perspective.* New York: Oxford University Press.

Birren, J. E., & Fisher, L. M. (1990). The elements of wisdom: Overview and integration. In R. J. Sternberg (Ed.), *Wisdom: Its nature, origins, and development* (pp. 317–332). New York: Cambridge University Press.

Burt, M. R., & Katz, B. L. (1987). Dimensions of recovery from rape: Focus on growth outcomes. *Journal of Interpersonal Violence, 2,* 57–81.

Calhoun, L. G. (1996, August). Posttraumatic growth: A functional descriptive model. In R. G. Tedeschi (Chair), *Posttraumatic growth: An overview of contemporary models.* Symposium conducted at the annual meeting of the American Psychological Association, Toronto.

Calhoun, L. G., & Tedeschi, R. G. (1989–1990). Positive aspects of critical life problems: Recollections of grief. *Omega, 20,* 265–272.

Calhoun, L. G., & Tedeschi, R. G. (1991). Perceiving benefits in traumatic events: Some issues for practicing psychologists. *The Journal of Training & Practice in Professional Psychology, 5,* 45–52.

Calhoun, L. G., Tedeschi, R.G., & Lincourt, A. (1992, August). *Life crises and religious beliefs: Changed beliefs or assimilated events?* Paper presented at the meeting of the American Psychological Association, Washington, DC.

Caplan, G. (1961). *An approach to community mental health.* New York: Grune & Stratton.

Caplan, G. (1964). *Principles of preventive psychiatry.* New York: Basic Books.

Collins, R. L., Taylor, S. E., & Skokan, L. A. (1990). A better world or a shattered vision? Changes in life perspectives following victimization. *Social Cognition, 8,* 263–285.

Cook, J., & Wimberley, D. (1983). If I should die before I wake: Religious commitment and adjustment to the death of a child. *Journal for the Scientific Study of Religion, 22,* 222–238.

Curbow, B., Somerfield, R., Baker, F., Wingard, J. R., & Legro, M. W. (1993). Personal changes, dispositional optimism, and psychological adjustment to bone marrow transplantation. *Journal of Behavioral Medicine, 16,* 423–443.

Dienstbier, R. A. (1992). Mutual impacts of toughening on crises and losses. In L. Montada, S. Filipp, & M. J. Lerner (Eds.), *Life crises and experiences of loss in adulthood* (pp. 367–384). Hillsdale, NJ: Lawrence Erlbaum Associates.

Draucker, C. (1992). Construing benefit from a negative experience of incest. *Western Journal of Nursing Research, 14,* 343–357.

Ebersole, P. (1970). Effects of nadir experiences. *Psychological Reports, 27,* 207–209.

Ebersole, P., & Flores, J. (1989). Positive impact of life crises. *Journal of Social Behavior and Personality, 4,* 463–469.

Edmonds, S., & Hooker, K. (1992). Perceived changes in life meaning following bereavement. *Omega, 25,* 307–318.

Elder, G. H., Jr., & Clipp, E. C. (1989). Combat experience and emotional health: Impairment and resilience in later life. *Journal of Personality, 57,* 311–341.

Epstein, S. (1990). The self-concept, the traumatic neurosis, and the structure of personality. In D. Ozer, J. M. Healy, Jr., & A. J. Stewart (Eds.), *Perspectives on personality* (Vol. 3, pp. 63–98). Greenwich, CT: JAI Press.

Fahlberg, L. L., Wolfer, J., & Fahlberg, L. A. (1992). Personal crisis: Growth or pathology? *American Journal of Health Promotion, 7*, 45–52.

Feeley, N., & Gottlieb, L. N. (1988). Parents' coping and communication following their infants' death. *Omega, 19*, 51–67.

Finkel, N. J. (1974). Strens and traumas: An attempt at categorization. *American Journal of Community Psychology, 2*, 265–273.

Finkel, N. J. (1975). Strens, traumas and trauma resolution. *American Journal of Community Psychology, 3*, 173–178.

Finkel, N. J., & Jacobsen, C. A. (1977). Significant life experiences in an adult sample. *American Journal of Community Psychology, 5*, 165–175.

Florian, V., Mikulincer, M., & Taubman, O. (1995). Does hardiness contribute to mental health during a stressful real-life situation? The roles of appraisal and coping. *Journal of Personality and Social Psychology, 68*, 687–695.

Frankl, V. (1961). Logotherapy and the challenge of suffering. *Review of Existential Psychology and Psychiatry, 1*, 3–7.

Frazier, P., & Burnett, J. (1994). Immediate coping strategies among rape victims. *Journal of Counseling and Development, 72*, 633–639.

Frazier, P. A., Byrne, C., & Klein, C. (1995, August). *Resilience among sexual assault survivors.* Poster presented at the annual meeting of the American Psychological Association, New York.

Fromm, E. (1976). *To have or to be?* New York: Harper & Row.

Garmezy, N. (1985). Stress resistant children: The search for protective factors. In J. Stevenson (Ed.), *Recent research in developmental psychopathology* (pp. 213–231). Oxford: Pergamon Press.

Gilbar, O., & Dagan, A. (1995). Coping with loss: Differences between widows and widowers of deceased cancer patients. *Omega, 31*, 207–220.

Hamera, E. K., & Shontz, F. C. (1978). Perceived positive and negative effects of life-threatening illness. *Journal of Psychosomatic Medicine, 22*, 419–424.

Harvey, M. R. (1996). An ecological view of psychological trauma and trauma recovery. *Journal of Traumatic Stress, 9*, 3–23.

Hogan, N., Morse, J. M., & Tason, M. C. (1996). Toward an experiential theory of bereavement. *Omega, 33*, 43–65.

Holahan, C. J., & Moos, R. H. (1990). Life stressors, resistance factors, and improved psychological functioning: An extension of the stress resistance paradigm. *Journal of Personality and Social Psychology, 58*, 909–917.

Holmes, G. R., Heckel, R. V., & Gordon, L. (1991). *Adolescent group therapy: A social competency model.* New York: Praeger.

Hull, J. G., Van Treuren, R. R., & Virnelli, S. (1987). Hardiness and health: A critique and alternative approach. *Journal of Personality and Social Psychology, 53*, 518–530.

Jaffe, D. T. (1985). Self-renewal: Personal transformation following extreme trauma. *Journal of Humanistic Psychology, 25*, 99–124.

Janoff-Bulman, R. (1992). *Shattered assumptions.* New York: The Free Press.

Joseph, S., Williams, R., & Yule, W. (1993). Changes in outlook following disaster: The preliminary development of a measure to assess positive and negative responses. *Journal of Traumatic Stress, 6*, 271–279.

Kast, V. (1990). *The creative leap: Psychological transformation through crisis.* (D. Whitcher, Trans.). Wilmette, IL: Chiron Publications. (Original work published 1987)

Kessler, B. G. (1987). Bereavement and personal growth. *Journal of Humanistic Psychology, 27,* 228–247.

Kierkegaard, S. (1983). *Fear and trembling.* (H. V. Long & E. H. Long, Trans.). Princeton, NJ: Princeton University Press.

Klass, D. (1986–1987). Marriage and divorce among bereaved parents in a self-help group. *Omega, 17,* 237–249.

Kobasa, S. C. (1979). Stressful life events, personality, and health: An inquiry into hardiness. *Journal of Personality and Social Psychology, 37,* 1–11.

Kobasa, S. C. (1982). Commitment and coping in stress resistance among lawyers. *Journal of Personality and Social Psychology, 42,* 707–717.

Kramer, D. A. (1990). Conceptualizing wisdom: The primacy of affect-cognition relations. In R.J. Sternberg (Ed.), *Wisdom: Its nature, origins, and development* (pp. 279–313). New York: Cambridge University Press.

Krook, D. (1969). *Elements of tragedy.* New Haven: Yale University Press.

Laerum, E., Johnsen, N., Smith, P., & Larsen, S. (1987). Can myocardial infarction induce positive changes in family relationships? *Family Practice, 4,* 302–305.

Lehman, D. R., Davis, C. G., Delongis, A., Wortman, C., Bluck, S., Mandel, D. R., & Ellard, J. H. (1993). Positive and negative life changes following bereavement and their relations to adjustment. *Journal of Social and Clinical Psychology, 12,* 90–112.

Lerner, M. J., & Gignac, M. A. M. (1992). Is it coping or is it growth? A cognitive-affective model of contentment in the elderly. In L. Montada, S. Filipp, & M. J. Lerner (Eds.), *Life crises and experiences of loss in adulthood* (pp. 321–337). Hillsdale, NJ: Lawrence Erlbaum Associates.

Lopata, H. Z. (1973). Self-identity in marriage and widowhood. *The Sociological Quarterly, 14,* 407–418.

Lund, D. A., Caserta, M. S., & Dimond, M. (1993). The course of spousal bereavement in later life. In M.S. Stroebe, W. Stroebe, & R. O. Hansson (Eds.), *Handbook of bereavement: Theory, research, and intervention* (pp. 240–254). New York: Cambridge University Press.

May, R. (1960). Existential bases of psychotherapy. *Journal of Orthopsychiatry, 30,* 685–695.

May, R. (1983). *The discovery of being: Writings in existential psychology.* New York: Norton.

McCrae, R. R. (1984). Situational determinanats of coping responses: Loss, threat, and challenge. *Journal of Personality and Social Psychology, 46,* 919–928.

McMillen, C., Zuravin, S., & Rideout, G. (1995). Perceived benefit from child abuse. *Journal of Consulting and Clinical Psychology, 63,* 1037–1043.

Meichenbaum, D. (1985). *Stress inoculation training.* New York: Pergamon.

Michela, J. L. (1987). Interpersonal and individual impacts of a husband's heart attack. In A. Baum & J. E. Singer (Eds.), *Handbook of psychology and health: Vol. 5. Stress* (pp. 255–301). Hillsdale NJ: Lawrence Erlbaum Associates.

Miles, M. S., & Crandall, E. K. B. (1983). The search for meaning and its potential for affecting growth in bereaved parents. *Health Values, 7,* 19–23.

Nerken, I. R. (1993). Grief and the reflective self: Toward a clearer model of loss and growth. *Death Studies, 17,* 1–26.

Neugarten, B. L. (1977). Personality and aging. In J. E. Birren & K. W. Schaie (Eds.), *Handbook of the psychology of aging* (pp. 626–649). New York: Van Nostrand Reinhold.

Nietzsche, F. (1955). *Beyond good and evil.* (M. Cowan, Trans.). Chicago, IL: Henry Regnery.

O'Connor, D., & Wolfe, D. M. (1991). From crisis to growth at midlife: Changes in personal paradigm. *Journal of Organizational Behavior, 12,* 323–340.

O'Leary, V., & Ickovics, J. R. (1995). Resilience and thriving in response to challenge: An opportunity for a paradigm shift in women's health. *Women's Health: Research on Gender, Behavior, and Policy, 1,* 121–142.

Orr, E., & Westman, M. (1990). Hardiness as a stress moderator: A review. In M. Rosenbaum (Ed.), *Learned resourcefulness: On coping skills, self-control, and adaptive behavior* (pp. 64–94). New York: Springer.

Overcash, W. S., Calhoun, L. G., Cann, A., & Tedeschi, R. G. (1996). Coping with crises: An examination of the impact of traumatic events on personal belief systems. *Journal of Genetic Psychology, 157,* 455–464.

Pargament, K. (1990). God help me: Toward a theoretical framework of coping for the psychology of religion. *Research in the Social Scientific Study of Religion, 2,* 195–224.

Pargament, K. I. (1996). Religious methods of coping: Resources for the conservation and transformation of significance. In E. P. Shafranske (Ed.), *Religion and the clinical practice of psychology* (pp. 215–240). Washington, DC: American Psychological Association.

Park, C. L., Cohen, L., & Murch, R. (1996). Assessment and prediction of stress-related growth. *Journal of Personality, 64,* 71–105.

Park, C. L. , & Stiles, W. B. (in press). Self-disclosure. In H. Friedman (Ed.), *Encyclopedia of mental health.* San Diego: Academic Press.

Pennebaker, J. W. (1995). *Emotion, disclosure and health.* Washington, DC: American Psychological Association.

Pierce, T. W. (1995). Skills training in stress management. In W. O'Donohue & L. Krasner (Eds.), *Handbook of psychological skills training* (pp. 306–319). Boston: Allyn & Bacon.

Ponzetti, J. J. (1992). Bereaved families: A comparison of parents and grandparents reactions to the death of a child. *Omega, 25,* 63–71.

Raphael, D. D. (1960). *The paradox of tragedy.* Bloomington: Indiana University Press.

Rutter, M. (1987). Psychosocial resilience and protective mechanisms. *American Journal of Orthopsychiatry, 57,* 316–331.

Sank, L. I. (1979). Community disasters: Primary prevention and treatment in a Health Maintenance Organization. *American Psychologist, 34,* 334–338.

Schaefer, J. A., & Moos, R.H. (1992). Life crises and personal growth. In B. N. Carpenter (Ed.), *Personal coping: Theory, research, and application* (pp. 149–170). Westport, CT: Praeger.

Schaubroeck, J., & Ganster, D. C. (1991). Associations among stress-related individual differences. In C. L. Cooper & R. Payne (Eds.), *Personality and stress: Individual differences in the stress process* (pp. 33–66). Chichester, England: John Wiley & Sons.

Scheier, M. F., Weintraub, J. K., & Carver, C. S. (1986). Coping with stress: Divergent strategies of optimists and pessimists. *Journal of Personality and Social Psychology, 51,* 1257–1264.

Schlesinger, B. (1982). Children's viewpoints of living in a one-parent family. *Journal of Divorce, 5,* 1–23.

Schwab, R. (1990). Paternal and maternal coping with the death of a child. *Death Studies, 14,* 407–422.

Schwartzberg, S. S. (1993). Struggling for meaning: How HIV-positive gay men make sense of AIDS. *Professional Psychology: Research & Practice, 24,* 483–490.

Showers, C. J., & Ryff, C. D. (1996). Self-differentiation and well-being in a life transition. *Personality and Social Psychology Bulletin, 22,* 448–460.

Shucter, S. R. (1986). *Dimensions of grief.* San Francisco: Jossey-Bass.

Silver, R. C., Boon, C., & Stones, M. H. (1983). Searching for meaning in misfortune: Making sense of incest. *Journal of Social Issues, 39,* 81–102.

Simon, R. I., & Blum, R. A. (1987). After the terrorist incident: Psychotherapeutic treatment of former hostages. *American Journal of Psychotherapy, 41*, 194–200.

Sledge, W. H., Boydstun, J. A., & Rabe, A. J. (1980). Self-concept changes related to war captivity. *Archives of General Psychiatry, 37*, 430–443.

Strentz, T. (1979). Law enforcement policy and ego defenses of the hostage. *FBI Law Enforcement Bulletin, 48*, 2–12.

Taylor, S.E., & Brown, J.D. (1988). Illusion and well-being: A social psychological perspective on mental health. *Psychological Bulletin, 103*, 193–210.

Taylor, S. E., Lichtman, R. R., & Wood, J. V. (1984). Attributions, beliefs in control, and adjustment to breast cancer. *Journal of Personality and Social Psychology, 46*, 489–502.

Taylor, V. (1977, October). Good news about disaster. *Psychology Today*, pp. 93–94, 124–126.

Tedeschi, R. G., & Calhoun, L. G. (1988, August). *Perceived benefits in coping with physical handicaps.* Paper presented at the meeting of the American Psychological Association, Atlanta.

Tedeschi, R. G., & Calhoun, L. G. (1995). *Trauma and transformation: Growing in the aftermath of suffering.* Thousand Oaks, CA: Sage.

Tedeschi, R. G., & Calhoun, L. G. (1996). The posttraumatic growth inventory: measuring the positive legacy of trauma. *Journal of Traumatic Stress, 9*, 455–471.

Tedeschi, R. G., Calhoun, L. G., & Page, L. (1992, August). *Possibilities for growth in positive and negative life events.* Paper presented at the meeting of the American Psychological Association, Washington, DC.

Tennen, H., Affleck, G., Urrows, S., Higgins, P., & Mendola, R. (1992). Perceiving control, construing benefits, and daily processes in rheumatoid arthritis. *Canadian Journal of Behavioral Science, 24*, 186–203.

Thomas, L. E., DiGiulio, R. C., & Sheehan, N. W. (1991). Identifying loss and psychological crisis in widowhood. *International Journal of Aging and Human Development, 26*, 279–295.

Thompson, S. C. (1985). Finding positive meaning in a stressful event and coping. *Basic and Applied Social Psychology, 6*, 279–295.

Tillich, P. (1952). *The courage to be.* New Haven: Yale University Press.

Veronen, L. J., & Kilpatrick, D. G. (1983). Rape: A precursor of change. In E. J. Callahan & K. A. McCluskey (Eds.), *Life span developmental psychology: Non-normative events* (pp. 167–191). San Diego, CA: Academic Press.

Wallerstein, J. S. (1986). Women after divorce: Preliminary report from a ten-year follow-up. *American Journal of Orthopsychiatry, 56*, 65–77.

Werner, E. E. (1989). High-risk children in young adulthood: A longitudinal study from birth to 32 years. *American Journal of Orthopsychiatry, 59*, 72–81.

Wiebe, D. J., & Williams, P. G. (1992). Hardiness and health: A social psychophysiological perspective on stress and adaptation. *Journal of Social and Clinical Psychology, 11*, 238–262.

Weisner, T. S., Betzer, L., & Stolze, L. (1991). Religion and families of children with developmental delays. *American Journal of Mental Retardation, 95*, 647–662.

Yalom, I. D. (1985). *The theory and practice of group psychotherapy* (3rd ed.). New York: Basic Books.

Yalom, I. D., & Lieberman, M. A. (1991). Bereavement and heightened existential awareness. *Psychiatry, 54*, 334–345.

2

Assessment of
Posttraumatic Growth

Lawrence H. Cohen
Tanya R. Hettler
Natalia Pane
University of Delaware

The belief that trauma can ultimately result in positive outcomes is documented in philosophical and religious writings since the beginning of recorded history (Tedeschi & Calhoun, 1995). Contemporary sources supporting the notion of growth from trauma include theories of psychotherapy (e.g., Frankl, 1963) and models of preventive psychiatry (e.g., Caplan, 1964). In fact, a cornerstone of modern crisis theory (Caplan, 1964) is the assumption that crises represent opportunities for growth, as well as for deterioration. Despite this very long history, it is only recently that behavioral scientists have begun to conduct empirical research on posttraumatic growth (PTG). As the preceding chapter illustrates, the conceptualization of PTG is not yet consensual, nor clearly explicated, and PTG theory is in its infancy. It is not surprising, then, that empirical research on PTG is scarce and, for the most part, methodologically primitive.

The purpose of this chapter is to review issues related to the assessment of PTG. We emphasize conceptual and methodological problems, although we present specific measurement strategies and research findings when appropriate. In particular, we describe the development and evaluation of two new self-report scales of PTG: the 50-item Stress-Related Growth Scale (SRGS; Park, Cohen, & Murch, 1996), and the 21-item Posttraumatic Growth Inventory (PTGI; Tedeschi & Calhoun, 1996).

MEASURES OF PTG

Interview Assessment of PTG

Some empirical studies assess PTG by interviewing victims about their experiences. In general, interrater agreement was reported in these studies to demonstrate that victims' responses were reliably categorized.

Collins, Taylor, and Skokan (1990) developed an a priori categorization of self-reported PTG outcomes. They studied more than 50 cancer patients, some of whom were still in treatment. In home interviews, participants were asked how their cancer experiences had affected their daily activities, plans/goals for the future, views of self, views of the world, and relationships with others. Raters further classified specific responses within each of these domains and also assigned a valence (positive vs. negative) to each response. Collins et al. found that there were more positive than negative changes in the activities and relationship domains, whereas the changes were balanced in the other domains.

A number of other interview studies reported categorization of PTG outcomes based on post hoc analyses of participants' responses. Affleck, Tennen, and Gershman (1985) interviewed approximately 40 mothers of newborns with serious medical problems. The mothers were asked if they had experienced any benefits, gains, or advantages from having newborns with serious problems. Responses were then classified into the following categories: better perspective on life, closer family relations, special appreciation for the child, emotional growth, and spiritual growth. Affleck et al. found that there was little difference among the first four categories, with approximately 20% of the mothers reporting positive changes in each and only about 7% of the mothers reporting positive changes in the spiritual domain.

Another example is Affleck, Tennen, Croog, and Levine (1987), who studied approximately 300 men who had experienced their first heart attacks. The men were interviewed 7 weeks after the attack and again approximately 8 years later. Their interview question was virtually identical to that asked by Affleck et al. (1985). Participants' responses were classified using the following categories: learned the value of health behavior, changed life to increase enjoyment, change in philosophy of life, insight concerning how to avoid stress and conflict, and change in family relations. Affleck et al. (1987) found that, at 7 weeks, the first two domains were mentioned by 25% to 30% of the respondents, whereas the other domains were mentioned by 12% or fewer of the respondents. At 8 years, the first two domains were still frequently mentioned (25% and 17%, respectively), as was the domain for changes in life philosophy (25%); the other two domains were mentioned by 13% or fewer of the respondents.

Still another example from this same research group is Mendola, Tennen, Affleck, McCann, and Fitzgerald (1990), who interviewed 65 women coping with infertility. Their interview question was also virtually identical to that asked by Affleck et al. (1985) and Affleck et al. (1987). The women's responses were classified as representing (a) a strengthening of their marriage, (b) personal growth, and (c) a greater appreciation of life. Mendola et al. found that the first category was mentioned by 48% of the respondents, whereas the other two categories were mentioned by approximately 20% of the respondents.

McMillen, Zuravin, and Rideout (1995) interviewed approximately 150 women who had experienced sexual abuse as children. They were asked to describe ways in which they benefited from the experience, and their verbal responses were then categorized as follows: (a) increased ability to protect children from abuse, (b) increased ability to protect themselves, (c) better knowledge of sexual abuse, and (d) increased personal strength. The authors found that the first category was mentioned most frequently, specifically by 29% of the women. McMillen et al. introduced their question about benefits with a statement that "some individuals can benefit from abuse." As the authors acknowledged, this statement might have inflated victims' reports of PTG.

Lehman et al. (1993) interviewed approximately 100 adults who had lost spouses or children in car accidents. Participants' responses were classified into 12 categories, which were seen as reflecting three major domains: (a) changes in self-perceptions (e.g., self-confidence), (b) changes in relationships, and (c) changes in life orientation (e.g., religion).

Paper-and-Pencil Assessment of PTG.   Other studies have used paper-and-pencil measures to assess PTG. Curbow, Somerfield, Baker, Wingard, and Legro (1993) surveyed more than 100 adult survivors of bone marrow transplantation. A mail survey assessed the occurrence and self-rated valence (positive vs. negative) of 20 life changes, which were classified into the following categories: (a) plans and activities (e.g., leisure activities, financial situation), (b) relationships, (c) physical changes (e.g., strength, appearance), and (d) existential issues (e.g., philosophy of life). Curbow et al. found differences between these PTG domains. Specifically, respondents reported more positive than negative changes in the relationship and existential domains, whereas they reported more negative changes in the physical domain, and balanced change in the plans/activities domain.

Thompson (1985) also conducted a mail survey in her study of adults whose apartments were damaged in a fire. The participants were primarily elderly and female. They were asked if they had used any of five ways of reevaluating the fire as positive (e.g., finding side benefits, imagining worse situations).

Ebersole and Flores (1989) administered a 1-item scale to college students, who were asked whether their most painful life experience had a positive versus negative impact on them. Aldwin, Levenson, and Spiro (1994) administered a 28-item scale (developed by Elder & Clipp, 1989) to male war veterans to assess positive and negative consequences of military service. Joseph, Williams, and Yule (1993) administered a 40-item questionnaire to 35 adult survivors of a sinking ship. Five judges rated each item as reflecting positive, negative, or unclear change. Eleven items were regarded as reflecting positive change (e.g., "I value my relationship much more now"). The internal reliability of this positive change scale was .83.

Burt and Katz (1987) conducted an ambitious study of 113 female rape victims. One of their newly created questionnaires was a 28-item scale to assess changes that came from efforts to recover from rape. A factor analysis revealed three factors: (a) self-value, (b) positive actions, and (c) interpersonal skills. Unfortunately, with 28 items and 113 subjects, their subject–item ratio (4:1) was low for a factor analysis. In any case, each subscale had an adequate internal reliability ($>.70$). In addition, Burt and Katz demonstrated the test–retest reliability of their measure over several weeks, and showed that it was not correlated with a measure of social desirability.

Critique of PTG Conceptualization and Assessment. As is evident from the preceding discussion, definitions of PTG have varied among studies. For the most part, these study-specific definitions have reflected the specific nature of the crisis under investigation. Although there are exceptions (e.g., Collins et al., 1990), most studies that assessed a priori PTG domains, or used total scores comprised of a priori dimensions, did not provide a theoretical or empirical justification for their specific conceptualization of PTG.

An interesting question for future research is how PTG domains might vary as a function of the type of crisis (e.g., medical vs. death of significant other vs. natural disaster), and the characteristics of victims (e.g., age, gender, religiousness, etc.). For example, certain types of events might inevitably result in positive changes in interpersonal relationships, whereas other types of events might result in positive changes in life philosophy. At a more complex level, the factor structure (composition) of PTG domains might also vary as a function of crisis and respondent. For example, for some respondents, positive changes in coping skills might covary with interpersonal changes, whereas for other respondents, these changes in coping skills might be associated with changes in life philosophy.

In those interview studies in which respondents were asked to report the benefits or positive consequences of their crisis (e.g., Affleck et al., 1987; McMillen et al., 1995), an obvious potential problem is the variability in respondents' definitions of such terms as *benefits*, *gains*, and *positive consequences*. For example, it is possible that some victims who experience improvements in their interpersonal relationships, or changes in life philosophy, would not report these as a benefit or gain in response to an open-ended interview question, whereas other victims would report these as a benefit.

PTGI AND SRGS

An awareness of these methodological problems in the assessment of PTG motivated the development of two new paper-and-pencil measures of stress-related growth (Park et al., 1996; Tedeschi & Calhoun, 1996). Although imperfect, these scales represent the state of the art in PTG assessment. (There are also unpublished preliminary data on a paper-and-pencil scale developed by Frazier, Byrne, & Klein, 1995.)

PTG: Unitary or Multidimensional? When developing the PTGI, Tedeschi and Calhoun (1996) began with 34 items, all positively worded, and all with a 0 to 5 response choice (0 = *I did not experience this change as a result of my crisis*, 3 = *I experienced this change to a moderate degree as a result of my crisis*, 5 = *I experienced this change to a very great degree as a result of my crisis*). Each item referred to growth that pertained to college students' most negative event in the past 5 years. The scale was administered to approximately 600 students.

Principal component analysis with orthogonal rotation led to the deletion of 13 items; the remaining 21 items comprised five factors (subscales) that accounted for about 60% of the variance: (a) relating to others (e.g., "A sense of closeness with others"), (b) new possibilities (e.g., "I developed new interests"), (c) personal strength (e.g., "A feeling of self-reliance"), (d) spiritual change (e.g., "I have a stronger religious faith"), and (e) appreciation of life ("My priorities about what is important in life").

When developing the SRGS, Park et al. (1996) administered 82 items to approximately 500 college students, who were instructed to complete the items as they pertained to their most negative event during the past year. Each item was rated a 0 (*not at all*), 1 (*somewhat*), or 2 (*a great deal*). Items reflect changes in social relationships, personal resources, including life philosophy, and coping skills.

Thirty-two items were deleted because of very skewed responses, leaving 50 items on the SRGS. A series of factor analyses were conducted on these 50 items ($N = 506$). Overall, most items loaded the highest on one general factor, and the factor structure was not consistent with expectations. For this reason, Park et al. (1996) used SRGS total scores in subsequent analyses. In any case, the items on the PTGI and SRGS are very similar; both scales have items that tap changes in social relationships, personal resources, and coping skills.

Hettler and Cohen (1996) recently completed one phase of a study of adult members ($N = 366$; 242 women and 124 men) of 12 Protestant churches in Delaware. The mean age was 47.44 ($SD = 14.74$). Subjects completed the SRGS for their most negative event in the past year, and also completed measures of coping with that negative event, and scales for optimism, depression, intrinsic religiousness, and perceived social support.

Principal component analysis of the SRGS items suggested the existence of one major factor and two minor factors. Overall, the analysis supported the computation of a total score: Most items loaded the highest on the first factor, and loadings on the other two factors were difficult to interpret.

Park, Cohen, and Murch (1995) examined the item-total correlations for the SRGS data with college students. They selected those 15 items that had the highest correlations with the total score. This was repeated by Hettler and Cohen (1996) for the SRGS data with adult church members. A comparison of the findings of Park et al. and Hettler and Cohen reveals good agreement on the SRGS items that are most highly related to the total score. From this work, a 15-item short form of the SRGS has been developed.

In any case, research to date supports the use of PTGI subscale scores, but only total scores for the SRGS. This is a definite advantage for the PTGI, because it allows researchers to test for varying effects on specific growth domains (e.g., personal relationships, religious beliefs) as a function of such variables as type of stressor and length of time since stressor occurrence. On the other hand, additional research with diverse samples is needed to confirm the factor structure of the PTGI.

Reliability of the PTGI and SRGS.   Both the full scale (.90) and the separate subscales (.67–.85) of the PTGI have good internal reliability. A small subsample of students was readministered the PTGI about 2 months later, and the test–retest reliability of the full PTGI was adequate (.71). However, for two of the PTGI subscales (personal strength, appreciation of life), the temporal stability was low ($r = .37$ and .47, respectively).

Cronbach's alpha for the 50-item SRGS was .94 in Park et al.'s (1996) sample of college students, and .96 in Hettler and Cohen's (1996) sample of adult church members. A subsample of Park et al.'s students were readministered the SRGS about 2 weeks later. The test–retest reliability was .81.

Therefore, both the PTGI and the SRGS appear to have adequate internal and test–retest reliability.

Validity of PTG Assessment: Corroboration of Self-Reports.

Empirical research on PTG has relied on crisis victims' reports of stress-related positive outcomes. However, researchers should be skeptical of the accuracy (validity) of victims' reports of PTG. If PTG is assessed in the early stage of a crisis, positive reports might reflect the denial typically seen at this time (Janoff-Bulman, 1992). On a more general level, Shedler, Mayman, and Manis (1993) criticized most self-report measures of "mental health" for their inability to identify individuals who are distressed but who engage in "defensive denial."

In their influential review, Taylor and Brown (1988) documented three types of positive illusions that are endemic to everyday life: (a) unrealistic positive self-evaluations, (b) unrealistic perceptions of control, and (c) unrealistic optimism about the future. These positive illusions are most evident during a severe stressor, when a situation is evaluated as threatening and important (Taylor & Brown, 1988). Although they contended that these illusions are adaptive—for dealing with everyday life as well as with tragedies—they are illusions nevertheless, and therefore victims' self-reports of PTG should not be taken at face value.

There are several ways to attempt to validate self-report measures of PTG. One is to obtain corroborating reports of PTG from victims' significant others. To our knowledge, Park et al.'s (1996) research with the SRGS is the only study that has used this strategy.

Park et al. (1996) sampled college students' close friends and family members, and requested their assessment of the PTG experienced by the students. Specifically, 140 college students gave their consent for a friend or family member to be contacted. Informants were asked to complete the SRGS, rating the types of changes that they had seen in the respective student as a result of a specific negative event that had occurred during the past year. In addition, informants were asked whether their perceptions were based on personal observation of the students, statements made by the student, and/or the report of a third party. They also reported the length of their relationship with the student, as well as the closeness of that relationship. Of the 140 friends and family members who were contacted, 73 (52%) agreed to participate.

Park et al. (1996) found that students' mean scores on the SRGS did not differ from those provided by their friends and relatives. There was a significant positive relationship between students' SRGS scores and those provided by their informants, r (72) $= .21, p < .05$. When this analysis was restricted to informants who reported to be extremely close to the students, the correlation increased to r (56) $= .31, p < .05$.

Park et al. (1996) computed additional subject–informant correlations for selected subjects (e.g., students whose informants reported direct observation of event-related changes), and for a selected subsample of SRGS items (those that represented observable change), and all correlations were approximately .30. The subject–informant correlation was virtually identical when informants were friends versus parents.

In addition, Park et al. (1996) computed the intrapair agreement rate, corrected for chance by using the kappa statistic, for each of the 50 SRGS items, for a total of 73 subject–informant pairs. In these analyses, SRGS responses were coded as 0 or 1 (*no or some growth*) versus 2 (*a great deal of growth*). Twelve of the SRGS items achieved significant agreement, with kappas ranging from .26 to .40.

Overall, Park et al. (1996) found that the correlation between SRGS scores provided by subjects and their informants was significant, but low ($r = .21$ to .31). This correlation is lower than that reported in life events-corroboration studies (Cohen, 1988), but this is not surprising. Most life events checklists include many events that are public, and for which corroboration from a significant other would be expected. Most of the SRGS items are very private issues, including changes in life philosophy and coping skills. Given these constraints, a significant correlation between the SRGS scores provided by college students and their informants is encouraging.

On a more general level, research on the corroboration of PTG is quite complex. Even if agreement between victims and significant others is high, it is unclear if this represents validation of a PTG measure, or corroborators simply commenting on the PTG that victims verbally reported to them. It is possible that corroboration will vary depending on the PTG domain (behavior vs. feelings), significant other (spouse vs. friend), and their interaction (Park et al., 1996).

Validity of PTG Assessment: Use of Control Analyses.   Another strategy to validate reports of PTG is to compare them to more established paper and pencil measures that are administered before and after a crisis. Park et al. (1996) used this strategy to validate college students' self-reports on the SRGS. Several measures were administered prior to and after the experience of a stressor, and SRGS scores were analyzed for their relationship to change on these measures. Specifically, Park et al. found that SRGS scores were positively related to residual change in optimism, positive affectivity, the number of socially supportive others, and satisfaction with social support, lending some support to the validity of this measure of PTG.

One problem with this analysis, however, is the failure to assess state affect at the Time 2 assessment, when both the SRGS and the other postevent measures were completed. It is possible that concurrent mood at Time 2 served as a "third" variable, influencing scores on the SRGS and the other measures. Findings obtained by Hettler and Cohen (1996) support this "third" variable explanation. In a similar set of analyses, but with Time 2 state affect statistically controlled, Time 2 SRGS was not significantly related to residual change in optimism and social support.

Some other analyses by Park et al. (1996) provided interesting contrasts, and served to test the construct validity of the SRGS. In one of their studies, more than 200 college students completed the SRGS twice, once for their most negative event in the past year, and again for their most positive event in the past year. SRGS scores were higher for positive events than for negative events ($p < .001$). This difference was seen as consistent with PTG theory: Positive changes in, for example, self-concept and social relationships are expected after an extremely positive life experience, whereas they may or may not occur after an extremely negative experience.

In an additional analysis, and concurrent with the data collection just described, Park et al. (1996) administered the SRGS to a new sample of approximately 100 college students, with the instructions to respond to the SRGS items as they pertained to the past 12 months. This was an attempt to study growth that stemmed from maturation, not from the experience of a specific life event. The SRGS scores for this sample were higher than those for the most positive event ($p < .05$) and the most negative event ($p < .001$) reported by subjects in the concurrent study. This too is logical: One would expect more growth from college students during a 12-month period than from one positive event, which occurred, on average, only about 6 months prior to data collection.

A similar comparison was conducted by Tedeschi and Calhoun (1996). They sampled 117 college students, some of whom had experienced a trauma in the past year, and others who had not. Students completed the PTGI for the past year, without reference to a specific event. The trauma group scored higher on the PTGI than did the no-trauma group. This finding appears to be inconsistent with the finding of Park et al. (1996), that 1-year growth on the SRGS, without reference to an event, exceeded growth linked to a specific negative event.

Validity of PTG Assessment: Distinguishing Outcomes From Coping. One of the most complicated issues in PTG research is distinguishing perceived PTG as an *outcome* from perceived PTG as cognitive reinterpretation *coping*. The ability to make this distinction is critical to the validity of PTG assessment. This distinction is especially problematical when the PTG construct involves self-perceptions that overlap with positive reinterpretation coping (e.g., reports of finding meaning in the event). With this in mind, it might make sense not to assess PTG at a time when positive reinterpretation coping is most likely to occur. Unfortunately, it is unclear when positive reinterpretation coping is most likely to occur—during the early, middle, or later stages of a crisis, or once the crisis is resolved. The answer to this question probably depends on characteristics of the crisis and the respondents.

Park et al. (1996) examined the correlates of PTG in two groups of college students: One group had rated their recent crisis as at least somewhat resolved, and the other group had rated their recent crisis as not being at least somewhat resolved. The rationale for this comparison was the assumption that the former group would be less likely to be coping with their crisis, including positive reinterpretation coping; therefore, their scores on PTG would be less confounded with coping. However, the correlational results were virtually identical for the two groups.

In retrospect, however, this comparison is difficult to justify. The students reported a wide range of recent stressors, some quite traumatic (e.g., death of a relative) and others relatively minor (e.g., failed an exam). For some events, positive reinterpretation coping might be more likely in the later stages of a crisis, whereas for others it might be more likely in earlier stages. In other words, attempts at disentangling PTG outcomes from positive reinterpretation coping will probably have to be event-specific, relying on "norms" concerning the course of a crisis and the typical sequence of coping strategies. At the same time, however, we are aware that very little is known about coping sequences, despite considerable research on the transactional model of stress and coping (Lazarus & Folkman, 1984).

A related validity issue concerns distinguishing perceived PTG as an outcome from perceived PTG as an individual difference variable. In one of Park et al.'s (1996) studies, college students completed the SRGS for their most negative event as well as their most positive event during the past year.

The two SRGS scores were strongly correlated ($r = .60, p < .001$). These same subjects also completed the SRGS 6 months later, for their most negative event during that interval. SRGS scores for negative events were fairly stable over time ($r = .59, p < .001$). These findings suggest that PTG responses reflect, in part, individual differences that are stable over time, and across situations. Results from Thompson (1985) and McRae (1989) are consistent with this conclusion.

Correlates of the PTGI and SRGS.   Neither scale is significantly correlated with a measure of social desirability. Women score higher than men on both the PTGI and the SRGS (Hettler & Cohen, 1996; Park et al., 1996; Tedeschi & Calhoun, 1996). In a cross-sectional analysis, Tedeschi and Calhoun found that PTGI scores were significantly positively related to optimism, religious participation, and the personality dimensions of extraversion, openness to experience, agreeableness, and conscientiousness.

In one of the studies reported by Park et al. (1996), college students completed questionnaires on two occasions, separated by about 6 months. At both Time 1 and Time 2, students completed the SRGS, rated their most negative event on a variety of dimensions (e.g., controllability), and completed measures of optimism, instrinsic religiousness, perceived social support, and dispositional affectivity (trait negative and positive affect). At Time 2, the students also completed measures of recent life events, coping (with their most negative event since time 1; 15 subscales), and the impact (avoidance, intrusion) of their most negative event since Time 1.

A multiple regression analysis ($N = 142$) was conducted to predict Time 2 SRGS scores (for the most negative event reported at Time 2). The order of predictors was (a) gender; (b) Time 1 scores on intrinsic religiousness, negative and positive affectivity, social support satisfaction, and optimism; (c) characteristics of the most negative event reported at Time 2, specifically its stressfulness at the time of occurrence, how long ago it occurred, and the controllability of its occurrence; (d) Time 2 scores on positive reinterpretation coping and acceptance coping with the most negative event reported at Time 2; (e) the degree to which the Time 2 negative event was resolved at the time of data collection; and (f) Time 2 number of negative life events and number of positive life events. This order of predictor blocks was based, in part, on Schaefer and Moos' (1992) model of stress-related growth.

When entered in this order, there were significant positive effects for intrinsic religiousness, social support satisfaction, acceptance coping, positive reinterpretation coping, and number of positive life events. In the full model, when all predictors were tested simultaneously, these predictors remained significant, and an additional variable emerged as significant (in the positive direction)—the stressfulness of the most negative event at the time of occurrence.

The finding that social support satisfaction and number of positive life events were significant predictors of growth is consistent with Hobfoll's (1989) resource conservation model of stress: Stress can produce increases in resources, but only for those individuals who begin with a large reservoir of preevent resources. In other words, the rich get richer. The positive relationship between event stressfulness and growth is consistent with the views of Tedeschi and Calhoun (1995), who hypothesized that PTG is, in part, the end product of struggling with a painful stressor.

Hettler and Cohen (1996), in their study of adult church members, also examined the correlates of the SRGS. Negative event characteristics (e.g., stressfulness, controllability) were not significantly related to the SRGS. Positive reinterpretation coping was significantly and positively related to the SRGS ($p < .001$), but acceptance coping was not. As expected, religious coping was strongly and positively related ($p < .001$) to stress-related growth in this sample.

The PTGI and SRGS are new scales. Preliminary analyses suggest that they have good psychometric properties, although additional research is needed. They represent the state of the art in the quantitative assessment of PTG. However, PTG is such a complex and personal construct that it makes sense for researchers to also consider *qualitative* approaches to PTG assessment. Specifically, some qualitative methods might be able to provide information about PTG that quantitative methods cannot.

Qualitative Assessment of PTG

Lincoln and Guba (1985) identified five approaches to qualitative research: interviewing, observation, nonverbal communication, documents and records, and other unobtrusive measures. Tedeschi and Calhoun (1995) suggested that unstructured interviews and analysis of narratives and accounts of experience are ideally suited for the qualitative assessment of PTG.

Unstructured Interviews. Open-ended interview questions do not restrict the respondent to the types of PTG that the researcher has defined in advance of the study. Consequently, the individual's responses will probably be genuine and unique, rather than a reaction to the demand characteristics of the research context.

An unstructured interview format allows the respondent to have an interactive role with the researcher in determining the direction of the interview. Such a format also allows the researcher to take unusual responses into account, whereas a more quantitative study would be forced to discard unusual and hard-to-categorize responses. In general, in qualitative research, there is a greater emphasis on taking the individual's perspective into account. There is usually more give and take between the respondent and researcher in an unstructured interview, which can lead to a better understanding of the respondent's point of view.

Another advantage of an unstructured interview is that, in the process of the respondent telling his or her story, it may become clear to the researcher how growth has occurred. In other words, the researcher may begin to understand whether the individual has integrated the event into his or her life story and has succeeded in "account-making" (Harvey, Weber, & Orbuch, 1990). In an unstructured interview, there is an excellent opportunity to analyze the language, form, and idiosyncracies of people's life stories. Many narrative analysts suggest that it is the manner in which a story is told that provides the most useful qualitative information (Riessman, 1993; Sarbin, 1986; Strauss, 1987). One of the cornerstones of Taylor's (1983) theory of cognitive adaptation is victims' natural motivation to seek meaning in a tragedy. An unstructured interview might provide rich qualitative data that contribute to the assessment of meaning.

Documents and Observation. Some qualitative data on PTG might also be obtained from documents and observation. If a respondent is in therapy, the therapist's process notes might document PTG. Similarly, school report cards and work evaluations might document PTG over time. If a respondent has kept a diary, entries could provide rich qualitative data on PTG.

Observations by others over time could also be useful in qualitative research on PTG. Psychotherapists, teachers, supervisors, and significant others (spouses, friends, parents) might be in a good position to provide interesting insights into how a respondent has changed as a result of a stressful life event.

Of course, one of the major limitations of qualitative research is the subjective and impressionistic nature of the data. However, at the least, qualitative research might prove very useful in the development of quantitative instruments of PTG. Specific interview questions, coding systems to be used in quantitative analyses of interview responses, and items on paper and pencil tests of PTG, can be based on qualitative data obtained from unstructured interviews, documents, and observations from others. For example, several items on the SRGS were based on qualitative data obtained by Park and Cohen (1993). In their study, college students were interviewed about their perceived growth from the recent death of a close friend. It is our hope that future attempts to assess PTG will reflect a more systematic integration of qualitative and quantitative strategies.

Unresolved Issues in PTG Assessment

Throughout this chapter, we have addressed a number of conceptual and methodological issues in the assessment of PTG. In this section, we attempt to tie up "loose ends" by presenting some additional aspects related to the measurement of PTG.

Time Frame of PTG Assessment.   One issue that remains unresolved is the time frame for the assessment of PTG. In other words, when should stress-related growth be measured? Should PTG be assessed weeks, months, or years after the occurrence of a stressful event?

The time frame for the assessment of PTG is dependent on the researcher's model of stress-related growth, which in turn can be influenced by the nature of the specific crisis, the characteristics of the respondents, and the specific growth-related constructs that will be measured. For some crises, and for some outcomes, PTG might be evident soon after the stressor occurs, and might even co-occur with distress. For example, evaluation of possible increases in social support might make sense weeks after a cancer diagnosis, whereas evaluation of changes in life philosophy might seem inappropriate at that time, because these changes would be more likely to occur only after months or years had elapsed. With this in mind, it is interesting to note the findings of Affleck et al. (1987). They interviewed several hundred men after they had experienced a heart attack. The first interview occurred approximately 7 weeks after the attack, and the second interview occurred approximately 8 years later. At the first interview, 12% of the men reported that they had experienced a positive change in life philosophy, whereas this percentage rose to 25% at the second interview.

In the empirical literature, the most frequent time frame for the assessment of PTG is *years* after the occurrence of an event. For example, Aldwin et al. (1994) and Elder and Clipp (1989) assessed the positive consequences of military experience *decades* after that experience. Silver, Boon, and Stones (1983) and McMillen et al. (1995) assessed perceived benefits from childhood sexual abuse approximately 20 years after the experience. Lehman et al. (1993) interviewed approximately 100 adults who had lost a spouse or child in an automobile accident. The interview was administered about 5 years after the accident. Most of the rape victims sampled by Burt and Katz (1987) completed measures at least 1 year post-rape. In the study by Joseph et al. (1993), participants completed questionnaires approximately 18 months after the sinking of their ship.

In their study of cancer patients, Collins et al. (1990) assessed positive consequences approximately 3 years after diagnosis. Zemore and Shepel (1989) also studied cancer patients, assessing emotional social support from family and friends approximately 2 years after diagnosis. In still another study of cancer patients, Curbow et al. (1993) surveyed survivors of bone marrow transplantation approximately 4 years after the operation.

The research of Affleck and colleagues is an exception, insofar as they assessed PTG weeks after the occurrence of a medical crisis. Specifically, Affleck et al. (1985) sampled 42 mothers of newborns with serious medical problems. The mothers were interviewed at home immediately after their infants were discharged from the hospital, several weeks after delivery. In addition, Affleck et al. (1987) interviewed several hundred adult men approximately 7 weeks (as well as 8 years) after their first heart attack.

For both the SRGS (Park et al., 1996) and PTGI (Tedeschi & Calhoun, 1996), the timing of their administration, by definition, delimits a specific time frame for PTG. In their initial series of studies, Park et al. (1996) administered the SRGS several months after the occurrence of a stressor. In the initial administration of the PTGI, subjects were college students who indicated that they had experienced a significant negative life event during the past 5 years.

In our opinion, an important topic for future research is the assessment of PTG as it relates to the amount of time that has elapsed since the occurrence of a trauma. As mentioned previously, some aspects of PTG might appear soon after the occurrence of a crisis, whereas other aspects might not be evident until years had elapsed. Also, the determinants (predictors) of PTG might vary as a function of time frame; for example, event severity might serve as a significant positive predictor of PTG, but only when growth is assessed years after the trauma.

Use of Control Groups. An interesting strategy to validate the assessment of PTG is to include a control group who did not experience a specific crisis, and to compare victims' and control subjects' scores on adjustment and so forth. In one of their studies, Tedeschi and Calhoun (1996) compared the growth scores of college students who either did or did not experience a major trauma in the previous year. Tedeschi and Calhoun did not focus on a specific stressor. There are, however, two studies that did, and they both have interesting implications for future research.

Lehman et al. (1993) used this strategy in their study of adults who had lost a spouse or child in the past several years. The control subjects were adults who were matched on such variables as sex, age, and income. They found that, compared to the control participants, the bereaved respondents reported more psychiatric symptoms and less happiness; this was true even for those bereaved respondents who, when interviewed about their tragedy, reported positive changes in their life.

But, it is possible that Lehman et al.'s (1993) outcome measures were insensitive to the types of changes reported or experienced by the bereaved respondents, which included changes in wisdom, maturity, coping flexibility, etc. Specifically, Lehman et al. administered the SCL-90R (Derogatis, Rickels, & Rock, 1976), which measures various psychological symptoms including depression, somatization, and anxiety, and a modified version of eight positive items from Bradburn's (1969) Affects Balance Scale, which assesses psychological well-being. The fact that the victims reported more symptoms than did the controls does not preclude the possibility that the victims also would have scored higher on such constructs as maturity and coping skills. As shown by Elder and Clipp (1989), in their study of the effects of military service, it is possible for a tragedy or hardship to simultaneously produce negative and positive outcomes. In addition, as acknowledged by Lehman et al., it is possible that because so much time had elapsed since the time of the spouse's or child's death (about 5 years), some respondents might have underreported growth because some positive changes were incorporated and were no longer perceived as event-related benefits.

Zemore and Shepel (1989) also used a control group. They sampled approximately 300 women who had a mastectomy in the past 2 years, and compared them to approximately 100 women who were evaluated for breast cancer (because of a lump) but with a negative medical finding. One of the major outcome measures was a three-item scale of emotional social support from family and friends. Zemore and Shepel found that the cancer patients had higher scores than the controls.

An ideal research design would include preevent and postevent assessment of a range of personality, coping, and adjustment measures, and would compare victims of a specific crisis with control participants. Lehman et al. (1993) and Zemore and Shepel (1989) included postevent assessment of victims and control subjects, but were unable to obtain baseline (preevent) measures for either group. Of course, preevent assessment is extremely difficult to accomplish, because it requires identification of crisis victims before the crisis has occurred. Preevent measurement is possible when a large group is assessed, and when the event is not uncommon (e.g., death of a relative). It is also possible in those situations in which individuals are identified as being at-risk for a specific problem, for example, medical screening (Zemore & Shepel, 1989).

When respondents report their PTG in an interview or on a paper and pencil scale, it is possible that they are comparing their current postevent functioning with their functioning during the peak of the crisis, and not with their functioning prior to the event (Tedeschi & Calhoun, 1995). This bias would result in inflated reports of PTG. Inclusion of both pre-event and post-event measures would serve as a check on this possible response tendency.

PTG in Children and Adolescents. Research on PTG in children and adolescents is an important topic that, to date, has been neglected (see Aldwin & Sutton, chap. 3, this volume). It is possible that for these samples, growth on some dimensions might require years to become evident. A consequence of this is the problem of how to assess constructs over time with equivalent instruments; for example, measures of coping or locus of control that are appropriate for middle school children are not appropriate for high school children. In addition, longitudinal research of PTG in children requires the ability to distinguish PTG from a specific event from PTG from other events, and from change that results from normal maturational processes. Because children are less resilient than adults, we assume that severe stressors experienced during childhood, as compared to adulthood, have less potential for producing PTG, although this is an empirical question.

PTG as a Group or Organizational Variable. Virtually all attempts to assess PTG have focused on the individual. However, it is easy to imagine PTG that occurs to a group, such as a family or classroom, an institution, such as a college or hospital, or larger social groups (see Bloom, chap. 8, this volume). For example, the death of a child will have profound effects on the family dynamics of the surviving family members, or on the climate in the classroom in which the child was a student. Assessment of PTG in these contexts requires scales that are designed to measure group or organizational variables.

CONCLUSION

We anticipate that in the next several years, there will be substantive advances in PTG theory, as researchers continue to develop and refine conceptual models of stress-related growth (e.g., Schaefer & Moos, 1992; Tedeschi & Calhoun, 1995). We also anticipate that, with the publication of the PTGI (Tedeschi & Calhoun, 1996) and the SRGS (Park et al., 1996), and the publication of this book, researchers will become more sophisticated in their assessment of PTG. In this chapter, we have attempted to identify the major issues and obstacles in the assessment of PTG, and to provide suggestions for improving assessment practices. At the same time, however, we realize the complexity of PTG assessment, because it includes the measurement of such variables as philosophy of life, values, and religious beliefs.

REFERENCES

Affleck, G., Tennen, H., Croog, S., & Levine, S. (1987). Causal attribution, perceived benefits, and morbidity after a heart attack: An 8-year study. *Journal of Consulting and Clinical Psychology, 55,* 29–35.

Affleck, G., Tennen, H., & Gershman, K. (1985). Mastery, meaning, and protection from future harm. *American Journal of Mental Deficiency, 89,* 653–656.

Aldwin, C., Levenson, M., & Spiro, A. (1994). Vulnerability and resilience to combat exposure: Can stress have lifelong effects? *Psychology and Aging, 9,* 34–44.

Bradburn, N. (1969). *The structure of psychological well-being.* Chicago: Aldine-Atherton.

Burt, M., & Katz, B. (1987). Dimensions of recovery from rape. *Journal of Interpersonal Violence, 2,* 57–81.

Caplan, G. (1964). *Principles of preventive psychiatry.* New York: Basic Books.

Cohen, L. H. (1988). Measurement of life events. In L. H. Cohen (Ed.), *Life events and psychological functioning: Theoretical and methodological issues* (pp. 11–30). Newbury Park, CA: Sage.

Collins, R., Taylor, S., & Skokan, L. (1990). A better world or a shattered vision: Changes in life perspectives following victimization. *Social Cognition, 8,* 263–285.

Curbow, B., Somerfield, M., Baker, F., Wingard, J., & Legro, M. (1993). Personal changes, dispositional optimism, and psychological adjustment to bone marrow transplantation. *Journal of Behavioral Medicine, 16,* 423–443.

Derogatis, L., Rickels, K., & Rock, A. (1976). The SCL-90 and the MMPI: A step in the validation of a new self-report scale. *British Journal of Psychiatry, 128,* 280–289.

Ebersole, P., & Flores, J. (1989). Positive impact of life crises. *Journal of Social Behavior and Personality, 4,* 463–469.

Elder, G., & Clipp, E. (1989). Combat experience and emotional health: Impairment and resilience in later life. *Journal of Personality, 57,* 311–341.

Frankl, V. (1963). *Man's search for meaning: An introduction to logotherapy.* New York: Pocket Books.

Frazier, P., Byrne, C., & Klein, C. (1995, August). *Resilience among sexual assault survivors.* Poster presented at the annual meeting of the American Psychological Association, New York.

Harvey, J., Weber, A., & Orbuch, T. (1990). *Interpersonal accounts.* Cambridge, MA: Basil Blackwell.

Hettler, T. R., & Cohen, L. H. (1996). *Stress-related growth among adult church members.* Unpublished raw data.

Hobfoll, S. (1989). Conservation of resources: A new attempt at conceptualizing stress. *American Psychologist, 44,* 513–524.

Janoff-Bulman, R. (1992). *Shattered assumptions.* New York: The Free Press.

Joseph, S., Williams, R., & Yule, W. (1993). Changes in outlook following disaster: The preliminary development of a measure to assess positive and negative responses. *Journal of Traumatic Stress, 6,* 271–279.

Lazarus, R., & Folkman, S. (1984). *Stress, appraisal, and coping.* New York: Springer.

Lehman, D., Davis, C., DeLongis, A., Wortman, C., Bluck, S., Mandel, D., & Ellard, J. (1993). Positive and negative life changes following bereavement and their relations to adjustment. *Journal of Social and Clinical Psychology, 12,* 90–112.

Lincoln, Y., & Guba, E. (1985). *Naturalistic inquiry.* Beverly Hills, CA: Sage.

McMillen, C., Zuravin, S., & Rideout, G. (1995). Perceived benefits from child sexual abuse. *Journal of Consulting and Clinical Psychology, 63,* 1037–1043.

McRae, R. (1989). Age differences and changes in the use of coping mechanisms. *Journal of Gerontology: Psychological Sciences, 44,* 161–169.

Mendola, R., Tennen, H., Affleck, G., & McCann, L., & Fitzgerald, T. (1990). Appraisal and adaptation among women with impaired fertility. *Cognitive Therapy and Research, 14,* 79–93.

Park, C. L., & Cohen, L. H. (1993). Religious and nonreligious coping with the death of a friend. *Cognitive Therapy and Research, 17,* 561–577.

Park, C. L., Cohen, L. H., & Murch, R. (1995). *Item-total correlations for the SRGS.* Unpublished raw data.

Park, C. L., Cohen, L. H., & Murch, R. (1996). Assessment and prediction of stress-related growth. *Journal of Personality, 64,* 71–105.

Riessman, C. (1993). *Narrative analysis.* Newbury Park, CA: Sage.

Sarbin, T. (Ed). (1986). *Narrative psychology: The storied nature of human conduct.* New York: Praeger.

Schaefer, J., & Moos, R. (1992). Life crises and personal growth. In B. Carpenter (Ed.), *Personal coping: Theory, research, and application* (pp. 149–170). Westport, CT: Praeger.

Shedler, J., Mayman, M., & Manis, M. (1993). The illusion of mental health. *American Psychologist, 48,* 1117–1131.

Silver, R., Boon, C., & Stones, M. (1983). Searching for meaning in misfortune: Making sense of incest. *Journal of Social Issues, 39,* 81–102.

Strauss, A. (1987). *Qualitative analysis for social scientists.* Cambridge, England: Cambridge University Press.

Taylor, S. (1983). Adjustment to threatening events. A theory of cognitive adaptation. *American Psychologist, 38,* 1161–1173.

Taylor, S., & Brown, J. (1988). Illusion and well-being: A social psychological perspective on mental health. *Psychological Bulletin, 103,* 193–210.

Tedeschi, R., & Calhoun, L. (1995). *Trauma and transformation.* Thousand Oaks, CA: Sage.

Tedeschi, R., & Calhoun, L. (1996). The Post-Traumatic Growth Inventory: Measuring the positive legacy of trauma. *Journal of Traumatic Stress, 9,* 455–471.

Thompson, S. (1985). Finding positive meaning in a stressful event and coping. *Basic and Applied Social Psychology, 6,* 279–295.

Zemore, R., & Shepel, L. (1989). Effects of breast cancer and mastectomy on emotional support and adjustment. *Social Science and Medicine, 28,* 19–27.

3

A Developmental Perspective on Posttraumatic Growth

Carolyn M. Aldwin
Karen J. Sutton
University of California at Davis

Some of the most fascinating aspects of the study of stress and trauma are its long-term outcomes—how is it that the same phenomenon can have tremendously different effects in different individuals? Although almost no one disputes the fact that psychosocial stress can have negative impacts on well-being, whether physical, psychological, or social, there is growing evidence of the positive concomitants of undergoing stress and trauma (for reviews, see Tedeschi, Park, & Calhoun, chap. 1, this volume). We have argued elsewhere that in order to understand this phenomenon, it is necessary to take a developmental perspective (Aldwin, 1994; Aldwin & Stokols, 1988). This can be done in two ways. The macro-perspective simply examines the long-term outcomes of organisms which have been stressed, especially vis-à-vis their ability to respond to later stressors, whereas the micro-perspective seeks to understand the processes through which stress can have long-term effects.

In this chapter we examine both macro- and micro-developmental processes. We review both the animal and the human literature looking at the positive long-term outcomes of stress, primarily in young organisms, and examine the processes by which these long-term outcomes may occur. First, however, we present the theoretical model that has guided our research.

TOWARD A DEVIATION
AMPLIFICATION MODEL

While early systems theory models focused on homeostasis (cf. von Bertalanffy, 1969), Maruyama (1963) was interested in how systems can promote change. He hypothesized two types of processes, deviation-countering and deviation-amplifying. Deviation-countering processes are best characterized in terms of negative feedback loops, such as those involved in thermostats or in regulating blood pressure. Namely, if a phenomenon deviates too much from baseline, negative feedback loops become activated to return the organisms to homeostasis. However, deviation-amplification models involve positive feedback loops, which results in the intensification of the change. It is likely that systems have both positive and negative feedback loops, and the relative proportion of these can result in either a countering or amplifying process.

Aldwin and Stokols (1988) sought to adapt this model to the long-term outcomes of stress. By definition, stressors involve a change of some sort in an individual's life (cf. Holmes & Rahe, 1967). However, in many (or perhaps most) situations, deviation-countering processes return the individual to homeostasis. In fact, in some situations, deviation-amplifying processes can result in either positive or negative long-term change. Aldwin and Stokols hypothesized that stressor characteristics may promote either deviation-amplifying or countering processes. Stressors which are less severe, have a gradual onset, and which are restricted to one domain of an individual's life (e.g., family, work, or health) are less likely to result in long-term change, whereas those which have a rapid onset, affect multiple domains, and are more severe are more likely to result in amplifying processes. Certainly, traumatic processes fit this definition. Note, however, that this model forms a framework only for specifying the conditions under which long-term change can result, but does not specify the factors which can lead to positive or negative change.

In subsequent publications (Aldwin, Sutton, & Lachman, 1996), we defined positive change as the development of coping resources (cf. Hobfoll & Lilly, 1993), and negative change as their depletion. Coping resources include emotional, tangible, and philosophical factors such as mastery, self-esteem, increases in coping repertoires, and positive changes in philosophy toward life. Aldwin (1994) hypothesized that a variety of person and situational factors may promote either positive or negative change. Drawing largely from the vulnerability and resilience literature, which generally studies children in largely dysfunctional families, factors such as social support, intelligence, a "sunny" disposition, effective coping, and determination coupled with flexibility in attitudes may result in the development of resources, whereas social isolation and/or negative social interactions, a difficult temperament, poor coping strategies, and lack of social and cultural resources may result in the depletion of resources and result in negative adaptive spirals (cf. Myrdal, 1962; Smith, 1968). Presumably, the development of resources leads to positive adaptive spirals, which may be indexed by increased resilience to future stress. Hobfoll and Lilly (1993) suggested that whether a stressful episode results in resource depletion or gain is in part dependent on an individual's initial resource level. However, as we shall see, the physiological studies of the positive and negative long-term effects of stress in young organisms focus more on stressor characteristics, such as their temporal sequencing.

PHYSIOLOGICAL STUDIES

This section draws on earlier reviews of the literature on the long-term physiological outcomes of stress in early childhood (Aldwin, 1994; Aldwin & Stokols, 1988). New research examining possible mechanisms will also be reviewed.

Studies of Stress in Early Life

The earliest models for studying the long-term physiological effects of stress subjected infant mice and rats in the first 10 days of life to environmental stressors such as handling or mild electric shock (Denenberg, 1964; Levine, 1966; Levine, Haltmeyer, Karas, & Denenberg, 1967). These animals matured at a more rapid rate than their non-stressed peers (for reviews see Dienstbier, 1989; Gray, 1981). They grew hair and opened their eyes earlier, showed better myelinization and locomotion, and reached puberty at younger ages. As adults, infant-handled rodents exhibit more exploratory behavior and are less likely to become immobilized during stress. They also have a different neuroendocrine response to stress, showing both heightened and more rapid response in epinephrine and norepinephrine, coupled with a faster return to baseline. Infant-handled rats may also exhibit stronger responses to immune challenges (Solomon & Amkraut, 1981).

Anthropologist J. Whiting and his colleagues examined cross-cultural data to determine whether there are similar effects of exposure to environmental stress in human infants (for a review, see Landauer & Whiting,

1981). In several samples, average adult physical stature was significantly higher in those cultures with stressful procedures in the first 2 years of life (such as circumcision, scarification, or sleeping apart from parents), than in those which did not subject infants to such stressful stimuli. Early vaccination may also enhance physical growth, apart from any effect on morbidity and mortality. More recent work by Belsky, Steinberg, and Draper (1991) also associated childhood stressors with the earlier onset of puberty. However, other work has shown that stressors in young organisms can suppress growth hormone levels, leading to poor growth and failure to thrive (see Field, 1992). Thus, in keeping with the deviation amplification model proposed above, stress may have either positive or negative consequences—even in the same system.

Even when enhanced growth occurs, however, it is by no means a completely positive outcome. Hilakivi-Clark, Wright, and Lippman (1993) confirmed that infant-handled rats showed better growth patterns and were more resistant to immobilization stress, but they also were more susceptible to mammary tumors. In part, the faster weight gain associated with higher fat levels may have put them at increased risk for estrogen-related tumors. Further, stress may enhance tumor growth (Romero et al., 1992). Glucocorticoids inhibit glucose transporters which can lead to higher levels of circulating glucose; however, some tumor cells are resistant to this suppression, so that "glucose stores throughout the body are, in effect, preferentially shunted to such tumors under stress" (Romero et al., 1992, p. 11084).

Stress can also lead to cell death, or apoptosis (Obeid & Hannun, 1995). However, by stopping cell proliferation, stress may allow time for DNA recovery mechanisms to work (Wu & Lozano, 1994). Some of the most controversial but fascinating research suggests that, under some conditions, exposure to stressors can lead to hormesis, or an increased resistance to death. Holtzman (1995) reviewed work showing that low levels of exposure to radiation may be associated with decreased levels of cancer deaths, in part because very low levels can stimulate DNA repair enzymes which may serve as a protective factor. Johnson and colleagues (Lithgow, White, Hinerfeld, & Johnson, 1994; Lithgow, White, Melov, & Johnson, 1995) have also shown that flat worms exposed to non-lethal increases in heat showed greater resilience to future heat stress, staying alive in temperatures that killed non-exposed flatworms.

Thus, stress appears to have complex and somewhat contradictory results. It can result in suppression or enhancement of growth, and promote or delay processes leading to death. Delineating the conditions under which these dichotomously opposed outcomes can occur is perhaps one of the most important areas for future stress research. Toward this end, some researchers have been examining contextual factors of stress. For example, Dienstbier (1989, 1992) developed a neuroendocrine model to delineate when vulnerability or resilience, which he terms "physiological toughness" results from exposure to stress. According to Dienstbier (1992, p. 367), "regular exposure to challenges and stressors followed by adequate recovery periods can cause peripheral and central physiological changes that increase one's future capacity for more positive forms of arousal and the suppression of more costly forms of arousal." Presumably, chronic stressors which do not allow for recovery may be associated with more negative forms of arousal.

Dienstbier (1992) distinguished between two types of arousal. The first involves hypothalamic stimulation of the sympathetic nervous system (SNS), leading to the arousal of the adrenal medulla, which releases noradrenaline. The second type of arousal depends on hypothalamic stimulation of the pituitary, which releases adrenocorticotropin (ACTH), which in turn releases cortisol. The first type of arousal is very short-lived, as peripheral catecholamines have a half-life of under 2 minutes, and is associated with better performance on cognitive and physical tasks, as well as emotional stability. The second type of arousal is less beneficial, has a slower onset, and lasts longer, as corticosteroids have a half-life of about 90 minutes, and may interfere with performance.

Early exposure to stressors can result in what Dienstbier terms the "ideal pattern" of SNS arousal in adulthood, characterized by low base rates of catecholamines, coupled with rapid increases in response to stress, and then a rapid return to baseline levels, while the optimal pattern for cortisol-mediated arousal is for low base rates coupled with delayed responses with challenge or stress. This pattern is associated with enhanced performance on a variety of tasks. For reasons that are not clear, short-term depletion of central catecholamines can lead to both an increased ability to generate catecholamines and long-term resistance to central catecholamine depletion for future stressors. Chronically elevated catecholamine base rates are associated with poorer psychological adjustment, as well as increased prevalence of health problems. Dienstbier (1992) also reviewed research showing that systematic aerobic training also results in both a greater sensitivity to catecholamines and as well as an increased capacity to generate them under maximal energy conditions.

Whether stress results in increased physiological resilience or vulnerability may depend on the temporal patterning of stressors. Intermittent stressors, allowing for recovery between episodes, are associated with more beneficial catecholamine and cortisol arousal patterns. However, continuous stressors do not allow the organism to recover, resulting in both catecholamine and cortisol depletion, similar to Selye's (1956) third stage in the General Adaptation Syndrome (exhaustion).

Dienstbier (1989) argued that similar patterns can be seen in the effect of stress on immune functioning. In adulthood, exposure to environmental stressors can retard tumor growth rates in mice and rats under certain circumstances (for reviews see Monjan, 1981; Riley, Fitzmaurice, & Spachman, 1981). Important factors in immunoenhancement versus immunosuppression appear to be the duration and timing of stress. Counterintuitively, chronic stress may enhance immune system functioning, if it occurs prior to exposure to chemical or biological carcinogens. However, if stress occurs after the exposure, immunosuppression may result (Joasoo & McKenzie, 1976; Monjan & Collector, 1977; Newberry, 1976; Newberry & Songbush, 1979; Rashkis, 1952; Solomon, 1969; Solomon & Amkraut, 1981).

The fact that stress appears to have contradictory effects on physiological development and senescence accords with the deviation-amplification model. Intermittent stress and/or challenges coupled with appropriate environmental resources may promote growth processes in young organisms, increase neuroendocrine resilience to future stress, and enhance DNA repair mechanisms, perhaps leading to protection against senescence. However, chronic stress, especially in the absence of resources which allow adequate recovery, may suppress growth hormones, enhance tumor growth, and hasten senescence. As shown in the following section, similar processes can be seen in psychosocial development.

STUDIES OF PSYCHOSOCIAL OUTCOMES IN CHILDREN

The notion that stress can have positive effects on development in children may, at first, sound counterintuitive as most research indicates that the effects are primarily negative. Nevertheless, long-term effects of stress are not always exclusively negative and some children thrive despite experiencing even extreme forms of stress. How, then, do these children differ from those who do not do as well? Can some children grow and develop in positive directions as a result of experiencing stress? In this section, we consider the possibility that stress-related growth occurs in developing children and explore the factors which predict the likelihood of this growth. First, however, we briefly review the literature on how children survive trauma, that is, studies of vulnerability and resilience.

Vulnerability and Resilience

A majority of studies have shown that stress has negative effects on children (Berlinsky & Biller, 1982; Furman, 1974; Rutter, 1981). Interest in the long-term effects of trauma in children has been propelled by incidents such as the school bus hijacking in Chowchilla and the grammar school shooting in Stockton, California (Armsworth & Holaday, 1993). These are examples of trauma that can affect, not only those directly involved, but those who are indirectly involved, such as family members. In addition to incidents of this type, children may experience traumatic stress in their homes and schools too often in the form of abuse, death, and violence. Experiencing trauma in childhood can have several major cognitive, emotional, behavioral, and physiological effects (Armsworth & Holaday, 1993; Roesler & McKenzie, 1994). Nevertheless, some children show resilience to major stresses like war, poverty, or family mental illness (Felsman & Vaillant, 1987; Garmezy, 1983; Murphy & Moriarty, 1976; Werner & Smith, 1982, 1992) and, in some cases, show enhanced functioning later in life (Anthony, 1987a, 1987b).

Vulnerable children show a high likelihood of becoming susceptible to psychological disorder in the presence of biological or psychosocial risk factors. However, protective factors can decrease the likelihood of negative developmental outcomes. They may operate in a way that is "catalytic" (Rutter, 1989) by attenuating the initial impact of a stressor or any negative chain reactions. Protective factors may support healthy coping, increase self-esteem and mastery, and lead to new opportunities for growth (see Aldwin, Sutton, & Lachman, 1996). Resilient children are those who have benefited from protective factors, show a pattern of successful adaptation, and are expected to continue to do well despite the presence of powerful risk factors (for a review, see Werner & Smith, 1992).

A number of studies have investigated the protec.tive factors that relate to high functioning in vulnerable children, including studies of children living with a mentally ill parent (Garmezy & Masten, 1986; Masten, Best, & Garmezy, 1990; Worland, Janes, Anthony, McGinnis, & Cass, 1984) or in poverty (Felsman & Vaillant, 1987; Long & Vaillant, 1984; Rutter, 1987; Werner & Smith, 1982, 1992). It is unusual for more than half of these children to develop serious or persistent problems and, surprisingly, a large percentage do quite well. Some factors seem to buffer stress and are universal as they emerge regardless of cohort, social class, or ethnicity. They fall into the following categories: gender, cognitive skills, temperament, and positive social interactions (Garmezy & Masten, 1986).

Boys are more vulnerable to stress than girls, both physiologically and psychologically (Rutter, 1979, 1983; Werner & Smith, 1982) and show a greater risk for developing disruptive behavior problems in response to stressful events like divorce (Wallerstein, 1991) and natural disaster (Garmezy & Rutter, 1983). However, girls are more likely to become depressed especially in adolescence (Nolen-Hoeksema, 1995), a negative outcome that may not be as readily apparent as the behavior problems of boys.

In addition to gender, high IQ predicts positive functioning, despite major stress, and resilient children are often more skilled and intelligent. There may be a variety of reasons why intelligence is a protective factor. Children with higher than average intelligence may develop more effective coping skills. In addition, functioning well at school and succeeding academically can provide a sense of achievement and self-esteem that, in turn, can buffer the effects of stress in other domains of life. One exception to this relationship between intelligence and resilience, however, was a study by Luthar (1991) showing that intelligent girls did worse than their peers during adolescence. However, this may be due to a cultural bias against intelligence in adolescent females.

Children with easy-going temperaments (Wyman, Cowen, Work, & Parker, 1991) and "sunny" dispositions (Garmezy, 1983) tend to function better overall both in childhood and later on in adulthood. These children may be less prone to depression and anxiety and, in turn, cope better with stress. They also tend to have higher levels of self-esteem and self-efficacy (Cowen, Wyman, Work, & Parker, 1990) that may contribute to psychological strength in the face of stress and protect them from developing the types of social and behavioral problems that less resilient children develop. How does the relationship between easygoing temperament and positive self-esteem operate? Having a pleasant disposition may increase the likelihood of soliciting positive interactions with adults and peers, thus contributing to the development of positive models of the self and the expectations of others.

Interestingly, the presence of positive social interaction in childhood is a factor which distinguishes resilient children from their less resilient peers. Research consistently shows that the presence of at least one supportive adult, either inside or outside of the immediate family can serve as a powerful protective factor (see Werner & Smith, 1992). For instance, in families with one mentally ill parent, identification with the healthy parent can provide a model of healthy functioning and a stable person on whom to rely for positive and appropriate feedback (Garmezy, 1983; Mosher, Pollin, & Stebenau, 1971). Further, in adolescence, finding a mate who is stable and supportive can help a vulnerable individual deal with a troubled past (Vaillant, 1993; Werner & Smith, 1992).

In summary, resilient children often possess characteristics which seem to protect them from developing problems later in life. Gender, intelligence, an easygoing temperament, and the quality of relationships with others, all contribute to the likelihood of positive adaptation despite the presence of powerful risk factors.

These factors provide a reasonable profile of the resilient child, yet how does the way in which one copes with stress relate to resilience? Wolin and Wolin (1993) found differences between vulnerable and resilient children in how they coped. For instance, vulnerable children tend to dwell more on their past, blame others (including parents) for their own failures, and subsequently see themselves as helpless victims. Resilient children, on the other hand, build on their strengths and deliberately strive to make better decisions than did their parents. They often make conscious, planned decisions to marry into strong, healthy families, and work hard to build a cohesive family of their own.

Although resilient children do better than we might expect, it is never-theless important to recognize that no child is completely invulnerable to stress and, although they appear to function quite well, resilient children may often pay a price in other areas (Anthony, 1987b). They may show a mixture of competence and vulnerability, the combination of which may change over time (Murphy & Moriarty, 1976). For instance, some children may develop competencies in some areas, such as social relationships or academics, but may suffer from symptoms of anxiety or depression (Cowen et al., 1990). It may be more useful to view resilience to stress as a process—an interaction between individuals and their environ-ment—rather than a static characteristic or personality trait (Rutter, 1987).

It is eminently reasonable that the age and developmental level of the child also contributes to the vulnerability and resilience process. Unfortu-nately, very few studies have systematically addressed this question. Waller-stein and Kelly (1980) examined age differences in the long-term effects of divorce. They found that very young children and teenagers did better emotionally, for very different reasons. Mothers of toddlers were more likely to remarry, and these young children, especially the little girls, often developed good relations with their step-fathers. Teenagers were old enough to separate from their troubled families and go their own ways, although many could not go to college due to lack of financial support from their parents. Pre-adolescents, however, often had the most problems. Most are as yet incapable of the cognitive complexity associated with post-formal operations, and thus tend to see the world in black and white. They may form destructive alliances with one parent and be unable to insulate themselves from their parents' emotional turmoil.

Elder and Caspi (1988) also found timing effects in the study of economic sites. Adolescents were more likely than younger children to develop positively from their families' economic stress, in terms of higher levels of maturity; the latter appeared to develop more vulnerabilities.

Thus, one can speculate that a child's cognitive, emotional, and developmental level will affect vulnerability and resilience to stress, probably in both generalized and stressor-specific ways. However, more research is needed in order to make definitive statements about the exact ways in which developmental stage interacts with stressors.

Evidence for PTG in Children

It is clear that all children do not necessarily suffer exclusively negative effects from stress. In fact, some highly stressed children seem to do very well and succeed despite it. In keeping with the theme of this volume, is it possible that some children may actually develop and grow in a positive way as a result of experiencing stress? To date, empirical evidence to support the possibility of PTG in children is sparse and weak, yet, it is nevertheless interesting. Collectively, evidence suggests that growth can be manifested in achievement motivation (Elder, 1974; Goertzel & Goertzel, 1962), mastery and effective coping skills (Murphy & Moriarty, 1976), and self-knowledge (Beardslee, 1989).

Much of what we know about the positive aspects of early childhood stress is derived from research on parental loss and genius (Cox, 1926; Roe, 1972). Children who lose one of their parents early in life usually show an increased vulnerability to psychological problems later on (for a review, see Laajus, 1984). However, among scientific and artistic geniuses, bereavement in childhood is fairly common (Albert, 1983; Eisenstadt, 1978; Simonton, 1984). One alternative explanation for this relationship is the possibility that children with older parents are more likely to excel academically but may also be more likely to lose a parent when they are still young. However, it is also possible that parental bereavement may serve as a developmental impetus under certain conditions.

Parental loss is only one example of an early trauma that can lead to positive outcomes. Goertzel and Goertzel (1962) studied more than 400 famous 20th-century men and women. Interestingly, 75% of these men and women were highly stressed in childhood by either physical handicaps, difficult parenting, or broken homes. However, no comparison group was used in their analyses so it is unclear just how common these types of traumas were in the lives of all children in the last century.

Nevertheless, assuming that this relationship provides some evidence for the relationship between stress and eminence, why would psychosocial and physical stressors in childhood relate to a higher level of achievement in adulthood? There are several possible pathways. First, creative achievement may serve as psychological compensation for other physical or social handicaps (Adler, 1956). Second, highly stressed children who happen to be very intelligent have the option of fleeing into creative or scientific endeavors in order to escape from painful experiences that other children may not have. It is possible that the ability to turn one's intelligence or talents toward coping with or escaping from the pain of trauma can actually serve to preserve the self during a time of great stress. Anthony (1987b) suggested that the creative individual's ability to venture off into fantasy and the possession of thin ego boundaries may serve as a buffer against stress rather than as a consequence of stress. However, it is possible that although intelligence and creativity are useful resources for coping with stress, the continued development of creativity is facilitated by a stressful environment. Hartmann (1950) suggested that the ability to see things differently from other people and to regress when warranted, in the service of the ego, is almost a requirement for those who become scientific or creative eminents.

It is interesting to speculate that children who have undergone high level of psychological stress may experience a certain amount of social isolation, which in turn may give rise to perspicacity and the ability to step outside of social conventions. In a recent talk at the University of California at Davis, author Isabelle Allende mentioned that as a child she had very few friends and simply didn't "see" things the way that "normal" people did. This process is graphically illustrated by the film *Muriel's Wedding*, in which the protagonist, a young girl who had always been a social outcast, was an observer rather than a participant at social gatherings, and thus observed many things that her peers overlooked. Social isolation, while undoubtedly stressful for children, can provide the freedom and motivation to observe, create, and fantasize.

What factors affect the probability of positive outcomes in the wake of stress? Very little research has focused on this question but we can speculate that many of the factors that predict resilience also contribute to the possibility of continued growth.

Whether or not children perceive benefits of stress, the degree to which they do, and the types of benefits gained depends on the context and the developmental stage of the child. For example, Elder, Foster, and Ardelt (1994) showed that economic hardship among farming families increased the likelihood of family discord and child behavior problems. Nevertheless, many children were seen as increasing in responsibility, largely due to taking on new chores and tasks in order to contribute to the maintenance of the farm. Indeed, in Elder's (1974) classic study of children of the Great Depression, economic deprivation had positive as well as negative effects. The type of effect depended on whether children were from middle or working class families. For example, economically deprived working class children were more poorly adapted and experienced difficulties in adulthood. Middle-class children, however, seemed to benefits from the hardships of the Depression. They matured faster psychologically and were more likely to be responsible and achievement-oriented. It seems as if experiencing the hardships of the Depression, although not in a way that severely compromised their survival, education, and development, taught them that hard work and industriousness could protect them from economic hardships in the future. In addition, since they were not as economically deprived as their working-class peers, they possessed more resources with which to pull themselves out of a difficult situation (perhaps through education and/or military service). This pattern has been demonstrated in other populations as well.

Beardslee (1989) offers some additional support that children may grow and develop in positive ways from stress. He found that adolescents who grew up in families with serious affective disorders, like major depression or alcoholism, but who were nevertheless resilient showed an exceptional understanding of themselves and their parents. In general they had made peace with their parents and had come to understand that they were not the cause of their parents' problems. They were able to talk about their concerns and how their perspective and behaviors changed over time in a way that their less resilient peers, who had not quite separated from their parents, were unable to do. However, it is unclear whether this increased insight and understanding is a consequence of their experience rather than a preexisting factor which contributed to their resilience. This insight may also be an aspect of advanced intelligence and highly developed cognitive skills.

Nevertheless, reports of self-perceived growth following traumatic events in children are largely anecdotal (see Tedeschi & Calhoun, 1995) and, again, often growth is perceived often in concurrence with substantial loss and/or compromise. What is needed is research that will unravel the influences of age, developmental level, and stress on growth as well as a clear delineation of which aspects develop: personality, social relationships, or mental health.

A DEVELOPMENTAL PERSPECTIVE ON PTG IN ADULTS

Other chapters in this volume review the literature on PTG in adults, and thus we will restrict this section to observations on possible developmental processes underlying this phenomenon—the micro approach mentioned earlier.

Elsewhere (Aldwin, 1992, 1994) we have argued that stress forms a context for personality development in adulthood. The most obvious developmental outcomes of stress include increases in coping skills, increases in self-confidence and self-esteem, changes in perspective, and increase in self-knowledge.

Increases in Coping Skills

Obviously, simple experience can result in an increase in coping skills. By definition, coping processes are activated in situations which are relatively novel or challenge an individual's capacities in some fashion (Folkman & Lazarus, 1980). One can acquire new coping skills through simple processes of trial and error, seeking information and advice, and observing others in similar situations. Aldwin and Brustrom (1997) argued that through the process of coping, one can develop management skills, or relatively rote means of handling tasks, which either serve to prevent the occurrence of stressors and/or decrease the stressfulness of routinely encountered problems. The management of chronic illnesses such as diabetes and asthma are good examples of this, as are routine problems in child care, work-related tasks, and caregiving for incapacitated relatives.

However, there are clearly individual differences in the ability to increase coping repertoires as a result of encountering stressful or traumatic experiences. In the development of good coping skills, one must differentiate between short- and long-term benefits. For example, hostile encounters with coworkers may allow one to achieve short-term goals, but result in long-term problematic relations and/or the creation of new problems. One can speculate that a certain modicum of intelligence and level of ego development (e.g., the ability to take others' perspectives and the ability to delay gratification) are necessary, but perhaps not sufficient, prerequisites for the development of good coping skills. A certain level of creativity and/or openness to new experience may also be helpful in this regard, as well as the ability to objectively examine one's own motivations and behaviors. For example, routinely blaming others for the existence of problems may forestall any attempts at individual change.

Increases in Self-Esteem and Self-Confidence

If one is able to handle a situation well, that is, achieve one's goals while minimizing psychological and physiological distress and maintaining good social relations, an increase in self-confidence and perhaps self-esteem is likely to result. Aldwin et al. (1996) showed that proportionately greater use of problem-focused coping, as well as the ability to perceive advantages in highly stressful situations, were associated with higher levels of mastery and lower levels of depression. The use of social support may aid this process. For example, Cook, Novaco, and Sarason (1982) showed that marine recruits with an initially external locus of control (LOC) developed a more internal LOC during basic training if their drill sergeants were supportive. We speculate that social support may result in increases in self-esteem in two ways. First, support may aid problem-focused efforts, increasing the likelihood of a positive outcome. Second, the provision of social support by others may reinforce an individual's sense of self-worth. This may explain why problematic social interactions (e.g., Rook, 1984) may greatly increase psychological distress for individuals coping with difficult problems.

Obviously, successful coping is more likely to lead to increases in self-esteem, and, unfortunately, whether or not a strategy is successful depends not only on the individual's efforts but also the exigencies of the situation and/or the reactions of others. For example, Aldwin and Revenson (1987) found that the use of the coping strategy of interpersonal negotiation interacted with perceived coping efficacy, such that individuals who used this strategy and thought it worked well showed decreases in psychological symptoms, whereas those who did not think it worked showed increases in symptoms. Further, individuals who exerted a great deal of effort, even if they did not think it worked very well, were more likely to maintain their psychological equilibrium than those individuals who did not exert themselves. Perhaps these individuals felt that they had done their best in the face of difficult circumstances, and thus were able to maintain a more positive image of themselves. Individuals who are more likely to use escapism as a coping strategy tend to evaluate their coping efficacy more negatively and may report more psychological distress—and, presumably, lower levels of self-esteem.

In any stressful situation, however, there is likely to be a variety of goals. We speculate that individuals who either maintain or increase in self-esteem in highly stressful situations may be more likely to focus on the goals that were successfully attained or managed. It is also possible that individuals may change their goals in order to maintain their self-image (Brandtstadter & Rothermund, 1994). Individuals who focus primarily on goals which were not achieved, however, may exhibit more psychological distress and increase their vulnerability (e.g., Taylor & Brown, 1988).

Changes in Perspective

Perhaps the most common finding in the literature on PTG is that individuals report a change in their perspective on life, either in terms of their hierarchy of values or in their perceptions of situations (for a review, see Aldwin, 1994). Close encounters with life-threatening situations, for example, may cause individuals to report that they now value their families or their health more, and also sometimes result in an increase in spirituality. Some speak of increases in empathy for others' suffering. Indeed, helping others may be a particularly healing way of dealing with one's own distress (as long as it is not used simply as an avoidance mechanism). How long these types of changes may last, however, is unclear.

Individuals may also use a personal trauma as a gauge or index against which they judge the relative stressfulness of other problems. For example, one man who had lost a daughter due to cancer felt that nothing could ever approach that level of stressfulness, and thus felt that he was more inclined to dismiss relatively minor problems (Aldwin et al., 1996). In the short term, trauma undoubtedly can increase irritability and magnify other problems, but, if successfully resolved, may help individuals gain more equilibrium in their lives. It is true, however, that some traumatized individuals may exhibit long-term increases in irritability to stress, especially if they have persistent cases of post traumatic stress disorder (PTSD). (See Friedman & Schnurr, 1995, for a review of the consequences of trauma and PTSD.)

However, not all individuals report positive changes in perspective. Some individuals can manifest long-term bitterness and suspiciousness. Individuals who feel that they have been unjustly harmed by their spouses, employers, or government may report increases in self-centeredness and an inability to trust others. Some may even adopt very self-limiting lifestyles in an attempt to ward off future harm. For example, one man we interviewed

(Aldwin et al., 1996) was very bitter about the intergenerational difficulties involved in parenting his baby-boomer children, never really forgave them for pursuing alternative lifestyles, and limited his contact with them. We speculate that initial levels of neuroticism, poor interpersonal skills, or the depression-related tendency to overgeneralize may contribute to negative changes in perspective. Alternatively, some types of trauma, such as rape or incest, may be particularly likely to result in long-term feelings of vulnerability, resentment, and hostility. Clearly, more research is needed to examine how and why positive and negative changes in perspectives occur.

Increases in Self-Knowledge

Epstein (1991) referred to trauma as the "atom smasher" of personality research. Trauma tends to "smash" basic assumptions about personal security, a just world, and the like. The process of healing a traumatized personality thus involves the reconstruction of a new self—individuals "pick up the pieces," as it were. Elsewhere (Aldwin, 1994) we have argued that almost by definition, stress creates uncertainty, and the greater the stress, the greater the uncertainty. Although some individuals may retreat into alcohol and drug abuse and other forms of mental illness, others apparently find the courage and support to reexamine to face themselves, sometimes in the midst of their worst nightmares.

Acredolo and O'Connor (1991) argued that uncertainty is a prerequisite for development. Working within the Piagetian framework, they showed that children first manifest uncertainty before making transitions in their cognitive schemata. Take, for example, conservation tasks. A very young child will be absolutely certain that a tall thin glass holds more liquid than a short wide one, despite all evidence to the contrary. A slightly older child is more likely to comprehend that empirical evidence challenges this belief, and manifests uncertainty in his or her prior understanding.

Cognitive and personal schemata form the structure of the self, and are generally so taken for granted that one may not even be consciously aware of them. It is not until one becomes uncertain of their veracity, often in the face of trauma, that one becomes aware of their existence and can examine them. Again, when faced with such uncertainty, some people may more rigidly adhere to old assumption systems or not be able to tolerate the stress levels that such uncertainty generates. However, stressful situations afford an almost unparalleled opportunity for self-examination and the development of self-knowledge (see Beardslee, 1989).

SUMMARY

Consistent with the deviation-amplification model of stress and coping described earlier in this chapter, it is clear that stress can lead to positive outcomes in the long run, whether one examines this phenomenon in biological or psychosocial processes, in childhood or adulthood. Several intriguing questions remain, however. First, it is clear that, in most circumstances, a combination of positive and negative sequellae can be identified. As Baltes (1987) stated, development in adulthood, at least, consists of a balance of gains and losses, and thus it is not surprising that the developmental effects of trauma also manifests this pattern. The next step will be to identify common or typical patterns of gains and losses, and determine which patterns appear to be more or less adaptive in which circumstances or contexts. Second, the need to differentiate between growth and denial is critical if individuals are to truly identify positive outcomes and specify their developmental course. Third, we hypothesized several possible processes through which stress can result in either positive or negative outcomes, but clearly much more empirical work is needed to address these hypotheses.

The implications of these types of research for both mental and physical health are immense. Very little research has examined hardiness on a physiological level. Understanding what patterns of stressors result in greater physiological toughness, or even hormesis, has exciting implications for our understanding of the adaptational process and perhaps even evolution. In addition, understanding vulnerability and resilience to stress has in many ways even greater implications for mental health research. The roots and definition of mental health (as opposed to mental illness) are still unclear, even after a century of psychological research, and we believe that studying the positive aspects of stress on developmental processes may finally shed important light on the origins, development, and maintenance of mental health throughout the lifespan.

ACKNOWLEDGMENT

Preparation of this chapter was supported by a grant from the National Institute on Aging, AG13006.

REFERENCES

Acredolo, C., & O'Connor, J. (1991). On the difficulty of detecting cognitive uncertain. Special Issue: Cognitive uncertainty and cognitive development. *Human Development*, *34*, 204–223.

Adler, A. (1956). *The individual psychology of Alfred Adler.* New York: Harper & Row.

Albert, R. S. (Ed.). (1983). *Genius and eminence.* New York: Pergamon Press.

Aldwin, C. M. (1992). Aging, coping, and efficacy: Theoretical framework for examining coping in a lifespan developmental context. In M. Wykle, E. Kahana, & J. Kowal (Eds.), *Stress and health among the elderly* (pp. 96–114). New York: Springer.

Aldwin, C. M. (1994). *Stress, coping, and development: An integrative perspective.* New York: Guilford.

Aldwin, C. M., & Brustrom, J. (1997). Theories of coping with chronic stress: Illustrations from the health psychology and aging literatures. In B. Gottlieb (Ed.), *Coping with chronic stress* (pp. 75–103). New York: Plenum.

Aldwin, C., & Revenson, T. (1987). Does coping help? A reexamination of the relationship between coping and mental health. *Journal of Personality and Social Psychology, 53,* 337–348.

Aldwin, C., & Stokols, D. (1988). The effects of environmental change on individuals and groups: Some neglected issues in stress research. *Journal of Environmental Psychology, 8,* 57–75.

Aldwin, C. M., Sutton, K., & Lachman, M. (1996). The development of coping resources in adulthood. *Journal of Personality, 64,* 91–113.

Anthony, E. J. (1987a). Children at high risk for psychosis growing up successfully. In E. J. Anthony & B. J. Cohler (Eds.), *The invulnerable child* (pp. 147–184). New York: Guilford.

Anthony, E. J. (1987b). Risk, vulnerability, and resilience: An overview. In E. J. Anthony & B. J. Cohler (Eds.), *The invulnerable child* (pp. 3–48). New York: Guilford.

Armsworth, M. W., & Holaday, M. (1993). The effects of psychological trauma on children and adolescents. *Journal of Counseling & Development, 72,* 49–56.

Baltes, P. (1987). Theoretical propositions of life-span development psychology: On the dynamics between growth and decline. *Developmental Psychology, 24,* 611–626.

Beardslee, W. R. (1989). The role of self-understanding in resilient individuals. *American Journal of Orthopsychiatry, 59,* 266–278.

Belsky, J., Steinberg, L., & Draper, P. (1991). Childhood experience, interpersonal development, and reproductive strategy: An evolutionary theory of socialization. *Child Development, 62,* 647–670.

Berlinsky, E. B., & Biller, H. B. (1982). *Parental death and psychological development.* Lexington, MA: D. C. Health.

Brandtstadter, J., & Rothermund, K. (1994). Self-percepts of control in middle and later adulthood: Buffering losses by rescaling goals. *Psychology & Aging, 9,* 265–273.

Cook, T. M., Novaco, R. W., & Sarason, I. G. (1982). Military recruitment training as an environmental context affecting expectancies for control of reinforcement. *Cognitive Therapy and Research, 6,* 409–428.

Cowen, E. L., Wyman, P. A., Work, W. C., & Parker, G. R. (1990). The Rochester Child Resilience Project: Overview and summary of first year findings. *Development and Psychopathology, 2,* 193–212.

Cox, C. (1926). *Genetic studies of genius: Vol. 2. The early mental traits of three hundred geniuses.* Stanford, CA: Stanford University Press.

Denenberg, V. H. (1964). Critical periods, stimulus input, and emotional reactivity: A theory of infantile stimulation. *Psychological Review, 71,* 335–357.

Dienstbier, R. A. (1989). Arousal and physiological toughness: Implications for mental and physical health. *Psychological Bulletin, 96,* 84–100.

Dienstbier, R. A. (1992). Mutual impacts of toughening on crises and losses. In S. Montada, H. Filippi, & M. J. Lerner (Eds.), *Life crises and experiences of loss in adulthood* (pp. 367–384). Hillsdale, NJ: Lawrence Erlbaum Associates.

Eisenstadt, J. M. (1978). Parental loss and genius. *American Psychologist, 33,* 211–223.

Elder, G. H., Jr. (1974). *Children of the Great Depression.* Chicago: University of Chicago Press.

Elder, G. H., Jr., & Caspi, A. (1988). Economic stress in lives: Developmental perspectives. *Journal of Social Issues, 44,* 25–45.

Elder, G. H., Jr., Foster, E. M., & Ardelt, M. (1994). Children in the household economy. In R. D. Conger, G. H. Elder, Jr., F. O. Lorenz, R. L. Simons, & L. B. Whitbeck (Eds.), *Families in troubled times: Adapting to change in rural America* (pp. 127–146). New York: Aldine de Gruyter.

Epstein, S. (1991). The self-concept, the traumatic neurosis, and the structure of personality. In D. Ozer, J. H. Healy, & A. J. Stewart (Eds.) *Perspectives in personality* (Vol. 3, pp. 63–98). London: Kingsley.

Felsman, J. K., & Vaillant, G. E. (1987). Resilient children as adults: A forty year study. In E. J. Anthony & B. J. Cohler (Eds.), *The invulnerable child.* New York: Guilford.

Field, T. (1992). Infants' and children's responses to invasive procedures. In A. M. La Greca, L. J. Siegel, J. L. Wallander, & C. Eugene Walker (Eds.), *Stress and coping in child health* (pp. 123–139). New York: Guilford.

Folkman, S., & Lazarus, R. S. (1980). An analysis of coping in a middle-aged community sample. *Journal of Health & Social Behavior, 21,* 219–239.

Friedman, M. J., & Schnurr, P. P. (1995). The relationship between trauma, post traumatic stress disorder, and physical health. In M. J. Friedman, D. S. Charney, & A. Y. Deutch (Eds), *Neurobiological and clinical consequences of stress: From normal adaptation to post-traumatic stress disorder* (pp. 507–524). Philadelphia, PA: Lippincott-Raven.

Furman, E. (1974). *A child's parent dies: Studies in childhood bereavement.* New Haven, CT: Yale University Press.

Garmezy, N. (1983). Stressors of childhood. In N. Garmezy & M. Rutter (Eds.), *Stress, coping, and development in children* (pp. 43–84).New York: McGraw-Hill.

Garmezy, N., & Masten, A. S. (1986). Stress, competence, and resilience: Common frontiers for therapist and psychopathologist. *Behavior Therapy, 17,* 500–521.

Garmezy, N., & Rutter, M. (Eds.) (1983). *Stress, coping, and development in children.* Baltimore: Johns Hopkins University Press.

Goertzel, V., & Goertzel, M. G. (1962). *Cradles of eminence.* Boston: Little-Brown.

Gray, J. A. (1981). *The physiopsychology of anxiety.* Oxford, England: Oxford University Press.

Hartmann, H. (1950). *Essays on ego psychology.* New York: International Universities Press.

Hilakivi-Clark, L., Wright, A., & Lippman, M. E. (1993). DMBA-Induced mammry tumor growth in rats exhibiting increased or decreased ability to cope with stress due to early postnatal handling or antidepressant treatment. *Physiology and Behavior, 54,* 229–236.

Hobfoll, S., & Lilly, R. (1993). Resource as a strategy for community psychology. *Journal of Community Psychology, 21,* 128–148.

Holmes, D., & Rahe, R. (1967). The Social Readjustment Rating Scale. *Journal of Psychosomatic Research, 11,* 213–218.

Holtzman, D. (1995). Hormesis: Fact or fiction? *Journal of Nuclear Medicine, 36,* 13–16.

Joasoo, A., & McKenzie, J. M. (1976). Stress and immune response in rats. *International Archives of Allergy and Applied Immunology, 50,* 659–663.

Laajus, S. (1984). Parental losses. *Acta Psychiatrical Scandinavia, 60,* 1–12.

Landauer, R. K., & Whiting, J. W. M. (1981). Correlates and consequences of stress in infancy. In R. H. Munroe, R. L. Munroe, & B. B. Whiting (Eds.), *Handbook of cross-cultural human development* (pp. 355–375). New York: Garland.

Levine, S. (1966). Sex differences in the brain. *Scientific American, 498,* 84–91.

Levine, S., Haltmeyer, G. G., Karas, C. G., & Denenberg, V. H. (1967). Physiological and behavioral effects of infant stimulation. *Physiology and Behavior, 2,* 55–59.

Lithgow, G. J., White, T. M., Hinerfeld, D. A., & Johnson, T. E. (1994). Thermotolerance of a long-lived mutant of Caenorhabditis elegans. *Journal of Gerontology, 49*, B270–B2766.

Lithgow, G. J., White, T. M., Melov, S., Johnson, T. E. (1995). Thermotolerance and extended life span conferred by single-gene mutations and induced by thermal stress. *Proceedings of the National Academy of Sciences of the United States of America, 92*, 7540–7544.

Long, J. V. F., & Vaillant, G. E. (1984). Natural history of male psychological health, XI: Escape from the underclass. *American Journal of Psychiatry, 141*, 341–346.

Luthar, S. (1991). Vulnerability and resilience: A study of high risk adolescence. *Child Development, 62*, 600–616.

Maruyama, M. (1963). The second cybernetics: Deviation-amplifying mutual causal processes. *American Scientist, 51*, 164–179.

Masten, A. S., Best, K. M., & Garmezy, N. (1990). Resilience and development: Contributions form the study of children who overcome adversity. *Development and Psychopathology, 2*, 425–444.

Monjan, A. A. (1981). Stress and immunological competence: Studies in animals. In R. Ader (Ed.), *Psychoneuroimmunology* (pp. 185–228). New York: Academic Press.

Monjan, A. A., & Collector, M. T. (1977). Stress-induced modulation of the immune response. *Science, 196*, 307–308.

Mosher, L., Pollin, W., & Stabenau, J. (1971). Families with identical twins discordant for schizophrenia. *British Journal of Psychiatry, 118*, 29–42.

Murphy, L., & Moriarty, A. (1976). *Vulnerability, coping, and growth: From infancy to adolescence.* New Haven, CT: Yale University Press.

Myrdal, G. (1962). *An American dilemma: The Negro problem and modern democracy.* New York: Harper & Row.

Newberry, B. H. (1976). Inhibitory effects of stress on experimental mammary tumors. *Abstracts of the International Symposium on Detection and Prevention of Cancer, 314*, 35.

Newberry, B. H., & Songbush, L. (1979). Inhibitory effects of stress on experimental mammary tumors. *Cancer Detection and Prevention, 2*, 222–223.

Nolen-Hoeksema, S. (1995). Epidemiology and theories of gender differences in unipolar depression. In M. V. Seeman (Ed.), *Gender and psychopathology* (pp. 63–87). Washington, DC: American Psychiatric Press.

Obeid, L. M., & Hannun, Y. A. (1995). Ceramide: A stress signal and mediator of growth suppression and apoptosis. *Journal of Cellular Biochemistry, 58*, 191–198.

Rashkis, H. A. (1952). Systemic stress as an inhibitor of experimental tumors in Swiss mice. *Science, 116*, 169–171.

Riley, V., Fitzmaurice, M., & Spackman, D. (1981). Psychoneuroimmunologic factors in neoplasia: Studies in animals. In R. Ader (Ed.), *Psychoneuroimmunology* (pp. 31–102). New York: Academic Press.

Roe, A. (1972). Patterns of productivity of scientists. *Science, 176*, 940–941.

Roesler, T. A., & McKenzie, N. (1994). Effects of childhood trauma on psychological functioning in adults sexually abused as children. *Journal of Nervous and Mental Disease, 182*, 145–150.

Romero, L. M., Raley-Susman, I. M., Redish, D. M., Brooke, S.M., Horner, H. C., & Sapolsky, R. (1992). Possible mechanism by which stress accelerates growth of virally derived tumors. *Proceedings of the National Academy of Science, 89*, 11084–11087.

Rook, K. (1984). The negative side of social interaction: Impact on psychological well-being. *Journal of Personality and Social Psychology, 46*, 1097–1108.

Rutter, M. (1979). Maternal deprivation, 1972–1978: New findings, new concepts, new approaches. *Child Development, 50*, 283–305.

Rutter, M. (1981). Stress, coping, and development: Some issues and questions. *Journal of Child Psychology, Psychiatry, and Allied Disciplines, 22*, 323–356.

Rutter, M. (1983). Stress, coping, and development: Some issues and some questions. In N. Garmezy & M. Rutter (Eds.), *Stress, coping, and development in children* (pp. 1–41). Baltimore, MD: Johns Hopkins University.

Rutter, M. (1987). Psychosocial resilience and protective mechanisms. *American Journal of Orthopsychiatry, 57*, 316–331.

Rutter, M. (1989). Pathways from childhood to adult life. *Journal of Child and Psychology and Psychiatry and Allied Disciplines, 30*, 23–51.

Selye, H. (1956). *The stress of life.* New York: McGraw-Hill.

Simonton, D. K. (1984). *Genius, creativity, and leadership: Histriometric inquiries.* Cambridge, MA: Harvard University Press.

Smith, M. B. (1968). Competence and socialization. In J. Clausen (Ed.), *Socialization and society* (pp. 270–320). Boston: Little-Brown.

Solomon, G. F. (1969). Stress and antibody in rats. *International Archives of Allergy and Applied Immunology, 35*, 97–104.

Solomon, G. F., & Amkraut, A. A. (1981). Psychoneuroendocrinological effects on the immune response. *Annual Review of Microbiology, 35*, 155–184.

Taylor, S., & Brown, J. D. (1988). Illusion and well-being: A social psychological perspective on mental health. *Psychological Bulletin, 103*, 193–210.

Tedeschi, R., & Calhoun, L. (1995). *Trauma and transformation: Growing in the aftermath of suffering.* Thousand Oaks, CA: Sage.

Vaillant, G. (1993). *The wisdom of the ego.* Cambridge, MA: Harvard University Press.

von Bertalanffy, L. (1969). *General systems theory: Foundations, development, applications.* New York: G. Brazilier.

Wallerstein, J. S. (1991). The long-term effects of divorce on children: A review. *Journal of the American Academy of Child and Adolescent Psychiatry, 30*, 349–360.

Wallerstein, J. S., & Kelly, J. B. (1980). *Surviving the breakup: How children and parents cope with divorce.* New York: Basic Books.

Werner, E. E., Smith, R. S. (1982). *Vulnerable but invincible: A longitudinal study of resilient children and youth.* New York: McGraw-Hill.

Werner, E. E., & Smith, R. S. (1992). *Overcoming the odds.* Ithaca, NY: Cornell University Press.

Wolin, S. J., & Wolin, S. (1993). *The resilient self: How survivors of troubled families rise above adversity.* New York: Ullard Books.

Worland, J., Janes, C., Anthony, E. J., McGinnis, M., & Cass, L. (1984). St. Louis Risk Research Project: Comprehensive progress report of experimental studies. In N. F. Watt, E. J. Anthony, L. C. Wynne, & J. Rolf (Eds.), *Children at risk for schizophrenia: A longitudinal perspective* (pp. 105–147). Cambridge, England: Cambridge University Press.

Wu, H., & Lozano, G. (1994). NF-$_k\beta$ activation of p53: A potential mechanism for suppressing cell growth in response to stress. *Journal of Biological Chemistry, 169*, 20067–20074.

Wyman, P. A., Cowen, E. L., Work, W. C., & Parker, G. R. (1991). Developmental and family milieu correlates of resilience in urban children who have experienced major life stress. *American Journal of Community Psychology, 19*, 405–426.

4

Personality and Transformation in the Face of Adversity

Howard Tennen
Glenn Affleck
University of Connecticut School of Medicine

Accounts of personal transformation abound in literature, biography, auto-biography, in the narratives of individuals who have been victims, and occasionally even among those who have victimized others (cf. Grass, 1990). Such changes are captured well in the reflections of a young father of an acutely ill newborn:

> Right after she was born, I remember having a revelation. Here she was, only a week old, and she was teaching us something—how to keep things in their proper perspective, how to understand what's important and what's not. I learned that everything is tentative, that you never learn what life is going to bring. I realized that I shouldn't waste any more time worrying about the little things. (unpublished)

In this observation, made by a woman with infertility:

> It has made me a stronger person, and has made me appreciate children so much more. It took determination and hard work to gain this strength, but it was worth the effort. (unpublished)

And in this description of personal transformation by a woman living with a painful chronic illness:

> Living with this disease has taught me so many precious things that I wouldn't have learned if I were healthy. I guess the most important things it has taught

me are to appreciate what life can hold for you every day and to be grateful for the loving relationships in your life. It's taken a long time for me realize this. (unpublished)

Changes such as these are reported regularly despite the contextual and interpersonal pressures against personal change (Baumeister, 1994) and people's tendencies to select social environments that homeostatically interrupt exceptional personal changes (Watzlawick, Weakland, & Fisch, 1974). Social psychologists have argued persuasively that the more stable a person's social environment, the more difficult it may be for him or her to experience personal change. The pervasive tendency to expect consistency in others (Jones & Nisbett, 1971) creates social pressure on us all, including those facing adversity, away from significant personal changes. In view of these potent homeostatic forces, any evidence of transformative experiences during life crises is all the more remarkable.

Although many people who face adversity report ensuing growth, the experience of growth is difficult to verify (Affleck & Tennen, 1996; Tedeschi, Calhoun & Gross, 1993), and we are not yet convinced that reports of positive change should be taken at face value. To our knowledge, the only published study to compare participant and informant ratings of stress-related growth found modest concordance (Park, Cohen, & Murch, 1996). And reports of personal change do not seem to stand up to scrutiny. For example, at the conclusion of a 6-year study of personality stability and change, Costa and McCrae (1989) asked participants how much their personality changed over the course of the study. Although a substantial minority reported "a good deal of change," these perceived changes were not substantiated by personality stability coefficients—personality was no less stable among individuals who experienced a good deal of change than among those who experienced little or no change. In this chapter we suspend judgment on the accuracy of personal growth experiences to examine the role of personality characteristics and processes in the initiation and main-tenance of perceived positive metamorphosis among individuals facing adversity. Although our focus is intrapersonal, we readily acknowledge the contextual (Folkman, 1992; Schaefer & Moos, 1992; chap. 5, this volume), interpersonal, and social forces (Bloom, chap. 8, this volume) that affect transformative experiences. We also appreciate that prior life experience, independent of personality, may influence adaptation during and after a personal crisis (Norris & Murrell, 1987; Ruch, Chandler, & Harter, 1980; Rutter, 1987).

PERSONALITY AND CRISIS RELATED TRANSFORMATION: ROUNDING UP THE USUAL SUSPECTS

In a now classic scene from *Casablanca*, Captain Louis Renault initiates a police investigation by demanding that the "usual suspects" be "rounded up." Psychological investigators, particularly those interested in personality processes, typically take the same approach to the study of new phenomena: We kickstart our inquiries by rounding up the usual moderational and mediational suspects without a fully developed theory of the phenomenon itself. So it has been in the study of personal growth following crisis. Thus, the personality moderators posited in the evolving crisis related growth literature, which we now describe, are identical to proposed moderators in totally unrelated areas of investigation (e.g., Hoorens, 1996), and are personal characteristics already suspected of being dimensions of one another (e.g., Marshall, Wortman, Kusulas, Hervig, & Vickers, 1992). Although there may be some benefits to sticking to the usual suspects, we believe there is the distinct risk of learning only what one already assumes. We now review the usual suspects that have been considered candidates for moderational status in the process of thriving (O'Leary & Ickovics, 1995), crisis induced personal transformation (Tedeschi & Calhoun, 1995), and stress-related growth (Park, Cohen, & Murch, 1996).[1]

Personality has great appeal as a potential moderator of adaptational outcomes during a trauma and in its aftermath. Although the life crisis literature suggests that personal growth may be more common than previously thought (Affleck, Tennen, Croog, & Levine, 1987; Affleck, Tennen, & Rowe, 1991; Wallerstein, 1986; Yarom, 1983) it is certainly not so prevalent as to span individual differences in personality traits. Many survivors of adversity do not experience positive consequences from their plight, and these individuals could well differ from their growth- experiencing counterparts in general or specific personality characteristics. Dispositional characteristics might also anticipate the nature of personal change.

Despite the intuitive appeal of linking pre-event personality with post-event personal growth, there are relatively few published empirical studies relating dispositional influences to thriving in the face of adversity. Over the years, authors have variously linked crisis-related benefit-finding and personal growth to an internal locus of control (Wollman & Felton, 1983);

---

[1]Portions of our discussion of "usual" personality moderators appear in Affleck and Tennen (1996). Construing benefits from adversity: Adaptational significance and dispositional underpinnings. *Journal of Personality.*

a persistent belief in a just world (Kiecolt-Glaser & Williams, 1987); dispositional optimism (Park, Cohen, & Murch, 1996; Tennen, Affleck, Urrows, Higgins, Mendola, 1992; Thompson, 1985); and extraversion and openness to experience (Tedeschi & Calhoun, 1996).

Because the empirical literature is limited, we focus on those personality dimensions that have received the greatest theoretical attention. We consider how dispositional optimism/pessimism, cognitive and self-complexity, and dispositional hope, each of which emphasizes the pursuit of personal goals in the face of obstacles, may figure in this process. We then address the potential role played by the "Big Five" constellation (McCrae, 1992) of personality organization.

Dispositional Optimism

Tennen, Affleck, and Mendola (1991a), Moos and Schaeffer (1990), O'Leary and Ickovics (1995), Tedeschi and Calhoun (1995), Tennen et al. (1991), and Thompson (1985) hypothesized that dispositional optimism, or the generalized expectancy for positive outcomes (Scheier & Carver, 1985, 1987), may anticipate growth following threatening events. Dispositional optimists, for example, display superior adaptation to medical stressors, including coronary artery bypass surgery (Fitzgerald, Tennen, Affleck, & Pransky, 1993; Scheier, Matthews, Owens, Magovern, Lefebvre, Abbot, & Carver, 1989), childbirth (Carver & Gaines, 1987), failed in-vitro fertilization (Litt, Tennen, Affleck, & Klock, 1992); and HIV-positive status (Taylor, Kemeny, Aspinwall, Schneider, Rodriguez, & Herbert, 1992). There is also good reason to believe that optimistic individuals might be more inclined than pessimists to extract a sense of benefit or gain from adversity: Their hopeful view of the future may well stem from a positive interpretation of the present.

Several studies using the Life Orientation Test (LOT) of dispositional optimism and pessimism (Scheier & Carver, 1985) already show that perceptions closely related to perceived growth or benefit-finding are related to optimistic expectations. For example, Fontaine, Manstead, and Wagner (1993) found that dispositional optimism was associated with positive reinterpretation as a strategy of coping with life stressors; Curbow, Somerfield, Baker, Winegard, and Legro (1993) reported that among individuals undergoing bone marrow transplantation, greater optimism was associated with reports of positive life changes and personal growth; and Carver et al., (1993) found that optimists were more likely to use positive reframing as a coping strategy before and after breast cancer surgery. In a study that measured situation specific optimism, an expected correlate of generalized optimism, Affleck, Tennen, and Rowe (1991) showed that mothers who maintained more optimistic expectancies for their premature infant's development were more likely to find benefits, including personal growth, in the neonatal intensive care crisis.

Tennen et al. (1992) examined how dispositional optimism and benefit-finding relate to one another and figure in the day-to-day symptoms, mood, and functioning of individuals with rheumatoid arthritis, a chronic, painful, and disabling illness. After completing the LOT and measures of perceived control over, and benefits from, their chronic pain drawn from the *Inventory of Perceived Control Beliefs* (IPCB: Mendola, 1990), research participants reported each day for 75 consecutive days their pain intensity, mood, and pain-related activity limitations (e.g., missing work, cutting back on planned social activities). As predicted, those scoring higher on the LOT were significantly more likely to endorse benefits from their illness, including the enhanced social and personal resources described by Schaefer and Moos (1992) as growth related outcomes of life crises. Optimists also reported significantly higher average levels of positive daily mood.

Perceiving benefits from living with chronic pain also correlated with these diary keepers' positive daily mood. Thus, we wondered whether the relationship between the enhanced social and personal resources described and daily mood might be explained by the tendency of dispositional optimists both to construe these benefits from their suffering and to experience more positive mood states. As expected, controlling for dispositional optimism did attenuate the significant relationship between benefit-finding and mood.

Is the association between experiencing personal benefits from adversity and emotional well-being due entirely then to differences in dispositional optimism? Enthusiasm for this hypothesis is dampened by refinements in the measurement of optimism since the study by Tennen et al., (1992) was published. First, there is compelling evidence that optimism, as measured by total scores on the LOT, is not a unitary construct. Instead, the LOT appears to measure two relatively orthogonal constructs: optimism *and* pessimism. Moreover, investigators have recently confirmed that optimism and pessimism may not have equivalent relationships with other personality and adaptational outcome measures (Marshall, Wortman, Kusulas, Hervig, & Vickers, 1992; Mroczek, Spiro, Aldwin, Ozer, & Bosse, 1993). Thus, the aforementioned analysis by Tennen et al. (1992) may be flawed because it fails to distinguish between optimism and pessimism as independent correlates of daily mood.

A second recent refinement of the LOT recommended by Scheier, Carver, and Bridges (1994) is even more critical to the specificity of the relationship between optimism and the experience of personal growth. Two of the four items originally claimed to measure optimism appear instead to measure the ability to extract positive value from negative circumstances: "I always look on the bright side of things" and "I'm a believer in the idea that 'every cloud has a silver lining'." Thus, any apparent relationship between optimism and the experience of personal growth may simply be due to overlapping measures of the capacity to extract something positive from an otherwise grim experience, one dispositional (as measured by these two items on the LOT) and the other more specific to the problem itself (as assessed by questions regarding personal growth or perceived personal benefits).

We re-analyzed the data reported by Tennen et al. (1992) to separate optimism from pessimism and the expectancy from the benefit-finding components of optimism. Although benefit-finding remained significantly correlated with the original 4-item optimism scale and remained significant even when pessimism was partialed from the association, the 2-item optimism scale without dispositional benefit-finding did not correlate significantly with the experience of enhanced personal resources from the illness. And the more narrowly operationalized measure of optimism did not confound the association between enhanced personal resources and well-being.

The rather modest though consistent association between optimism and posttraumatic growth (PTG) has recently been interpreted as an indication that "the tendency to experience growth is not 'simply' optimism" (Tedeschi & Calhoun, 1995, p. 48). Although we certainly agree in principle, the available evidence suggests that whatever shared variation exists between optimism and growth may be attributable to item overlap in indicators of the presumed predictor (optimism) and the criterion (perceived growth). Both published findings and the reanalysis of previously published data render equivocal the role of dispositional optimism in the experience of personal growth, at least among those facing major medical problems. Because of recent, and welcome, refinements in the LOT, some of the findings linking optimism and pessimism to personal growth and benefit-finding should be reconsidered and revisited in future research.

Although the relationship between optimism and perceived growth remains uncertain, investigators and theorists have not been reticent to propose mechanisms mediating the relationship. These purported mediators converge on the idea that optimists experience growth in adversity because they try harder: optimists are active, problem-oriented copers (Tedeschi & Calhoun, 1995), who because of these efforts, have an edge in dealing with acute challenges (Moos & Schaeffer, 1990). The effort optimists exert to reframe negative experiences in a positive light (O'Leary & Ickovics, 1995) similarly propels them toward positive transformations. That the experience of PTG is related to effortful strategies is an untested assumption to which we will return in our discussion of growth-inducing processes.

Cognitive and Self-Complexity

Cognitive complexity shares with dispositional optimism/pessimism the ability to achieve personal goals despite barriers imposed by aversive events. More than 30 years ago, Harvey (1965) theorized that the more complex one's conceptual system, the greater should be one's ability to achieve "adequate means of fate control … And a greater mastery over what would otherwise be a capricious, unpredictable, and overwhelming environment" (p. 249). The logic of this argument turns on the contention that in the face of adversity, cognitively complex individuals should be better able to pursue alternative goals and find more flexible ways of achieving them. This is one way of interpreting the redefinition of threatening experiences that occurs when people see the threat as an opportunity to change their life goals, values, or priorities in desirable ways.

Linville's (1985, 1987) more recent elaboration of the concept of self-complexity refines this argument. Linville documented that individuals who display high self-complexity—reflecting a greater number of discrete roles or identities used to organize self-schemas—adapt better to adversity, presumably because they are less likely to suffer global effects on self-representation. Bringing additional specificity to this hypothesis, Morgan and Janoff-Bulman (1994) suggested that not all forms of complex self-representations should have equivalent effects on adaptation to threat. Rather, it is the complexity of *positively* valenced self-representations that should best predict adaptation to events that threaten personal identities and roles. Their test of this hypothesis revealed that psychological adjustment to lifetime traumas (e.g., death of a parent, physical abuse, sexual assault) was superior among those who continued to hold many more independent positive self-representations (e.g., hard-working, focused, imaginative, motivated) than among trauma survivors with fewer independent positive self-representations. Along with Schaefer and Moos (1992) and clinical investigators (McCann & Pearlman, 1990) who conjecture that the capacity to view oneself from multiple perspectives enhances adjustment to trauma, we believe that self-complexity may hold considerable promise as a personality moderator of crisis-related growth. But as we will highlight, the promise of cognitive complexity in relation to trauma-related growth will only be realized through fully prospective inquiries.

Dispositional Hope

Dispositional hope is yet another personality construct that rests on the perceived accessibility of desired goals. Hope differs from optimism/pessimism in that it encompasses not only one's expectancy that desired goals can be achieved but one's ability to imagine avenues for goal attainment (Snyder, Irving, & Anderson, 1991).

We are uncovering evidence of the key role that dispositional hope plays in experiencing personal growth from living with fibromyalgia, a syndrome of unknown origin which combines widespread pain with unusual tenderness in multiple tender point sites and is often accompanied by sleep disturbance. Our study affords a test of the relative importance of dispositional optimism/pessimism and dispositional hope as measured by the LOT and HOPE (Snyder et al., 1991) scales respectively, in experiencing growth in the context of fibromyalgia pain.

The results from our first 35 participants suggest that neither the LOT pessimism scale, nor the revised LOT optimism scale correlate with perceived growth from living with fibromyalgia. Instead, it is individuals with greater dispositional hope who cite more benefits from living with their chronic pain. In particular, those scoring higher on the HOPE scale endorsed greater agreement with the IPCB items "I have learned a great deal about myself from living with my pain," and "dealing with my pain has made me a stronger person." The ability of dispositional hope to predict these facets of perceived growth, controlling for differences in the related constructs of optimism and pessimism, is strong evidence of its unique role in shaping positive appraisals of adversity. In a later section, we summarize additional data concerning its ability to predict how often fibromyalgia patients actually use their conviction of personal growth as a daily cognitive coping strategy for contending with their pain.

The Big Five Dimensions of Personality

No discussion of the personality underpinnings of coping with adversity would be complete without mentioning the potential contribution of second-order personality traits that are captured by the "Big Five" constellation of *neuroticism, extraversion, openness to experience, conscientiousness,* and *agreeableness* (McCrae, 1992). McCrae and Costa (1986) found that individuals low in neuroticism, high in extraversion, and high in openness do tend to rely to a greater extent on drawing strength from adversity as a style of coping with threat. These broad dimensions of personality may account more efficiently for the variance in crisis-related growth shared by more specific traits that emphasize goal attainment in the face of obstacles. They may also provide a template for predicting the types of benefits people will construe from adversity.

Specific benefits attributed to misfortune could match the characteristic approaches to the self, the world, and others associated with major dimensions of personality. For example, the typical negative self-perceptions associated with neuroticism/negative affectivity would lead to the hypothesis that individuals high on this trait would be less able to find adversity as a source of personal growth. Those scoring higher on measures of extraversion, who are more gregarious, cheerful, and seekers of social contact, might be especially likely to cite positive consequences of adversity for social relationships. The individual who is more open to experience—imaginative, emotionally responsive, and intellectually curious—might be particularly likely to meet the challenge of adversity through a philosophical re-orientation and a new direction in life plans.

Only a single study (Tedeschi & Calhoun, 1996), to our knowledge, examined the full range of personality prediction of specific benefits found in adversity. More than 600 college students who reported recent major life stressors, such as the death of a parent, criminal victimization, or accidental injuries, completed the *NEO Personality Inventory* (NEO; Costa & McCrae, 1985) and the *Posttraumatic Growth Inventory* (PTGI; Tedeschi & Calhoun, 1996), which measures characteristic forms of positive change claimed from adversity, such as the emergence of new possibilities, spiritual growth, and better relationships. NEO scores for extraversion, openness, agreeableness, and conscientiousness each correlated significantly with the total PTG score. Although a multivariate analysis of personality predictors was not reported, it appears that extraversion is the most likely candidate to maintain an independent prediction of overall benefit-finding. It correlated highest with benefit-finding and was the only dimension to be associated significantly with each of the subscales of the PTGI. Extraversion, as might be predicted, correlated most strongly with the report of improved relationships. Openness to experience was also an expectedly strong correlate of the PTGI subscale labeled *new possibilities*, which concerns the emergence of new interests and new life paths.

Tedeschi and Calhoun (1995) proposed several other personality factors that they believe might set the stage for personal growth amidst crisis. One such factor is an *internal locus of control* (LOC). Individuals with an internal LOC find rewards for their behavior in internal rather than external sources. This orientation might give them a sense of control in threatening circumstances that might infuse these circumstances with the sense of meaning and coherence associated with growth in adversity. Along with Moos and Schaefer (1990), Tedeschi and Calhoun also propose that *self-efficacy* or confidence in one's coping capacities (Bandura, 1982), a *sense of coherence*, which includes a recognition that even catastrophic events are comprehensible and that life experiences are manageable and meaningful (Antonovsky, 1987), and *hardiness* (Kobasa, 1979) position individuals to extract growth from personal crisis. In a fashion akin to LOC, the posited "salutogenic" (Antonovsky, 1987) effects of self-efficacy, sense of coherence and hardiness derive from cognitive or behavioral effort. Self-efficacy leads individuals to try to master challenges. A sense of coherence promotes *active search* for meaning during threatening events, which in turn orients one to view these events as comprehensible and to muster the resources needed to master them. And hardiness requires active involvement, a sense of personal influence, and an inclination to actively derive meaning from stressful events. These are all strategic, effortful processes.

The foregoing research and speculation views personality factors as independent variables in the process of perceiving growth in aversive life experiences. However, a case could be made that construing personal benefits mediates a change in personality among at least some of those who are contending with acute or chronic adversities. Researchers are just beginning to address this issue, and the prospect of personality change arising from a single experience, no matter how momentous, might be rejected by many personality theorists. Nonetheless, a recent study by Park et al. (1996) raises the possibility of personality change after encounters with adverse life events. College students who reported more personal growth stemming from their most negative event during a 6-month span displayed significant increases in both dispositional optimism and trait positive affectivity during that time. Later in this chapter we return to the issue of personality change in response to crisis.

LIMITATIONS OF CURRENT CONCEPTIONS OF PERSONALITY AND CRISIS-RELATED GROWTH

Each of the personality constructs we have described may well play a role in PTG. Yet there are reasons to question the associations reported thus far.

One reason is that an adequate test of the personality hypothesis requires that we assess personality prior to the traumatic event. Diathesis-stress models of psychopathology have struggled with this demanding requirement, and investigators have reached a general consensus that there is no satisfactory alternative to measuring hypothesized risk factors prior to the stressful event (e.g., Abramson, Metalsky, & Alloy, 1989). Researchers are aware that fully prospective designs are the only way to investigate thriving or crisis-related growth adequately (O'Leary & Ickovics, 1995), but with very few exceptions (Park et al., 1996), retrospective designs have been employed.

In support of retrospective designs in which both personality and an aversive event are measured some time after the event, investigators have argued (mostly by implication, although occasionally explicitly) that because personality demonstrates temporal stability during adulthood (Costa & McCrae, 1988), we can assume that precrisis personality, particularly the Big Five factors, can be accurately inferred from postcrisis assessments. This is simply not so. Using a simulated data set, Weinberger (1994) demonstrated what we should already know: Moderately high test–retest correlations and no mean difference for a cohort on a personality factor does *not* rule out even dramatic change for certain individuals within the cohort. As Pervin (1994; see also Ramey, Lee, & Burchinal, 1989) reminds us: " … overall stability, as reflected in correlation coefficients, may mask significant gains in functioning …. By the same token, stable means may mask significant individual differences" (p. 321).

The literature on adaptation to serious illness provides abundant evidence for personal growth, including what many might view as changes in personality. This evidence comes from studies of heart attack survivors (Affleck, Tennen, Croog, & Levine, 1987); women with breast cancer (Taylor, Lichtman, & Wood, 1984); survivors of spinal cord injuries (Bulman & Wortman, 1977); individuals who have lost their sense of taste and smell (Tennen, Affleck, & Mendola, 1991b); women with impaired fertility (Abbey & Halman, 1995; Tennen, Affleck, & Mendola, 1991a); patients with chronic rheumatic diseases (Affleck, Tennen, Pfeiffer, & Fifield, 1988; Liang, et al., 1984); stroke victims and their caregivers (Thompson, 1991); parents of infants hospitalized on newborn intensive care units (Affleck, Tennen, & Gershman, 1985; Affleck, Tennen, & Rowe, 1991); and mothers of children with insulin-dependent diabetes (Affleck, Allen, Tennen, McGrade, & Ratzan, 1985), among others. A prominent theme in this literature (as well as in the literature on non-medical crises described by Janoff-Bulman, 1992; Tedeschi & Calhoun, 1995; and Thompson, 1985) is the perception of positive personality change, including the development of greater patience, tolerance, empathy, and courage, or a valued change in life's priorities and personal goals. Therefore, it seems incongruous for investigators to point to the prevalence of significant personal changes in the aftermath of crisis while making the case for retrospective designs on grounds of personality stability. Rather than starting down methodological paths that have already shown themselves to be dead ends in vulnerability studies, investigators of postcrisis growth need to bite the proverbial bullet and define fully prospective methods as necessary (though not sufficient) to reliable inquiry.

The concerns we raise regarding the "usual suspects" have been primarily methodological: indicators of some of these personality predictors overlap with one another and with the phenomenon of PTG they ostensibly predict; they have not been put to the rigorous requirements of fully prospective studies; and they are assumed to remain stable whereas the models of PTG and thriving in which they are embedded predict significant personal change. Perhaps what is most limiting about rolling out these same personality characteristics to explain individual differences in PTG is not methodological. Rather, it is the implication that those who are already well functioning are most likely to benefit further from a crisis. Individuals who already experience a sense of personal control, who are optimistic about the future, who are outgoing and open to new experience, who are confident in their coping capacities, and who view the world as meaningful and its slings and arrows as manageable are, according to current theory, most likely to emerge from a crisis or traumatic experience in some way better than they were prior to the experience. With only one exception (Tedeschi & Calhoun, 1995), no attempt has been made to address this conceptual dilemma.[2]

It may well be that these personal characteristics, which admirably serve those who demonstrate them in their everyday lives, are also fertile ground for further personal growth in the face of adversity. Individual differences seem to be magnified in times of transition or crisis, as people rely on those personal characteristics and well-practiced behavioral strategies that have

---

[2]McCrae (personal communication, May 13, 1996) suggests that the experience of personal growth may represent a mechanism for restoring an individual's characteristic hedonic level (cf. Brickman, Coates, & Janoff-Bulman, 1978). Consider a well-adjusted extrovert who tends to be happy regardless of her circumstances. If she experiences trauma yet continues to feel happy, she may need to explain her continued positive emotional state. Her explanation may be that she appreciates the little things in life, or is grateful for past good fortune, and she would appear to have experienced PTG. McCrae believes that she may be rationalizing her temperament: "[d]istressing events will be most incompatible with high hedonic levels, and thus the people who are most likely to engage in cognitive restructuring [experience growth] are *those who are already well functioning*. People who are chronically distressed have no need to rethink the world when they experience adversity—it already makes sense."

worked in the past (Caspi & Moffit, 1993). Yet the personality moderators incorporated into current models of crisis-related growth make no distinctions between characteristics that successfully guide our daily lives and those that might turn out to benefit us in crisis (Gould, 1993). Instead, these models seem to describe paragons of mental heath and personal development as the sole beneficiaries of growth following adversity, a perspective which fails to explain the most interesting and dramatic instances of growth documented in accounts of such change, such as the heroin addicts described by Biernacki (1986) who decided to give up their identity as an addict and successfully did so without treatment. These were by all accounts pessimistic, hopeless, fatalistic individuals who nonetheless managed to experience profound personal growth in the process of intentionally changing a central component of their identities (Kiecolt, 1994). Current visions of growth-moderating personality characteristics also fail to capture descriptions of change offered by the many research participants who lacked the postulated personality characteristics prior to their traumatic experience. Miller and C'de Baca (1994) and Lifton (1993) describe individuals who were certainly not optimistic, hardy, or extraverted. They were not particularly open to experience, and lacked a sense of coherence and meaning in life. And from all evidence they maintained an external control orientation. Yet they changed dramatically in the face of personal crisis. A more complete understanding of the role of personality in PTG requires an extended discussion of how personality psychologists define personality, including aspects of personality more amenable to change.

LEVELS OF PERSONALITY AND POSSIBILITIES FOR CHANGE

McAdams (1994a) draws from the work of McClelland (1951), Hogan (1987), and Cantor (1990) to distinguish three levels of personality: *dispositional traits, personal concerns,* and *life narratives.* He argues that the answer to the question of whether people can psychologically grow in adulthood depends on which level of personality we consider. Traits are "relatively nonconditional, relatively decontextualized, generally linear, and explicitly comparative dimensions of personality" (McAdams, 1994a, p. 300). Their noncontingent quality has led McAdams (1994b) to refer to the trait perspective as "the psychology of the stranger."

There is converging and abundant evidence that traits remain stable, particularly in adulthood (McCrae & Costa, 1990), and even in the face of dramatic changes in personal circumstances (Caspi & Moffit, 1993). The consistency of traits may derive in part from their genetic base (Dunn & Plomin, 1990), and from the tendency of individuals to select social environments that support their dispositions (Buss, 1987). Among the many critiques of trait conceptions of personality, those most relevant to our discussion of crisis-related growth have been offered by Thorne (1989) and Mischel and Shoda (1995; Shoda, Mischel, & Wright, 1994). They argue convincingly that personality defined as traits leaves no room for "conditional patterns" (Thorne, 1989) or "*if ... then ...* situation–behavior relations as signatures of personality" (Mischel & Shoda, 1995). These conditional relationships between the person and her world are captured in the statements: "I lose my sense of control when I'm threatened" and "Life seems to lose its meaning when someone important in my life leaves." The notion of conditional patterns opens new opportunities not available in trait conceptions for the study of crisis-related growth.

Personal concerns is McAdams' (1994) second level of personality. This level includes a person's current life tasks (Cantor, 1990), strivings (Emmons, 1986), personal projects (Palys & Little, 1983), and current concerns (Klinger, 1977). Personal concerns refer to what individuals want at a particular point in life, and how they plan to get what they want. Buss and Cantor (1989) referred to this level of personality as *middle-level units*, whereas McCrae and Costa (1996; Costa & McCrae, 1994) preferred the term *characteristic adaptations*. These are neither traits nor epiphenomena of a more fundamental aspect of personality. People are quite aware of this second level of their personalities because personal concerns guide everyday activities. McAdams' second level appears to correspond to what Costa and McCrae (1994; Weinberger, 1994) called *characteristic adaptations*. Unlike Level 1, Level 2 is contextual and motivated. Although there is scant evidence regarding stability and change in Level 2, McAdams (1994) made a strong case for the ebb and flow of personal concerns throughout life.

Much of what investigators describe as PTG seems to reflect changes in this second level of personality, although as we will argue, another level of change may be even more closely related to growth experiences. When a research participant states that since she received a life-threatening diagnosis, personal relationships have become a focus of her everyday life in a way that is new and rewarding, she is describing a change in personality at Level 2. Or consider a young man who notes how since his son's death he has shifted his priorities from his work to the community. He now organizes a community program for chronically ill children, volunteers at a local hospital, and shares freely his time and expertise with the town Little League.

These generative efforts have given his life renewed purpose and reflect a change in personality at Level 2. Similarly, the middle-aged heart attack victim who in response to his newfound appreciation of life makes radical lifestyle changes (Affleck et al., 1987) is also a Level 2 personality change.

Personality at Level 3 concerns the individual's attempt to shape an identity by finding unity and purpose in life. This level of inquiry into personality processes has gained momentum among those who are interested in personality across the life cycle (McAdams, 1993), those with an interest in psychotherapeutic change (Hermans & Hermans-Jansen, 1995), as well as those with an interest in affective experience (Landman, 1993), investigators interested in personal crisis (Harvey, Orbuch, Chwalisz, & Garwood, 1991), and theoreticians interested in trauma (Herman, 1992; Pearlman & Saakvitne, 1995). McAdams (1994) and others who draw on the narrative tradition to understand personality consider identity as an "evolving story that integrates a reconstructed past, perceived present, and anticipated future into a coherent and vitalizing life myth" (p. 306). Personal myth, which McCrae and Costa (1996; Costa & McCrae, 1994) view as part of the self-concept, cannot be reduced to traits or personal concerns. It is an internalized, unfolding narrative that is revised so as to give life a sense of direction, meaning and continuity.

The most stable feature of a personal narrative is its tone and form. Drawing on literary scholarship (Frye, 1957), McAdams distinguishes four general narrative forms: comedy, romance, tragedy, and irony. Comedy and romance supply a hopeful, optimistic, narrative tone, whereas tragedy and irony offer a more hopeless, pessimistic tone. Comedy as personal narrative need not be funny. Rather, it is based on the notion that happy endings are possible and that pain can be avoided. Romance, like comedy, is optimistic, but rather than emerging from life's obstacles happy, the romantic hero emerges "wiser and more virtuous" (McAdams, 1993, p. 51). The person confronts and overcomes challenges.

Tragic personal narratives are, of course, pessimistic. Tragic myths involve facing life's inherent absurdities with an awareness that happiness and pleasure are never unalloyed. Ironic narratives are also pessimistic, characterized by confusion and sadness, along with an awareness that we can never fully comprehend life's complexities. Although each person's narrative is a mixture of these four forms, one or two are typically emphasized.

McAdams (1993) speculates that whereas traits remain stable throughout adulthood and personal concerns change in response to circumstances and life stage, identity is continuously being shaped—both consciously and without awareness—to provide narrative coherence and a sense of meaning and purpose to life, and to fit personal experiences into this coherent account. Personal trauma or crisis (called *nuclear episodes* or *nadirs* in McAdams' scheme) provides the individual an opportunity to fit the experience into the form and tone of her/his life narrative and even to use the incident to affirm personal transformation. Citing Taylor's (1989) concept of "positive illusions," McAdams (1994) described how narrative explanations of serious illness and other forms of adversity shape and reshape personal identity.

The identity level of personality, with its goal of coherence and meaning, seems most closely related to the growth experiences described by individuals who have come through major crises. A goal of the prominent theories of adaptation to adversity, to which we now turn briefly, is to explicate how people create and maintain meaning and purpose in times of crisis.

THE PLACE OF PERCEIVED PERSONAL GROWTH IN THEORIES OF COPING WITH ADVERSITY

The most influential theories of psychological re-organization in the wake of adversity reserve an important role for victims' perceptions of crisis-related benefits, including personal growth. For example, Taylor, Wood, and Lichtman (1983) viewed construing such benefits from the event as a selective evaluation that helps victims to "devictimize" themselves by mitigating feelings of stigmatization and restoring their self-esteem. In a similar vein, Thompson (1985) included the discovery of perceived growth and other experienced benefits in her taxonomy of methods of psychological control which mitigate the aversiveness of threatening events. These theories conceptualize perceived growth as one of many possible self-enhancing appraisals.

To understand the adaptive value of appraisals of personal growth under threat requires an appreciation of the ways in which major adversities can threaten our most treasured assumptions about ourselves and the world. Janoff-Bulman and Frieze (1983) reminded us that "from day to day ... [we] operate on the basis of assumptions and personal theories that allow [us] to set goals, plan activities and order [our] behavior" (p. 3). These basic assumptions—also referred to as our higher order postulates (Janoff-Bulman & Schwartzberg, 1991) and assumptive world (Parkes, 1975)—include seeing ourselves as having control over events and being relatively invulnerable to harm; viewing the things that happen to us as orderly, predictable, and meaningful; and regarding ourselves as worthy and other people as benevolent. These worldviews are what Watzlawick (1978) called "second-order realities" as opposed to the first-order reality of the world that exists independently of our appraisals, and as such belong squarely in the constructivist tradition of psychological functioning and change (von Glaserfeld, 1984).

According to these theories, we are rarely aware of the fundamental elements of our assumptive world; the minor disappointments and failures of everyday life seldom bring them to light. Fundamentally, they are conservative cognitive schemas that resist change and disconfirmation (Janoff-Bulman & Schwartzberg, 1991). They are revealed and questioned, however, when a personal catastrophe challenges their validity (McCann & Pearlman, 1990; Pearlman & Saakvitne, 1995). As both Janoff-Bulman and Taylor have so eloquently documented in numerous works, much of the shock and confusion people experience in the immediate aftermath of victimization appear to stem from threats to cherished assumptions of mastery, meaning, and self-worth.

This very questioning of basic assumptions is what sets the stage for deep-seated personal change through the task of rebuilding an assumptive world accommodated to new realities (Janoff-Bulman & Schwartzberg, 1991). "By engaging in interpretations and evaluations that focus on the benefits and lessons learned," wrote Janoff-Bulman, "survivors emphasize benevolence over malevolence, meaningfulness over randomness, and self-worth over self-abasement" (Janoff-Bulman, 1992, p. 133). Positive appraisals are what Taylor (1983) has made the centerpiece of her theory of cognitive adaptation to threatening events.

Another view of the cognitive reappraisal process, which includes perceived growth, can be found in Rothbaum, Weisz, and Snyder's (1982) two-factor model of personal control. They view the discovery of positive meaning in adversity as a secondary control appraisal, one that provides a comforting alternative to feelings of helplessness from the loss of a sense of primary or direct personal control over an uncontrollable event. Rothbaum et al.'s prediction that secondary control appraisals should wax as primary control wanes has received initial empirical support (McLaney, Tennen, Affleck, & Fitzgerald, 1995).

Janoff-Bulman (1992) described three aspects of adaptive posttraumatic reappraisal: lessons about life, lessons about the self, and benefits to others (see also Greenberg, 1995). The lessons victims construe about themselves are in many ways comparable to the experience of PTG. These lessons can involve greater awareness of existing strengths or the development of admirable characteristics. Some people come to appreciate for the first time their courage, strength, or wisdom. Others believe that they developed one or more of these characteristics as a result of the crisis they experienced. Although this and the other theories embrace the concept of PTG it is not always clear if, and under what circumstances, they consider self-attributed growth to be a belief, an active coping effort, or an adaptational outcome. Assuming that such growth is an adaptational outcome (see Tedeschi, Park & Calhoun, chap. 1, this volume), an unresolved issue for the study of personality and PTG is the extent to which such growth is the outcome of a strategic, effortful process or the result of a spontaneously emerging change in self-perception. This distinction is important because the personality characteristics that facilitate effortful, goal-oriented personal growth may differ from those which facilitate automatic or unintended change. Another unresolved issue, equally important but obscured in current theory and research, is whether PTG is abrupt or gradual. Gradual change may well require different personality characteristics and processes than abrupt change. To genuinely understand how personality is involved in PTG, we need more fully developed models of the processes that determine growth as an adaptational outcome. It is to these two issues—whether such growth is a result of coping efforts and whether it is gradual or abrupt—that we now turn our attention.

POSTTRAUMATIC GROWTH: OUTCOME OF EFFORTFUL OR AUTOMATIC PROCESSES?

Descriptions of personal growth offered by individuals in clinical settings and by research participants suggest that such changes may reflect both efforts to change and automatic processes. Consider the comments of our research participants presented at the beginning of this chapter. The young father of an acutely ill newborn had a revelation about keeping things in perspective. His description suggests no effort or intention to change. The woman with impaired fertility, on the other hand, explicitly mentions that her newfound personal strength required hard work and effort.

We distinguish these experiences of personal growth in terms of their relation to coping efforts. The young father appears to have experienced growth independent of coping, whereas the woman experienced coping-contingent growth. We are not suggesting that her growth is itself a coping strategy, but that it *is* the consequence of an effortful, goal-directed process.

There are certainly circumstances in which an individual intentionally tries to view her/his crisis as an opportunity for personal growth (positive reappraisal), and these efforts may lead to positive personal change. But the effort (coping strategy) must not be confused with the adaptational outcome of personal growth.

Our distinction between coping-independent growth and coping-contingent growth turns on the notion that coping requires effort and that effortless adaptive behaviors are unrelated to coping (Tennen & Affleck, 1997). The effortful nature of coping is central to Lazarus and Folkman's (1984) definition of coping and is captured well in Haan's (1992) conclusion that "the hallmark of coping is conscious choice" (p. 268). Other investigators, including Aldwin (1994), Parker and Endler (1996), and Zeidner and Saklofske (1996) share the view that coping reflects conscious decision making. Although not all theorists agree that coping strategies require conscious effort (Coyne & Gottlieb, 1996; Houston, 1987), we maintain the distinction between coping and other adaptational behaviors that do not require conscious effort, because we believe that it is critical to understanding the relation between personality and PTG.

Current theories of adaptation to traumatic events describe both automatic processes and deliberate efforts. In Horowitz's (1986) influential theory, the process of adjustment to trauma includes "dosing," that is, controlling the timing, frequency, and duration of trauma-related thoughts and images, and choosing what information about the trauma will be considered or disregarded at any moment in time, including information about one's newly discovered strengths. Although some aspects of dosing are automatic, Horowitz (1986) did not exclude from his model conscious efforts to manage threatening images and information. Janoff-Bulman (1992), building on Horowitz's theorizing, explicitly distinguished two cognitive processes that help victims rebuild their assumptive worlds: automatic patterns for processing potentially threatening information and deliberate efforts to reconstruct cherished assumptions. Denial and numbing are examples of automatic processes that help individuals pace their cognitive integration of the traumatic experience (see Greenberg, 1995). Trying to re-evaluate the trauma as imparting personal strength, wisdom, or other growth-related characteristics is an example of deliberately trying to reinterpret the event so as to maintain cherished assumptions about oneself, the world, and the future.

Janoff-Bulman's (1992) distinction between automatic processes and intentional efforts to restructure one's assumptive world appears to have important implications for how personality figures in the experience of PTG.

More hopeful individuals, particularly those who anticipate more pathways to desired goals, may well work toward personal growth following trauma. Their intentional coping efforts become automatic routines and finally progress to the growth outcomes referred to in the PTG literature. But they begin with coping efforts intended to change oneself in a positive way. Making resolutions may be another way people begin to grow from crisis. Some of our research participants described resolving to change in some positive way, including revising their personal projects, current concerns or strivings in ways we would call PTG. Others consciously decided to revise their personal narratives. But (as smokers and dieters will attest) resolve alone is not sufficient for change. Perhaps conscientious individuals hold the edge when resolve must be transformed into persistent effort.

Although the concept of efforts toward personal growth following trauma is not incompatible with PTG as an adaptational outcome, the literature has paid scant attention to the possibility that the experience of personal growth, which we call *growth conclusions*, is distinct from the coping strategy in which an individual consciously reminds himself or herself of positive personal changes, which we call *growth reminding*. Whereas only those who have already discovered personal growth from their adversity may be able to use this knowledge to actively comfort themselves in difficult times, there is nothing about the experience of growth *per se* which implies that growth-related cognitions will be used as effortful coping strategies. For some people, growth conclusions may actually mitigate the need for growth reminding strategies.

In our study in progress on fibromyalgia pain (Affleck & Tennen, 1996), we are exploring this and related questions, which concern the overlapping and unique adaptational functions of perceived growth that refer to conclusions or that function as daily coping strategies. Although our study investigates the broader concept of perceived benefits, the vast majority of pain-related benefits endorsed by our participants capture very well the construct of personal growth, including realizing "what is important in life," experiencing "life as more precious," and having "become a stronger person." This investigation is unique in its measurement of growth-related cognitions, in its daily process design that permits within-person analysis of relations among variables over time, and in its combination of idiographic and nomothetic methods (see Tennen & Affleck, 1996, and Larsen & Kasimatis, 1991, for detailed discussions of the benefits of this design).

The time-intensive self-monitoring methodology used in this study, patterned after that of Shiffman and colleagues (e.g., Shiffman, Fischer, Paty, Gnys, Hickcox, & Kassel, 1994) combines a nightly structured diary with a computer-assisted real-time assessment of pain intensity and mood several times each day. A palmtop computer is programmed to deliver auditory signals to complete an on-screen interview at randomly selected times during the mid-morning, mid-afternoon, and mid-evening.

One item on the nightly questionnaire measured benefit-reminding: Participants used a 0 (*not at all*) to 6 (*very much*) scale to describe how much that day they had "reminded [themselves] of some of the benefits that have come from living with their chronic pain." There were considerable individual differences in how frequently these individuals actually reminded themselves of any benefits they had construed from their illness. Some who cited many benefits at the start of the study never reminded themselves of these during a month's time span, whereas some who had cited only one or a few reported benefit-reminding on many days.

Personality Correlates of Benefit-Reminding

As expected, individuals who scored higher on the IPCB subscale on benefit-finding—which measures such growth-related changes as finding new faith, having become a stronger person, and positively restructuring priorities as a result of the pain experience—did report more days of benefit-reminding. Neuroticism, extraversion, and optimism were unrelated to the frequency of daily benefit-reminding.

The personality measures that did correlate with benefit-reminding were the LOT pessimism subscale and the HOPE pathways subscale. We noted earlier that the HOPE pathways scale also correlated with benefit-finding in this sample. Because the relationship between benefit-finding and benefit-reminding became nonsignificant when HOPE pathways scores were partialed from this association, it appears that this psychological disposition—the ability to plan alternative avenues for successful goal attainment—may be a stable individual difference underlying growth-related conclusion *and* the use of benefit-reminding as a daily pain coping strategy.

The design of our study enables within-person analysis of day to day differences in benefit-reminding and other daily processes. We found that days characterized by more benefit-reminding did not differ in pain intensity, but were accompanied by significant differences in mood, specifically increased levels of pleasant (i.e., happy, cheerful) mood; increased levels of aroused-pleasant (i.e., peppy, stimulated) mood; and decreased levels of unaroused (passive, quiet) mood. Thus, on days when these chronic pain sufferers made greater efforts to remind themselves of the benefits that have come from their illness, they were especially more likely to experience pleasurable mood, regardless of how intense their pain was on these days.

This preliminary within-person analysis of efforts to remind oneself of the benefits of living with chronic pain strengthens the hypothesis that benefit-reminding, which typically involves reminders of personal growth, can improve one's emotional well-being on more difficult days. The literature, with its focus on "variables," has essentially ignored the daily experience of personal growth and growth reminding, and the processes through which reminding might change to and subsequently reinforce, the experience of PTG.

It seems less clear how nonintentional change relates to personality. Unlike the process of intentional change, for which there is a considerable theoretical literature (Prochaska, DiClemente, & Norcross, 1992), the characteristics and processes that give rise to revelatory experiences and, in turn, changes in current concerns, strivings, and personal narratives, have not been a focus of theoretical or empirical inquiry. The processes involved in self-directed, intentional change may be irrelevant to nonintentional change, and the role of personality may differ distinctly between these two forms of personal growth in the wake of crisis. One possible difference between these forms of growth is that intentional growth may need to unfold over time, whereas revelatory growth, by its very nature, may emerge rather suddenly. We now turn to the poorly understood distinction between gradual and abrupt personal transformation and how personality influences and is influenced by these processes.

PTG: GRADUAL OR ABRUPT?

Just as distinctions between effortful and automatic posttraumatic growth processes have been infrequent, so has the distinction between gradual and abrupt personal transformations. The concepts employed in the theoretical literature suggest that positive psychological adaptation to trauma unfolds at a gradual pace and tempo. Constructs such as "working through" and moderated "dosing" of traumatic material into awareness (Greenberg, 1995; Horowitz, 1986) convey a lengthy and unfolding process. The very notion of "rebuilding" shattered assumptions (Janoff-Bulman, 1992) reflects well this sense of gradual change. Individuals "pace their recovery" (Janoff-Bulman, 1992, p. 100) "over the course of coping and adjustment" (p. 110). Repeated comparisons of an experienced trauma with existing schemas produce *gradual* changes in one's view of oneself and the world. Some theories of personal change are explicit about its protracted course (Prochaska et al., 1992). Indeed, the literature on coping has come to equate the term *process* with something that requires time to unfold. The comments at the beginning of this chapter by our research participant experiencing chronic pain seem to be describing just such gradual change.

Yet the young father of an acutely ill newborn quoted at the beginning of this chapter appears to be describing a very different process: a revelatory, abrupt change in current concerns. There exists a rather compelling though relatively unappreciated theoretical and empirical literature beyond (Eldredge & Gould, 1972; Gould & Eldredge, 1977) and within (Franklin, Allison & Gorman, 1996) psychological inquiry on dramatic transformations that occur abruptly and through mechanisms that are not yet fully appreciated. We believe that for individuals in crisis or facing prolonged adversity, these "quantum" changes (Miller & C'deBaca, 1994) may be the most dramatic, and include changes in personality that cannot be easily incorporated into current conceptions of trait stability or notions of a gradual rebuilding of cherished assumptions. In a series of studies that are insufficiently cited in the coping literature, Finkel (1974, 1975; Finkel & Jacobsen, 1977) discovered that some people were able to metamorphose a trauma into an opportunity for personal growth. Although the experiences he studied may be considered less than traumatic by most investigators, Finkel's theory and findings are relevant to trauma researchers. He used the term *stren* to describe events that catalyze growth, and documented the qualities of the trauma-to-stren transformation. Traumas that become opportunities for growth seemed to depend more on individual resources than on the nature of the event—which suggests a potentially important role for personality—and the transformation is typically abrupt and described as an insight or revelation. The implications of these findings were not lost on Greenberg (1995), who suggested that change in leaps rather than unfolding increments presents a distinct challenge to current conceptions of adaptation to trauma. We would add the challenge it presents to how to construe the role of personality in this type of change.

From their fascinating review of what is known about abrupt personal changes, Miller and C'deBaca (1994) concluded that dramatic change, including what appeared to be fundamental personality change, sometimes occurred quite abruptly. Their preliminary study of quantum change produced a number of challenging findings related to personality. Most of the individuals who reported quantum change described finding a new sense of meaning in life and a different view of the world. They described equally dramatic changes in what McAdams (1993) called Level 2 personality characteristics: Their personal goals shifted from achievement, adventure, and the pursuit of pleasure to personal peace and spirituality. As a group, they had experienced far more negative events in the year prior to their transformation than one would expect from normative data. Although the retrospective methodology of this study places restraints on interpretation, the overall pattern of findings related to personality supports our position that this type of change must be considered as distinct from the incremental change described in the coping literature.

Miller and C'deBaca (1994) did not measure LOC. But they did ask participants to rate how much they felt in control of their lives before their transformation, after the transformation, and at the time of the interview. This question, which captures the essence of the LOC construct if not the psychometric elegance of its formal measurement, revealed that participants experienced only a modest degree of control of their lives prior to their conversion. This is in direct contrast to current theorizing about personality characteristics associated with incremental transformation, but perfectly consistent with James' (1902) contention that the "perception of external control" (p. 195) is essential to abrupt personal transformations. Similarly, formal indicators of optimism and hope were not available. But most participants noted that they were at a relatively low point in their lives (McAdams' "nadir"), suggesting, at least, that as a group they were not particularly hopeful about the future. Whereas current conceptualizations of PTG associate optimism with positive change in adversity, James (1902) suggested that such change, at least abrupt change, is preceded by despair. Premack (1970) suggested that a sense of humiliation and conscience pangs may trigger abrupt personal changes. Humiliation and conscience pangs are more common among field-dependent individuals (Lewis, 1971). We find the idea appealing that a personality characteristic like field-dependence, which increases the likelihood of distress during times of relative stability, might, at stressful times, trigger abrupt personal growth (see Gould, 1993, for an evolutionary counterpart), and we hope such findings move investigators beyond "the usual suspects."

GENDER DIFFERENCES IN PTG:
A CALL TOO EARLY TO MAKE

Throughout this chapter we have ignored possible gender differences in PTG. This was not an unintended omission, but rather a reflection of the absence of reliable gender differences in the literature we reviewed. Many studies that examined PTG have recruited only men or only women as participants. For example, the loss of an infant to SIDS has been studied among women (McIntosh, Silver, & Wortman, 1993); studies of rape, breast cancer (Carver et al., 1993), and infertility (Tennen et al., 1991a) also employ women. Other studies have begun with samples too small to allow meaningful comparisons between men and women (Borden & Berlin, 1990), or have been limited to examining gender differences in distress following traumatic experiences (Vrana & Lauterbach, 1994). The few studies that have examined the interactive effect of gender and personality on coping (e.g., Amirkhan, Risinger, & Swickert, 1995) have typically reported no significant findings.

Where gender differences have been reported, contradictory findings have been the rule rather than the exception. The psychological well-being literature, for example, has found that in unselected adult samples, women report more personal growth, including feelings of continued development, self-improvement, and increased self-knowledge (Ryff, 1991; Ryff & Keyes, 1995; Ryff, Lee, Essex, & Schmutte, 1994). Yet in other unselected adult samples (Vingerhoets & Van Heck, 1990), men more than women endorse personal growth as a coping strategy. This difference may reflect the distinction we made earlier between growth-related conclusions and coping efforts toward growth.

Even generally accepted gender differences in coping, such as women seeking more support and men engaging in more problem-focused activities (Miller & Kirsch, 1987), have recently been challenged by Porter and Stone (1995), who found that these differences are minimal and appear to reflect differences in the kinds of stressful encounters experienced by men and women. The two studies which have most carefully examined gender differences in stress-related growth suggest that reliable gender differences may exist, but that these differences may be elusive. Tedeschi and Calhoun (1996) found that women endorsed more trauma-related benefits than did men, whereas Park et al. (1996) found that such gender differences were inconsistent over a span of 6 months. Although we suspect that women and men may differ in the nature of their PTG experiences if not in the prevalence of these experiences, even this is a call too soon to make. We encourage investigators to examine more carefully the role of gender in crisis-related transformation.

SUMMARY AND CONCLUSIONS

One's view of how personality influences transformative experiences, and how personality is in turn transformed by those experiences turns on how both personality and the transformative process are construed. Current conceptions have relied explicitly on trait notions of personality and implicitly on an incremental model of transformation. The usual suspects from the coping and well-being literatures have been examined as moderators of transformation. But the closer we looked, the less impressed with the findings we became, particularly those related to optimism. We suspect that some of the usual supects will maintain an important role in our understanding of crisis-related transformation, and that some more unusual candidates will become increasingly prominent in our conceptual models and investigations. One such factor is *intrinsic religiousness* (Gorsuch & McPherson, 1989; Park & Cohen, 1992), which is the integration of religion as a guiding framework for one's life. But we will first have to disentangle the effects of the importance of religion from those of religious participation and the support of the religious community (McIntosh, Silver, & Wortman, 1993). Nonetheless, only after we abandon the strategy of marching out variables and begin instead to examine processes will any personality related constructs gain explanatory power.

A process conceptualization of transformation demands fully prospective studies. We believe that daily process studies are particularly well suited to furthering our understanding of the ebb and flow of change. But to appreciate fully the place of personality in the experience of PTG, we need to define personality to include traits, current concerns, and personal narratives. These conceptions of personality can enrich our understanding of just what changes during transformation while extricating investigators from the quagmire of predicting changes in aspects of personality that resist characterizations of change. Many of the personal changes described in the literature appear to reflect concerns and narratives. But to conclude that traits set the stage for changes in concerns and narratives would be to miss the point we most want to make: We cannot appreciate the place of personality in these transformations until we appreciate the nature of the changes themselves. We have proposed that people experiencing trauma, crisis, or prolonged adversity can make an effortful, consciously controlled change, or they may change without awareness of the process. The change may be incremental or abrupt. There may be circumstances in which effortful change is abrupt (Premack, 1970), yet we suspect that such change is gradual, and that our current conceptualizations best explain gradual, intentional change. Abrupt transformations that occur unintentionally probably involve different personality characteristics than do gradual, intentional transformations, and may involve aspects of personality that do not necessarily enhance individual functioning in the absence of adversity.

Some investigators (Loder, 1981; Miller & C'deBaca, 1994) believe that abrupt transformations influence not only our concerns and personal narratives, but even our temperament and perceptual style. We need to continue to seek insight into the way personality influences people's attempts to reorganize basic assumptions in the wake of adversity, but we must also allow the possibility of profound changes in personality, which may occur in the absence of effort and through nonincremental processes.

ACKNOWLEDGMENTS

The findings we report in this chapter related to fibromyalgia come from studies funded by National Institute of Arthritis, Musculoskeletal, and Skin Diseases Grant #AR-20621 to the University of Connecticut Multipurpose Arthritis Center. We are indebted to Jeff Siegel of National Technology Services for his assistance in programming the electronic diaries used in these studies, and to Robert McCrae, Dan McAdams, and Laurie Pearlman for their comments on an earlier version of this chapter.

REFERENCES

Abbey, A., & Halman, L. (1995). The role of perceived control, attributions, and meaning in members' of infertile couples well-being. *Journal of Social and Clinical Psychology, 14,* 271–296.

Abramson, L. Y., Metalsky, G. I., & Alloy, L. B. (1989). Hopelessness depression: A theory-based subtype of depression. *Psychological Review, 96,* 358–372.

Affleck, G., Allen, D., Tennen, H., McGrade, B., & Ratzan, S. (1985). Causal and control cognitions in parent coping with a chronically ill child. *Journal of Social and Clinical Psychology, 3,* 367–377.

Affleck, G., & Tennen, H. (1996). Construing benefits from adversity: Adaptational significance and dispositional underpinnings. *Journal of Personality, 64,* 899–922.

Affleck, G., Tennen, H., Croog, S., & Levine, S. (1987). Causal attribution, perceived benefits, and morbidity following a heart attack: An eight-year study. *Journal of Consulting and Clinical Psychology, 55,* 29–35.

Affleck, G., Tennen, H., & Gershman, K. (1985). Cognitive adaptations to a high risk infant: The search for mastery, meaning and protection from future harm. *American Journal of Mental Deficiency, 89,* 653–656.

Affleck, G., Tennen, H., Pfeiffer, C., & Fifield, J. (1988). Social comparisons in rheumatoid arthritis: Accuracy and adaptational significance. *Journal of Social and Clinical Psychology, 6,* 219–234.

Affleck, G., Tennen, H., & Rowe, J. (1991). *Infants in crisis: How parents cope with newborn intensive care and its aftermath.* New York: Springer-Verlag.

Aldwin, C. (1994). *Stress, coping, and development: An integrative perspective.* New York: Guilford.

Amirkhan, J. H., Risinger, R. T., & Swickert, R. J. (1995). Extraversion: A "hidden" personality factor in coping? *Journal of Personality, 63*, 189–210.

Antonovsky, A. (1987). *Unraveling the mystery of health: How people manage stress and stay well.* San Francisco: Jossey-Bass.

Bandura, A. (1982). Self-efficacy mechanism in human agency. *American Psychologist, 37*, 122–147.

Baumeister, R. F. (1994). The crystallization of discontent in the process of major life change. In T. F. Heatherton & J. L. Weinberger (Eds.), *Can personality change?* (pp. 281–297). Washington, DC: American Psychological Association.

Biernacki, P. (1986). *Pathways from heroin addiction: Recovery without treatment.* Philadelphia: Temple University Press.

Borden, W., & Berlin, S. (1990). Gender, coping, and psychosocial well-being in spouses of older adults with chronic dementia. *American Journal of Orthopsychiatry, 60*, 603–610.

Brickman, P., Coates, T., & Janoff-Bulman, R. (1978). Lottery winners and accident victims: Is happiness relative? *Journal of Personality and Social Psychology, 36*, 917–927.

Bulman, R., & Wortman, C. (1977). Attributions of blame and coping in the "real world": Severe accident victims react to their lot. *Journal of Personality and Social Psychology, 35*, 351–363.

Buss, D. M. (1987). Selection, evocation, and manipulation. *Journal of Personality and Social Psychology, 53*, 1214–1221.

Buss, D. M., & Cantor, N. (1989). Introduction. In D.M. Buss & N. Cantor (Eds.), *Personality psychology: Recent trends and emerging directions* (pp. 1–12). New York: Springer-Verlag.

Cantor, N. (1990). From thought to behavior: "Having" and "doing" in the study of personality and cognition. *American Psychologist, 45*, 735–750.

Carver, C., & Gaines, J. (1987). Optimism, pessimism, and post-partum depression. *Cognitive Therapy and Research, 11*, 449–462.

Carver, C., Pozo, C., Harris, S., Noriega, V., Scheier, M., Robinson, D., Ketcham, A., Moffat, F., & Clark, K. (1993). How coping mediates the effect of optimism on distress: A study of women with early stage breast cancer. *Journal of Personality and Social Psychology, 65*, 375–390.

Caspi, A., & Moffit, T. E. (1993). When do individual differences matter?: A paradoxical theory of personality coherence. *Psychological Inquiry, 4*, 248–273.

Costa, P., & McCrae, R. (1985). *The NEO Personality Inventory manual.* Odessa, FL: Psychological Assessment Resources.

Costa, P. T., Jr., & McCrae, R. R. (1988). Personality in adulthood: A six-year longitudinal study of self-reports and spouse ratings on the NEO Personality Inventory. *Journal of Personality and Social Psychology, 54*, 853–863.

Costa, P. T., Jr., & McCrae, R. R. (1989). Personality continuity and the changes of adult life. In M. Storandt & G. R. VandenBos (Eds.), *The adult years: Continuity and change* (pp. 45–77). Washington, DC: American Psychological Association.

Costa, P. T., Jr., & McCrae, R. R. (1994). Set like plaster? Evidence for the stability of adult personality. In T. F. Heatherton & J. L. Weinberger (Eds.), *Can personality change?* (pp. 21–40). Washington, DC: American Psychological Association.

Coyne, J. C., & Gottlieb, B. H. (1996). The mismeasure of coping by checklist. *Journal of Personality, 64*, 959–992.

Curbow, B., Somerfield, M. R., Baker, F., Wingard, J. R., & Legro, M. W. (1993). Personal changes, dispositional optimism, and psychological adjustment to bone marrow transplantation. *Journal of Behavioral Medicine, 16*, 423–443.

Dunn, J., & Plomin, R. (1990). *Separate lives: Why siblings are so different.* New York: Basic Books.

Eldredge, N., & Gould, S. J. (1972). Punctuated equilibria: An alternative to phyletic gradualism. In T. J. M. Schoph (Ed.), *Models of paleobiology* (pp. 82–115). San Francisco: W. W. Freeman.

Emmons, R. (1986). Personal strivings: An approach to personality and subjective well-being. *Journal of Personality and Social Psychology, 51,* 1058–1068.

Finkel, N. J. (1974). Strens and traumas: An attempt at categorization. *American Journal of Community Psychology, 2,* 265–273.

Finkel, N. J. (1975). Strens, traumas and trauma resolution. *American Journal of Community Psychology, 3,* 173–178.

Finkel, N. J., & Jacobsen, C. A. (1977). Significant life experiences in an adult sample. *American Journal of Community Psychology, 5,* 165–275.

Fitzgerald, T., Tennen, H., Affleck, G., & Pransky, G. (1993). Quality of life after coronary artery bypass surgery: The importance of initial expectancies and control appraisals. *Journal of Behavioral Medicine, 16,* 25–43.

Folkman, S. (1992). Making the case for coping. In B. N. Carpenter (Ed.), *Personal coping: Theory, research, and application* (pp. 31–46). Westport, CT: Praeger.

Fontaine, K., Mastead, A., & Wagner, H. (1993). Optimism, perceived control over stress, and coping. *European Journal of Personality, 27,* 267–281.

Franklin, R. D., Allison, D. B., & Gorman, B. S. (Eds.) (1996). *Design and analysis of single-case research.* Mahwah, N. J.: Lawrence Erlbaum Associates.

Frye, N. (1957). *Anatomy of criticism.* Princeton, N. J.: Princeton University Press.

Gorsuch, R., & McPherson, S. (1989). Intrinsic/extrinsic measurement: I/E-revised and single-item scales. *Journal for the Scientific Study of Religion, 28,* 348–354.

Gould, S. J. (1993). *Eight little piggies: reflections on natural history.* New York: W.W. Norton.

Gould, S. J., & Eldredge, N. (1977). Punctuated equilibria: The tempo and mode of evolution reconsidered. *Paleobiology, 3,* 115–151.

Greenberg, M. A. (1995). Cognitive processing of traumas: The role of intrusive thoughts and reappraisals. *Journal of Applied Social Psychology, 25,* 1262–1296.

Grass, G. (1990). *Two states, one nation?* New York: Harcourt Brace Jovanovitch.

Haan, N. (1992). The assessment of coping, defense, and stress. In L. Goldberger & S. Breznitz (Eds.), *Handbook of stress: Theoretical and clinical aspects* (2nd ed., pp. 258–273). Toronto: The Free Press.

Harvey, J. (1965). Cognitive aspects of affective arousal. In S. Tomkins & C. Izard (Eds.), *Affect, cognition, and personality: Empirical studies* (pp. 242–262). New York: Springer.

Harvey, J. H., Orbuch, T. L., Chwalisz, K. D., & Garwood, G. (1991). Coping with sexual assault: The roles of account-making and confiding. *Journal of Traumatic Stress, 4,* 515–531.

Herman, J. L. (1992). *Trauma and recovery: The aftermath of violence from domestic abuse to political terror.* New York: Basic.

Hermans, H. J. M., & Hermans-Jansen, E. (1995). *Self-narratives: The construction of meaning in psychotherapy.* New York: Guilford Press.

Hogan, R. (1987). Personality psychology: Back to basics. In J. Aronoff, A. I. Rabin, & R. A. Zucker (Eds.), *The emergence of personality* (pp. 79–104). New York: Springer.

Hoorens, V. (1996). Self-favoring biases for positive and negative characteristics: Independent phenomena? *Journal of Social and Clinical Psychology, 15,* 53–67.

Horowitz, M. J. (1986). *Stress response syndromes* (2nd ed.). Northvale, NJ: Aronson.

Houston, B. K. (1987). Stress and coping. In C. R. Snyder & C. Ford (Eds.), *Coping with negative life events: Clinical and social-psychological perspectives* (pp. 373–399). New York: Plenum.

James, W. (1902). *The varieties of religious experience.* Cambridge, MA: Harvard University Press.

Janoff-Bulman, R. (1992). *Shattered assumptions: Toward a new psychology of trauma.* New York: The Free Press.

Janoff-Bulman, R., & Frieze, I. (1983). A theoretical perspective for understanding reactions to victimization. *Journal of Social Issues, 39,* 1–17.

Janoff-Bulman, R., & Schwartzberg, S. (1991). Toward a general model of personal change. In C. R. Snyder & D. R. Forsyth (Eds.), *Handbook of social and clinical psychology: The health perspective* (pp. 488–508). New York: Pergamon Press.

Jones, E. E., & Nisbett, R. E. (1971). *The actor and the observer: Divergent perceptions of the causes of behavior.* Morristown, NJ: General Learning Press.

Kiecolt, K. J. (1994). Stress and the decision to change oneself: A theoretical model. *Social Psychology Quarterly, 57,* 49–63.

Kiecolt-Glaser, J., & Williams, D. (1987). Self-blame, compliance, and distress among burn patients. *Journal of Personality and Social Psychology, 53,* 187–193.

Klinger, E. (1977). *Meaning and void: Inner experience and the incentives in people's lives.* Minneapolis: University of Minnesota Press.

Kobasa, S. C. (1979). Stressful life events, personality, and health: An inquiry into hardiness. *Journal of Personality and Social Psychology, 37,* 1–11.

Landman, J. (1993). *Regret: The persistence of the possible.* New York: Oxford University Press.

Larsen R., & Kasimatis, M. (1991). Day-to-day physical symptoms: Individual differences in the occurrence, duration, and emotional concomitants of minor daily illnesses. *Journal of Personality, 59,* 387–424.

Lazarus, R., & Folkman, S. (1984). *Stress, appraisal and coping.* New York: Springer.

Lewis, H. B. (1971). *Shame and guilt in neurosis.* New York: International Universities Press.

Liang, M., Rogers, M., Larson, M., Eaton, H., Murawksi, B., Taylor, J., Swafford, J., & Schur, P. (1984). The psychosocial impact of systemic lupus erythematosus and rheumatoid arthritis. *Arthritis and Rheumatism, 27,* 13–19.

Lifton, R. J. (1993). *The protean self: Human resilience in an age of fragmentation.* New York: Basic Books.

Linville, P. (1985). Self-complexity and affective extremity: Don't put all of your eggs in one basket. *Social Cognition, 3,* 94–120.

Linville, P. (1987). Self-complexity as a cognitive buffer against stress-related illness and depression. *Journal of Personality and Social Psychology, 52,* 663–676.

Litt, M., Tennen, H., Affleck, G., & Klock, S. (1992). Coping and cognitive factors in adaptation to in vitro fertilization failure. *Journal of Behavioral Medicine, 15,* 119–126.

Loder, J. E. (1981). *The transforming moment: Understanding convictional experiences.* New York: Harper & Row.

Marshall, G., Wortman, C., Kusulas, J., Hervig, L., & Vickers, R. (1992). Distinguishing optimism from pessimism: Relations to fundamental dimensions of mood and personality. *Journal of Personality and Social Psychology, 62,* 1067–1074.

McAdams, D. P. (1993). *The stories we live by: Personal myths and the making of the self.* New York: William Morrow.

McAdams, D. P. (1994a). Can personality change? Levels of stability and growth in personality across the life span. In T. F. Heatherton & J. L. Weinberger (Eds.), *Can personality change?* (pp. 299–313). Washington, DC: American Psychological Association.

McAdams, D. P. (1994b). A psychology of the stranger. *Psychological Inquiry, 5,* 145–148.

McCann, I. L., & Pearlman, L. A. (1990). *Psychological trauma and the adult survivor: Theory, therapy, and transformation.* New York: Bruner/Mazel.

McClelland, D. (1951). *Personality.* New York: Holt, Rinehart & Winston.

McCrae, R. R. (1992). The five-factor model: Issues and applications. *Journal of Personality,* 60.

McCrae, R. R., & Costa, P. T., Jr. (1986). Personality, coping, and coping effectiveness. *Journal of Personality, 54,* 385–405.

McCrae, R. R., & Costa, P. T., Jr. (1990). *Personality in adulthood.* New York: Guilford.

McCrae, R. R., & Costa, P. T., Jr. (1996). Toward a new generation of personality theories: Theoretical contexts for the five-factor model. In J. S. Wiggins (Ed.), *The five-factor model of personality: Theoretical perspectives* (pp. 51–87). New York: Guilford.

McIntosh, D. N., Silver, R. C., & Wortman, C. B. (1993). Religion's role in adjustment to a negative life event: Coping with the loss of a child. *Journal of Personality and Social Psychology, 65,* 812–821.

McLaney, A., Tennen, H., Affleck, G., & Fitzgerald, T. (1995). Reactions to impaired fertility: The vicissitudes of primary and secondary control appraisals. *Women's Health: Research on Gender, Behavior, and Policy, 1,* 143–160.

Mendola, R. (1990). *Coping with chronic pain: Perceptions of control and dispositional optimism as moderators of psychological distress.* Unpublished doctoral dissertation, University of Connecticut, Storrs.

Miller, S. M., & Kirsch, N. (1987). Sex differences in cognitive coping with stress. In R. C. Barnett, L. Biener, & G. K. Baruch (Eds.), *Gender and stress* (pp. 278–307). New York: The Free Press.

Miller, W. R., & C'deBaca, J. (1994). Quantum change: Toward a psychology of transformation. In T. F. Heatherton & J. L. Weinberger (Eds.), *Can personality change?* (pp. 253–280). Washington, DC: American Psychological Association.

Mischel, W., & Shoda, Y. (1995). A cognitive-affective system theory of personality: Reconceptualizing situations, dispositions, dynamics, and invariance in personality structure. *Psychological Review, 102,* 246–268.

Moos, R. H., & Schaefer, J. A. (1990). Coping resources and processes: Current concepts and measures. In H. S. Friedman (Ed.), *Personality and disease* (pp. 234–257). New York: Wiley.

Morgan, H., & Janoff-Bulman, R. (1994). Positive and negative self-complexity: Patterns of adjustment following traumatic versus non-traumatic life experiences. *Journal of Social and Clinical Psychology, 13,* 63–85.

Mroczek, D., Spiro, A., Aldwin, C., Ozer, D., & Bosse, R. (1993). Construct validation of optimism and pessimism in older men: Findings from the normative aging study. *Health Psychology, 12,* 406–409.

Norris, F. H., & Murrell, S. A. (1987). Transitory impact of life events stress on psychological symptoms in older adults. *Journal of Health and Social Behavior, 28,* 197–211.

O'Leary, V. E., & Ickovics, J. R. (1995). Resilience and thriving in response to challenge: An opportunity for a prardigm shift in women's health. *Women's Health: Research on Gender, Behavior, and Policy, 1,* 121–142.

Palys, T. S., & Little, B. R. (1983). Perceived life satisfaction and the organization of personal project systems. *Journal of Personality and Social Psychology, 44,* 1221–1230.

Park, C., & Cohen, L. H. (1992). Religious beliefs and practices and the coping process. In B. Carpenter (Ed.), *Personal coping: Theory, research, and application* (pp. 185–198). Westport, CT: Praeger.

Park, C., Cohen, L., & Murch, R. (1996). Assessment and prediction of stress-related growth. *Journal of Personality, 64,* 71–105.

Parker, J. D. A., & Endler, N. S. (1996). Coping and defense: A historical overview. In M. Zeidner & N. S. Endler (Eds.), *Handbook of coping: Theory, research, applications* (pp. 3–23). New York: Wiley.

Parkes, C. (1975). What becomes of redundant world models? A contribution to the study of adaptation to change. *British Journal of Medical Psychology, 48,* 131–137.

Pearlman, L. A., & Saakvitne, K. W. (1995). *Trauma and the therapist: Countertransference and vicarious traumatization in psychotherapy with incest survivors.* New York: Norton.

Pervin, L. A. (1994). Personality stability, personality change, and the question of process. In T. F. Heatherton & J. L. Weinberger (Eds.), *Can personality change?* (pp. 315–330). Washington, DC: American Psychological Association.

Porter, L. S., & Stone, A. A. (1995). Are there really gender differences in coping?: A reconsideration of previous data and results from a daily study. *Journal of Social and Clinical Psychology, 14,* 184–202.

Premack, D. (1970). Mechanisms of self-control. In W. A. Hunt (Ed.), *Learning mechanisms in smoking* (pp. 107–123). Chicago: Aldine.

Prochaska, J. O., DiClemente, C. C., & Norcross, J. C. (1992). In search of how people change: Applications to addictive behaviors. *American Psychologist, 47,* 1102–1114.

Ramey, C. T., Lee, M. W., & Burchinal, M. R. (1989). *Developmental plasticity and predictability: Consequences of ecological change.* In M. H. Bornstein & N. A. Krasnegor (Eds.), Stability and continuity in mental development (pp. 217–233). Hilldale, NJ: Lawrence Erlbaum Associates.

Rothbaum, F., Weisz, J., & Snyder, S. (1982). Changing the world and changing the self: A two-process model of perceived control. *Journal of Personality and Social Psychology, 42,* 5–37.

Ruch, L., Chandler, S., & Harter, R. (1980). Life change and rape impact. *Journal of Health and Social Behavior, 21,* 248–260.

Rutter, M. (1987). Psychosocial resilience and protective mechanisms. *American Journal of Orthopsychiatry, 57,* 316–331.

Ryff, C. D. (1991). Possible selves in adulthood and old age: A tale of shifting horizons. *Psychology and Aging, 6,* 286–295.

Ryff, C. D., & Keyes, L. M. (1995). The structure of psychological well-being revisited. *Journal of Personality and Social Psychology, 69,* 719–727.

Ryff, C. D., Lee, Y. H., Essex, M.J., & Schmutte, P. S. (1994). My children and me: Midlife evaluations of grown children and self. *Psychology and Aging, 9,* 195–205.

Schaefer, J. A., & Moos, R. H. (1992). Making the case for coping. In B. N. Carpenter (Ed.), *Personal coping: Theory, research, and application* (pp. 149–170). Westport, CT: Praeger.

Scheier, M., & Carver, C. (1985). Optimism, coping, and health: Assessment and implications of generalized outcome expectancies. *Health Psychology, 4,* 219–247.

Scheier, M., & Carver, C. (1987). Dispositional optimism and physical well-being: The influence of generalized outcome expectancies on health. *Journal of Personality, 55,* 169–210.

Scheier, M., Carver, C., & Bridges, M. (1994). Distinguishing optimism from neuroticism (and trait anxiety, self-mastery, and self-esteem): A reevaluation of the Life Orientation Test. *Journal of Personality and Social Psychology, 67,* 1063–1078.

Scheier, M., Matthews, K., Owens, J., Magovern, G., Lefebvre, R., Abbot, R., & Carver, C. (1989). Dispositional optimism and recovery from coronary artery bypass surgery: The beneficial effects on physical and psychological well-being. *Journal of Personality and Social Psychology, 57,* 1024–1040.

Shiffman, S., Fischer, L., Paty, J., Gnys, M., Hickcox, M., & Kassel, J. (1994). Drinking and smoking: A field study of their association. *Annals of Behavioral Medicine, 16,* 203–209.

Shoda, Y., Mischel, W., & Wright, J. C. (1994). Intra-individual stability in the organization and patterning of behavior: Incorporating psychological situations into the idiographic analysis of personality. *Journal of Personality and Social Psychology, 67,* 674–687.

Snyder, C., Harris, C., Anderson, J., Holleran, S., Irving, L., Sigmon, S., Yoshinobu, L., Gibb, J., Largelle, C., & Harney, P. (1991). The will and the ways: Development and validation of an individual difference measure of hope. *Journal of Personality and Social Psychology*, 60, 570–585.

Snyder, C., Irving, L., & Anderson, J. (1991). Hope and health. In C. R. Snyder & D. R. Forsyth (Eds.), *Handbook of social and clinical psychology: The health perspective* (pp. 285–305). New York: Pergamon Press.

Taylor, S. (1983). Adjustment to threatening events: A theory of cognitive adaption. *American Psychologist*, 38, 624–630.

Taylor, S. E. (1989). *Positive illusions: Creative self-deception and the healthy mind.* New York: Basic Books.

Taylor, S. E., Kemeny, M., Aspinwall, L., Schneider, S., Rodriguez, R., & Herbert, M. (1992). Optimism, coping, psychological distress, and high-risk sexual behavior among men at risk for AIDS. *Journal of Personality and Social Psychology*, 63, 460–473.

Taylor, S. E., Lichtman, R., & Wood, J. (1984). Attributions, beliefs about control, and adjustment to breast cancer. *Journal of Personality and Social Psychology*, 46, 489–502.

Taylor, S., Wood, J., & Lichtman, R. (1983). It could be worse: Selective evaluation as a response to victimization. *Journal of Social Issues*, 39, 19–40.

Tedeschi, R. G., & Calhoun, L. G. (1995). *Trauma and transformation: Growing in the aftermath of suffering.* Thousand Oaks, CA: Sage.

Tedeschi, R., & Calhoun, L. (1996). The post-traumatic growth inventory: Measuring the positive legacy of trauma. *Journal of Traumatic Stress*, 9, 455–471.

Tedeschi, R., Calhoun, L., & Gross, B. (1993, August). *Construing benefits from negative events: An examination of personality variables.* Paper presented at the Annual Meeting of the American Psychological Association, Toronto, Canada.

Tennen, H. & Affleck, G. (1996). Daily processes in coping with chronic pain: Methods and analytic strategies. In M. Zeidner & N. Endler (Eds.), *Handbook of coping* (pp. 151–177). New York: Wiley.

Tennen, H., & Affleck, G. (1997). Social comparison as a coping process: A critical review and application to chronic pain disorders. In B. Buunk & R. Gibbons (Eds.), *Health, coping and well-being* (pp. 263–298). Mahwah, NJ: Lawrence Erlbaum Associates.

Tennen, H., Affleck, G., & Mendola, R. (1991a). Causal explanations for infertility: Their relation to control appraisals and psychological adjustment. In A. Stanton & C. Dunkel-Schetter (Eds.), *Infertility: Perspectives from stress and coping research* (pp. 109–132). New York: Plenum.

Tennen, H., Affleck, G., & Mendola, R. (1991b). Coping with smell and taste disorders. In T. Getchell, R. Doty, L. Bartoshuk, & J. Snow (Eds.), *Smell and taste in health and disease.* (pp. 787–801). New York: Raven.

Tennen, H., Affleck, G., Urrows, S., Higgins, P., & Mendola, R. (1992). Perceiving control, construing benefits, and daily processes in rheumatoid arthritis. *Canadian Journal of Behavioral Science*, 24, 186–203.

Thompson, S. (1985). Finding positive meaning in a stressful event and coping. *Basic and Applied Social Psychology*, 6, 279–295.

Thompson, S. (1991). The search for meaning following a stroke. *Basic and Applied Social Psychology*, 12, 81–96.

Thorne, A. (1989). Conditional patterns, transference, and the coherence of personality across time. In D. M. Buss & N. Cantor (Eds.), *Personality psychology: Recent trends and emerging directions* (pp. 149–159). New York: Springer-Verlag.

Vingerhoets, A. J. M., & Van Heck, G. L. (1990). Gender, coping and psychosomatic symptoms. *Psychological Medicine*, 20, 125–135.

von Glaserfeld, E. (1984). An introduction to radical constructivism. In P. Watzlawick (Ed.), *The invented reality* (pp. 17–40). New York: Norton.

Vrana, S., & Lauterbach, D. (1994). Prevalence of traumatic events and post-traumatic psychological symptoms in a nonclinical sample of college students. *Journal of Traumatic Stress, 7*, 289–302.

Wallerstein, J. S. (1986). Women after divorce: Preliminary report from a ten-year follow-up. *American Journal of Orthopsychiatry, 56*, 65–77.

Watzlawick, P. (1978). *The language of change*. New York: Basic Books.

Watzlawick, P., Weakland, J. H., & Fisch, R. (1974). *Change: Principles of problem formation and problem resolution*. New York: Norton.

Weinberger, J. L. (1994). Can personality change? In T. F. Heatherton & J. L. Weinberger (Eds.), *Can personality change?* (pp. 333–350). Washington, DC: American Psychological Association.

Wollman, C., & Felton, B. (1983). Social supports as stress buffers for adult cancer patients. *Psychosomatic Medicine, 45*, 321–331.

Yarom, N. (1983). Facing death in war: An existential crisis. In S. Breznitz (Ed.), *Stress in Israel* (pp. 3–38). New York: Van Nostrand Reinhold.

Zeidner, M., & Saklofske, D. (1996). Adaptive and maladaptive coping. In M. Zeidner & N. S. Endler (Eds.), *Handbook of coping: Theory, research, applications* (pp. 505–531). New York: Wiley.

5

The Context for Posttraumatic Growth: Life Crises, Individual and Social Resources, and Coping

Jeanne A. Schaefer
Rudolf H. Moos
Department of Veterans Affairs and Stanford University Medical Centers

Common crises such as physical illness, bereavement, and divorce, and dramatic events such as natural disasters and war each shape the lives of the people they touch in unique and lasting ways. Most of the growing body of research on traumatic events and peoples' adaptation to them emphasizes the painful emotions and physical and psychological symptoms that these events typically produce, at least in the short run (Bromet & Dew, 1995; Rubonis & Bickman, 1991). But, in the aftermath of adversity, people often show tenacious resilience and eventually experience personal growth. For many people, life crises are the catalyst for enhanced personal and social resources and the development of new coping skills.

Why do life crises lead to greater self-reliance and maturity, better relationships with family and friends, and new problem-solving skills for some people, but shatter the lives of others? To what extent do characteristics of the crisis itself, such as its severity, determine whether people emerge better or worse off? What role do social and community resources play in bringing about personal transformations? How do people's personal resources and coping skills contribute to successful adaptation and personal growth? We focus on these questions here.

In a quest to understand individuals' positive adaptation to life crises, researchers have emphasized factors that enable people to confront stressors and maintain healthy functioning and have begun to identify specific resources that may engender personal growth. We developed a conceptual model (Fig. 5.1) to encompass the most important sets of relevant variables and to conceptualize the determinants of positive outcomes of crises (Schaefer & Moos, 1992). The model posits that environmental and personal system factors (Panels I and II) shape life crises and their aftermath (Panel III) and influence appraisal and coping responses (Panel IV), and thereby contribute to the development of positive outcomes or personal growth (Panel V). This model is consistent with our resources perspective on coping in which coping functions as one essential mechanism through which personal and social resources foreshadow improved psychological functioning after a person experiences a life crisis (Holahan & Moos, 1994).

The personal system encompasses individuals' sociodemographic characteristics and such personal resources as self-efficacy, resilience, motivation, health status, and prior crisis experience. The environmental system comprises individuals' relationships with and social support from family members, friends, and coworkers, as well as aspects of their financial, home, and community living situation. Event-related factors include the severity, duration, and timing of a crisis as well as its scope, that is, whether it affects an individual or a group of people.

We separate the coping responses that people use to manage life crises into approach and avoidance coping. Approach coping involves trying to analyze the crisis in a logical way, reappraising the crisis in a more positive

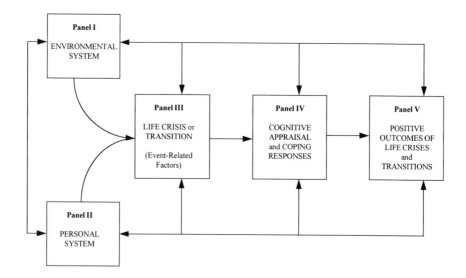

FIG. 5.1. A conceptual model for understanding positive outcomes of life crises and transitions.

light, seeking support, and taking actions to solve the problem. Avoidance coping includes trying to minimize the problem, deciding that nothing can be done to change the problem itself, seeking alternative rewards, and venting emotions (Moos & Schaefer, 1993).

Three major types of positive outcomes may emerge after a person experiences a crisis: (a) enhanced social resources, such as better relationships with family and friends and new support networks and confidant relationships, (b) enhanced personal resources, such as more cognitive differentiation, assertiveness, self-understanding, empathy, altruism, and maturity; and (c) the development of enhanced coping skills, such as the ability to think through a problem logically, to seek help when needed, and regulate affect (Schaefer & Moos, 1992).

In this chapter, we review selected life crises that may be associated with successful adaptation and PTG, and use our model to identify factors that provide the context for growth. We focus on how features of the life crisis and individuals' environmental and personal resources influence appraisal and coping strategies. We then examine how these factors affect individuals' adaptation to life crises and the extent to which they experience PTG. We conclude by identifying challenging areas for future research on PTG.

LIFE CRISES AND POSTTRAUMATIC GROWTH

In principle, any life crisis can spark posttraumatic growth. Here, we focus on how people are transformed by and may eventually develop some benefits through their experience of life-threatening physical illness, divorce, bereavement, natural disasters, and war and combat. With the exception of divorce, people rarely choose to confront these types of life crises. Nevertheless, after an interval of painful emotional reactions and heightened distress, most people adapt successfully to their new circumstances and many emerge from the crisis stronger and wiser than before. Such positive outcomes are quite common; more than 50% of people who experience life crises report some benefits from them (Schaefer & Moos, 1992).

Illness

In his book *A Whole New Life*, the well-known writer, Reynolds Price (1994), succinctly captured the metamorphosis in personal identity that often occurs after confronting the physical and psychological changes wrought by an illness. At age 50, Price developed a cancerous spinal cord tumor and recounted his often harrowing struggle with surgery and radiation, loss of control of his lower body, severe pain, and the long, slow process of rehabilitation. Personal characteristics of determination and humor; a strong network of friends, coworkers, and caretakers; and a coping style characterized by self-analysis, religious faith, and positive reappraisal helped Price to continue with his creative writing and to conclude:

> So *disaster* then, yes, for me for a while—great chunks of four years. *Catastrophe* surely, a literally upended life with all parts strewn and some of the most urgent parts lost for good, within and without. But if I were called on to value honestly my present life beside my past—the years from 1933 till '84 against the years after—I'd have to say that, despite an enjoyable fifty-year start, these recent years since full catastrophe have gone still better. They've brought more in and sent more out—more love and care, more knowledge and patience, more work in less time. (p. 179)

As in this example, the threat of a shortened lifespan often prompts individuals to reexamine their values, change their priorities, and gain insights into how to live a more meaningful life. Pain and loss of function frequently trigger empathy for others with similar problems. By forcing individuals to rely on others, the vulnerability and increased dependence that illness often brings can stimulate an increase in social resources. Moreover, caregiving tasks that arise from attending to the needs of an ill family member and from the threatened loss of the individual may strengthen family relationships. New relationships may be developed and new coping skills learned in support and educational groups. Individuals also frequently develop enhanced information seeking skills and new knowledge in an attempt to learn more about an illness and its treatment. For example, many people with AIDS develop sophisticated knowledge about alternative drug therapies, and then develop closer relationships with other affected individuals when they share this information.

Human Immunodeficiency Virus (HIV) Infection.   HIV-positive individuals may experience personal growth as they cope with an uncertain future and try to make sense of it. In-depth clinical interviews (Schwartzberg, 1994) found that a majority of HIV-positive gay men identified some positive aspects in their situation. For some men, being HIV positive was a transformative experience—it brought out their talents, strengths, and internal resources. The possibility of a shortened lifespan compelled the men to appreciate time, focus on the here and now, accomplish personal goals, and live life to the fullest. Some men became more compassionate and empathic; one physician described how his HIV-positive status had helped him become a better AIDS doctor, while an HIV-positive minister felt he could empathize more with others' pain. Relationships between positive outcomes were evident in Schwartzberg's descriptions of the benefits that the men reported. For example, some men engaged in altruistic behavior, such as helping less experienced HIV-positive men and AIDS patients. In turn, this altruism served as a way for the men to derive meaning from their illness.

For many men, the HIV diagnosis produced a greater sense of kinship with humanity and a feeling of community, especially with the gay community and with other HIV-positive people. The sense of community flowed, in part, from coping efforts that led the men to seek out support groups for HIV-positive men. Likewise, Gaskins and Brown (1992) found that being diagnosed with HIV helped some men to accept their sexual orientation. Individuals who learned they were HIV positive also developed a new perspective on life and changed their lifestyle. They eliminated high-risk behaviors that compromised their health, such as excessive alcohol consumption and drug abuse.

Cancer.   Many studies have focused on cancer's impact on individuals and their families (Kristjanson & Ashcroft, 1994). PTG, reflected in enhanced personal and social resources, is quite common among persons with cancer. Many cancer patients report better attitudes toward themselves, others, and life. The experience of having a life-threatening illness can help patients put their life in perspective, stimulate a new appreciation of and closer relationships with family and friends, renew patients' religious faith, and foster a greater appreciation of nature (O'Connor, Wicker, & Germino, 1990; Welch-McCaffrey, Hoffman, Leigh, Loescher, & Meyskens, 1989).

A number of studies of women with breast cancer have identified positive changes. For example, Northouse (1994) found that the quality of many young women's marital relationships improved after mastectomy. Similarly, Zemore, Rinholm, Shepel, and Richards (1989) noted that many women with breast cancer experienced closer family ties and a more positive outlook on life. The experience of coping with cancer also strengthened the women's character, brought them closer to God, and helped them to better understand others' feelings.

Similar findings have been noted among men with advanced testicular cancer. More than half of the men that Rieker, Edbril, and Garnick (1985) studied reported that important aspects of their life functioning had improved after the cancer was diagnosed. Patients had a better outlook on life, more self-respect, better relationships with their spouse and children, and less fear of death. A number of patients viewed cancer as a challenge; they considered it an accomplishment to have endured the treatment and saw the loss of sexual function and infertility associated with treatment as a distressing but reasonable tradeoff for potential freedom from cancer.

Bone Marrow Transplant (BMT). BMT is a drastic, life-threatening cancer treatment that is emotionally taxing for patients and their families; the uncertain future that plagues these patients may contribute to depression and severe distress. Nevertheless, Fromm, Andrykowski, and Hunt (1996) found that adult BMT patients' turmoil and fear were matched by a corresponding number of positive psychological outcomes that contributed to their quality of life. The most common outcomes that patients reported were acquiring a new philosophy and greater appreciation of life, becoming less selfish or more outgoing, and experiencing improved family relationships and more family support. Similarly, Curbow, Legro, Baker, Wingard, and Somerfield (1993) found that the majority of BMT survivors reported finding new meaning and value in life; increased self-esteem, self-confidence, and independence; new life goals and direction; increased compassion; and better family relationships.

Divorce

The typically painful, permanent rupture of a relationship that is signaled by divorce often foreshadows positive life changes. Wallerstein (1986) found that more than 40% of women showed long-term improvements in psychological functioning 10 years after their divorce. In the postdivorce period, the women became more assertive and developed more realistic views of themselves. Some women who did not work while they were married developed successful careers after their divorce that contributed to increases in their self-esteem.

In another longitudinal study, Nelson (1989, 1994) examined the changes that separated and married women experienced at four points in time over a 6-year interval. More of the separated women reported positive changes, such as reduced conflict, abuse, and distress, and increased independence, control over their life, self-confidence, and optimism. Changes continued to occur over time. At the 6-year follow-up, more of the separated women had developed new social resources. In contrast, women who remained married experienced positive changes in their relationships with their husbands, most probably because these women focused more on enhancing existing family resources than on developing new resources.

Bereavement

Perhaps because of the challenges it presents, experiencing the death of a family member or friend can engender a personal metamorphosis. In interviews with bereaved individuals, Kessler (1987) noted that many of them showed enhanced personal resources, especially wisdom and maturity and changes in their perspective on life. After their loss, bereaved people discovered new personal strengths; they became more independent, compassionate, emotionally stronger, and more purposeful. Greater independence and self-reliance emerged as individuals who were now alone faced the prospect of having to do things on their own and handle new responsibilities. A number of the bereaved indicated that they had become more aware of the fragility of life, of their vulnerability to tragedy, and of their inability to predict the future. They came to recognize that each moment of life provides an opportunity and they tried to live life more fully.

Calhoun and Tedeschi (1989/1990) identified comparable changes in bereaved individuals' personal resources. These individuals saw themselves as more mature, independent, wise, and better able to cope with future crises. They were more accepting of their mortality and their religious beliefs deepened.

Disasters

The literature on disasters has proliferated as researchers seek to understand individuals' responses to the dramatic and often abrupt changes wrought by fires, floods, hurricanes, earthquakes, volcanic eruptions, and nuclear power plant explosions. Although most of the research on disasters has focused on posttraumatic stress disorder (PTSD) as the outcome of interest (Rubonis & Bickman, 1991), some studies have focused on successful adaptation and the positive outcomes that may ensue following successful coping with a disaster and its aftermath.

Coffman (1994) examined the experiences of school-age children who endured Hurricane Andrew. She found that children grew closer to parents, siblings, extended family members, and neighbors. Children also reached out to others and expressed concern and sadness for those who were less fortunate than themselves. Similarly, Saylor, Swenson, and Powell (1992) reported that parents of preschool children who lived in the area hit by Hurricane Hugo noted positive changes in their children, such as increased concern for others, insight into people's needs for basic necessities such as food, shelter, fuel, and clothing, and a beginning understanding of the roles of people who may help survivors cope with the aftermath of a disaster, such as insurance adjusters and contractors.

When rescue workers confront massive death and destruction from disasters, they often find that their lives change as a result. For example, when the skywalks at the Kansas City Hyatt Hotel collapsed, killing over 100 people and injuring nearly 200, the majority of rescue workers at the disaster changed their view of life. The experience left some workers with an increased understanding of the fragility of life; others became more altruistic and compassionate (Miles, Demi, & Mostyn-Aker, 1984).

War and Combat

Military nurses who served during the Vietnam War indicated that their experiences contributed to their personal and professional growth (Scannell-Desch, 1996). The danger and uncertainty that characterized the nurses' daily lives fostered a special camaraderie and teamwork. The trauma of war nurtured deep and lasting friendships, some of which endured many years after the war ended. The nurses found that they valued life, people, and freedom more and had a deeper feeling of pride and patriotism toward their country. They also had a better sense of their capabilities and limitations and were less judgmental toward others. Many of the nurses described their time in Vietnam as the most rewarding professional experience in their career. The work was challenging and they gained advanced clinical knowledge and skills.

The extreme demands of combat and the threat of death that Israeli soldiers who fought on the front line in the Yom Kippur War faced made them aware of their vulnerability and mortality. Consequently, they developed closer relationships with their spouse, children, and others, enjoyed life more, and tried to live more meaningful lives (Yarom, 1983).

The civilian population may also undergo positive changes after they confront and survive the horrors of war. Rosenthal and Levy-Shiff (1993) examined Israeli mothers' perceptions of their infants' and toddlers' reactions to stressors associated with the Gulf War, such as the sound of wailing sirens that warned of missile attack, having to sleep in sealed cots, or wearing gas masks to protect against attacks by chemical missiles. Although more than half of the children displayed adjustment problems such as prolonged crying, sleep disturbances, and temper tantrums, 30% became more helpful and assumed more responsibility. The uncertainty posed by the threat of Scud missile attacks also took its toll on adult family members, who experienced intense emotional responses during the early attacks. Nevertheless, more than 75% of the mothers identified eventual positive consequences of these experiences, especially renewed awareness of their family's closeness, and commitment.

THE CONTEXT FOR SUCCESSFUL ADAPTATION AND GROWTH

The context for effective adaptation to life crises and PTG comprises a dynamic interplay of factors—the nature of the crisis, personal and environmental resources, and how individuals perceive and choose to cope with the crisis.

Characteristics of the Crisis

People's responses to crises vary immensely. In part, this variation may reflect fundamental differences in what appears to be similar crises, as well as differences in individuals' crisis experiences and short-term outcomes. Life crises may differ in their severity, individuals' proximity to and amount of exposure to them, extent of loss, and scope, that is, whether an individual, family, or whole community experiences the event. Crises also vary in their duration, predictability, and suddenness of onset.

Some of these event-related factors have been linked to crisis outcomes. For example, terminal illnesses of longer duration that afford spouses the opportunity to prepare for their partner's death tend to result in better postbereavement outcomes (Schaefer & Moos, 1992). By influencing the coping tasks individuals confront and their psychological adaptation, event-related factors may affect the likelihood of PTG.

Intensely personal crises, such as a life-threatening illness, may induce individuals to value life more. This type of crisis may also elicit support from family and friends, strengthen emotional ties between family members, and, in turn, facilitate an individual's adaptation. In contrast, PTG may be less likely following large scale disasters and epidemics that affect entire families and communities and deplete the family's or community's ability to provide support.

Physical Illness.   The studies that have examined illness-related factors imply that the initial severity of the threat and the short-term outcome are important factors in long-term adjustment to life crises. A successful medical outcome in the face of a poor prognosis and more threat to life seems to enhance the prospects for PTG, whereas disfigurement and loss of key aspects of functioning reduces them.

Fromm et al. (1996) found that individuals who had a poorer prognosis prior to BMT reported more psychosocial benefits following successful BMT, such as a greater appreciation of life and improved family relationships. A high degree of threat posed by an individual's illness is likely to cause substantial distress, which when alleviated, may be a stimulus for positive change. Patients who have more advanced disease and a poor prognosis and still survive in the face of these odds may be especially motivated to seek meaning in their illness experience, and thus, to show positive changes in their quality of life. Such patients may also want to justify their good luck and feel compelled to keep their part of the "bargain" for a new life, which typically entails a more mature and helpful personal orientation.

Among men treated for testicular cancer, those who were left with nonimpaired sexual functioning were more likely to link the cancer and its treatment with positive psychosocial outcomes, such as increased self-respect, a greater ability to enjoy themselves, and strengthened marital relationships (Rieker et al., 1985). Taylor and her colleagues (1985) found that women who had a poorer prognosis and more radical surgery for breast cancer experienced poorer psychological adjustment. However, even in the light of these risk factors, when women experienced less sense of disfigurement and stability in affection and sexual activity in their marriage, they showed better adjustment. For women and men who undergo cancer treatment, better physical functioning and less disfigurement may make them and their spouse more able to maintain a positive marital relationship, and, consequently, to view their experience in a positive light.

People who suffer more devastating life crises may experience more positive outcomes because these crises trigger an outpouring of support from others. In this vein, Tempelaar and colleagues (1989) found that cancer patients in the worst medical condition experienced the most help and support. A severe, life-threatening illness may elicit more support from family members and friends and thus lead the ill person to experience positive personal and social changes. In contrast, some illnesses are so severe or present such immense burdens that they deplete individual and family resources and lead to continuing distress and depression.

Disasters.   The findings on exposure to life-threatening natural disasters are quite different from those on exposure to life-threatening illness. In general, there is a dose–response relationship such that more severe exposure is associated with more psychological symptoms and distress (Carr et al., 1995; Lonigan, Shannon, Taylor, Finch, Sallee, 1994; Pynoos et al., 1993). A high level of distress may foreclose some opportunities for growth, especially when no support is forthcoming. Alternatively, people who experience more immediate distress may mobilize more support and thus be more likely to undergo long-term personal transformations.

Adaptation to large-scale disasters appears to depend not only on individuals' personal resources, but on the extent of community destruction and the death toll as well. When disasters wreak havoc on an entire community, few people may be left with the resources available to provide aid and emotional support. Among older adults in southeastern Kentucky who confronted two floods during the span of 3 years, those who were exposed to a combination of personal loss and high levels of community destruction (a high number of homes destroyed in their county relative to the population) experienced the greatest increase in psychological symptoms (Phifer & Norris, 1989).

Disasters that result in high death rates also are associated with more psychological problems for their victims (Rubonis & Bickman, 1991). High casualties leave a large number of bereaved people in the community. In turn, communitywide bereavement may lead to high levels of distress that prolong recovery and postpone PTG among members of the community.

War and Violent Crime.   As with disasters, proximity and exposure to war zones and violent crime have been shown to affect people's psychological adaptation. Rosenthal and Levy-Shiff (1993) found that during the Gulf War, Israeli children living farther from the target zone for Scud missile attacks displayed fewer changes in routine habits and adjustment problems than those near areas hit by missiles. Likewise, among children whose elementary school was the site of a fatal playground sniper attack, Nader, Pynoos, Fairbanks, and Frederick (1990) found that children who were somewhat protected from the violence by being inside the school, off the school grounds, or on vacation when the attack occurred, had fewer PTSD symptoms 1 year later than those who were on the playground during the attack.

Environmental Resources

People made vulnerable by stressors may benefit from the resources that their social networks provide. Social resources may enable individuals to muster effective coping strategies and to redefine an event in a more positive light. Social support, a positive family environment, community resources, and new life events in the postcrisis environment are key environmental resources that we address here.

Social and Family Support. Event-related factors (severity of illness, extent of loss), personal resources (marital status and education), and environmental resources (size of pre-existing social network) influence the amount and type of support individuals receive following a life crisis.

With respect to event-related factors, people who experience more severe events often receive more support. Thus, Zemore and Shepel (1989) found that women with breast cancer experienced more social support than women with benign breast lumps. Likewise, Kaniasty and Norris (1995) noted that people who experienced more impact from Hurricane Hugo received more tangible, informational, and emotional support. Moreover, prior stressors were also important: People who experienced more life events in the year prior to the hurricane received more help. Similarly, individuals who had larger pre-existing social networks received more support, as did those who were married and who had more education. These findings suggest that people who experience more severe stressors, and those who have more prior personal and social resources, are likely to obtain more social support.

By influencing coping behavior and fostering successful adaptation to life crises, social resources may be precursors of personal growth. According to Zemore and Shepel (1989), social support was related to better adjustment among women with breast cancer and among those with benign breast lumps. Women who were able to share their concerns with their spouse, family, or friends developed more self-esteem and better social and emotional adjustment than women who were not able to talk to others. Similarly, individuals with AIDS who had more family support experienced better psychological adjustment (Grummon, Rigby, Orr, & Procidano, 1994).

Individuals who have more social resources, especially from family and friends, tend to rely more on approach coping. In turn, people who employ more approach coping tend to adjust better to life stressors and to have fewer psychological symptoms (Moos & Schaefer, 1993). In a 1-year follow-up of middle-aged persons with cardiac illness, Holahan, Moos, Holahan, and Brennan (1995) examined the protective roles of social support and approach coping skills in psychological adjustment. Individuals who experienced more social support and who employed more approach-coping strategies had fewer symptoms of depression 1 year later. Social support was directly related to fewer subsequent depressive symptoms; it also enhanced approach coping, which, in turn, was associated with less depression.

In a subsequent study, Holahan, Moos, Holahan, and Brennen (1997) prospectively analyzed the impact of cardiac patients' social context and coping strategies on their psychological functioning 4 years later. They found that a more positive social context, in both family and extrafamily domains, predicted less depression among cardiac patients. In addition, ongoing social support enhanced approach-coping efforts, whereas ongoing social stressors created demands that hindered coping efforts.

More generally, a stable and cohesive family is a critical stress-resistance factor that may enable adults and children to confront life crises and prosper in their aftermath. Waltz, Badura, Pfaff, and Schott (1988) examined the role of marital factors on cardiac patients' long-term psychological responses to heart attack. High levels of marital intimacy were associated with less depressed mood in these patients. And, among women with rheumatoid arthritis, those with supportive husbands relied more on coping strategies such as cognitive restructuring and information seeking, which were associated with better psychological adjustment (Manne & Zautra, 1989).

The family environment has also been linked to childrens' adaptation to natural disasters and divorce. Green and her colleagues (1991) assessed PTSD symptoms in children who were exposed to the Buffalo Creek dam collapse and flood. When the family environment was characterized by a relatively conflict-free and/or optimistic atmosphere, and parents were moderately well-adjusted, the children experienced fewer PTSD symptoms. Likewise, in a 14-month follow-up of children who endured Hurricane Hugo, Swenson and her colleagues (1996) found that children whose mothers experienced less distress had fewer behavioral difficulties after the hurricane. Over time, the children's behavioral problems decreased. Children whose mothers' sadness and depression and feelings of being shocked and dazed were of shorter duration adjusted more quickly.

Among children of divorce, the quality of parental relationships and household stability during adolescence predict better adjustment. In a 10-year follow-up of daughters of divorced families, Wallerstein and Corbin (1989) found that young women who had good relationships with their custodial mothers and with their fathers (mutual affection, support, firm limits, and clarity of generational boundaries) adjusted better psychologically. Overall, girls who grew up in smoothly functioning households during adolescence had better outcomes at the 10-year follow-up than those who lived in disorganized households.

Community Groups and Resources. Community resources can also foster better adaptation and thereby contribute to PTG. Self-help and mutual support groups may be particularly valuable in promoting successful adaptation and positive outcomes for people who are ill. Leserman, Perkins, and Evans (1992) found that HIV-positive men who participated in more

AIDS support groups and organizations engaged in more active coping strategies, such as adopting a fighting spirit and reframing stressors to maximize PTG.

Community services that encourage family communication can pave the way for PTG in bereaved families. In a study that compared children with a sibling who died at home after being treated in a home care program with those whose sibling died while hospitalized, children in the home care group reported more positive outcomes (Lauer, Mulhern, Bohne, & Camitta, 1985). Children in the home care group received information about their dying sibling and support from their parents. Subsequently, 85% of these children described increased family closeness and enhanced relationships with their parents, whereas this was true of less than 20% of the children with hospitalized siblings.

The Post-Crisis Environment. Once the acute phase of a crisis is past, the quality of the postcrisis environment can have a potent effect on outcome. A postcrisis period that is marked by chronic problems that stem from acute stressors may thwart successful adaptation. In contrast, postcrisis events that result in positive changes in personal relationships or other life circumstances, such as separation from an abusive spouse or mentally ill parent or finding a new job, may aid adaptation and be decisive factors in determining whether individuals undergo a positive transformation.

Leenstra, Ormel, and Giel (1995) found that positive life changes helped to facilitate primary care patients' recovery from depression or anxiety. Compared with nonrecovered patients, recovered patients reported twice as many positive life events in the prior 3-month period. These positive life events included ones that led to a reduction in difficulties (ending of financial problems), neutralized difficulties (getting a job after unemployment), or eliminated barriers toward difficulty reduction (divorcing a violent husband).

A reduction of difficulties and "fresh start" events may generate a new sense of hope and aid recovery by leading depressed individuals to believe that their life will improve (Brown & Harris, 1989). Sometimes, however, a threatening event, such as a serious illness or death of a family member, may contribute to recovery. For example, one woman was jolted out of her depression when her sister-in-law died and left a young child. The woman realized that she had to be strong in order to help her family. Coping with the death of her family member appeared to raise her self-confidence and enabled her to change jobs and improve her life. This example shows that a new life crisis can be a precursor of positive changes in adaptation.

Personal Resources

The personal system in our model encompasses demographic characteristics such as age, gender, and marital and socioeconomic status, and other resources such as self-confidence, resilience, optimism, and prior crisis and coping experience. These factors provide one part of the context for coping, and, as such, influence how individuals appraise and confront life crises.

Sociodemographic Characteristics.   In general, demographic characteristics that are associated with more personal and social resources, such as being married and better educated are related to better outcomes. For example, developmental maturity as reflected in age appears to serve children well. Among Israeli children who endured the Gulf War, those who were older coped better with its stressors than did younger children (Rosenthal & Levy-Shiff, 1993). Older children also showed an increased sense of responsibility and were more likely to be helpful to their family.

Among adults, the impact of age on adaptation depends on the type of crisis and the person's resources for coping with it. A review of research on the emotional impact of breast cancer led Northouse (1994) to conclude that older women tended to experience less emotional distress from cancer than younger women did. Younger women may have more at stake, in addition to special concerns regarding their young children and family that contribute to their distress.

When Wallerstein (1986) studied adults 10 years after their divorce, she discovered that four times as many women as men reported psychological growth. Women in their 20s and 30s did better than those in their 40s. The younger women exhibited more resilience and demonstrated more economic and emotional improvement. These findings may be due to the enhanced freedom the women experienced and to the fact that younger women had more job opportunities and educational resources.

Carr et al. (1995) found that men and younger individuals experienced less psychological distress after the Newcastle earthquake than did women and older people. Effects of threat (injury or the possibility of injury) were more marked among people 46 years of age or older. The authors speculated that the earthquake was particularly difficult for the older people because, without warning, it devastated familiar surroundings that had provided a sense of security and safety. In a massive disaster, younger people may do better because they possess the physical stamina to cope with injury and they have a lifetime ahead of them to rebuild whatever is destroyed.

Sociodemographic characteristics may also influence the specific types of PTG that people experience. Curbow et al. (1993) discovered that among long-term survivors of BMT, younger survivors more frequently redirected their lives, whereas older survivors were more likely to find new meaning in life, to place increased value on family relationships, and to take more time for themselves. Compared to single survivors, those who were married or living with a partner reported that the experience led to finding new meaning in life and to improved family relationships.

Optimism.   When optimists confront life crises, they tend to rely on coping strategies that are more apt to promote favorable outcomes; in turn, these outcomes may foster personal growth (Moos & Schaefer, 1993). Friedman and her associates (1992) noted that, among cancer patients, dispositional optimism was associated with more approach coping and less avoidance coping and stronger expectations of good outcomes. In turn, these coping strategies and positive expectations may promote better psychological well-being.

Optimism has been linked to faster recovery from surgery and better quality of life in people with life-threatening illness. Scheier and his colleagues (1989) found that, after coronary artery bypass surgery, optimistic patients used more problem-focused coping strategies and less denial, recovered more rapidly from surgery, and resumed normal life more quickly when they returned home. Carver and his colleagues (1994) noted that women with breast cancer who were more optimistic reported more subjective well-being and life satisfaction. In addition, the women's optimism predicted increased well-being 3 and 6 months after surgery. Better quality of life in the aftermath of serious illness may be a precursor for positive change and growth. (For a more in-depth discussion of dispositional optimism and PTG, see Tennen & Affleck, chap. 4, this volume).

Self-Confidence and an Easygoing Disposition.   Self-confidence and an easygoing disposition are two other personal characteristics that help people confront life crises. In a study of a community sample, Holahan and Moos (1987) found that self-confidence and an easygoing disposition predicted better mood over a 1-year period, even after controlling for individuals' mood at baseline. Subsequently, they found that self-confidence and an easygoing disposition operated prospectively over 4 years along with family support to help prevent depression (Holahan & Moos, 1991). Among people who encountered no new negative life events, these personal and social resources directly predicted subsequent psychological health. Among people who experienced two or more new negative events, these resources predicted more reliance on approach coping strategies which, in turn, were associated with better mental health.

Ego-Resiliency.   Resilience is another personal resource that has been linked to people's ability to adapt to life crises and transitions. Klohnen, Vandewater, and Young (1996) found that women's ego-resiliency in early middle age (at age 43) predicted subsequent psychological well-being and life satisfaction and psychological distress at two follow-ups in later middle age (at age 48 and age 52). Compared with women who were less resilient at age 43, those who were more resilient saw themselves as more attractive and reported more relationship and work satisfaction and better health. Women who entered middle age with high levels of ego-resiliency were more likely to experience it as a time of opportunity for change and growth. They showed increases in life and work satisfaction, better marital relationships, and better general health.

Prior Crisis Experience.   Prior experience with and mastery of life crises can boost people's self-efficacy and enhance their coping resources. Individuals who triumph over small stressors in day-to-day life may acquire resilience that serves to protect them when future crises arise (Rutter, 1987).

When Phifer and Norris (1989) examined the psychological functioning of people who experienced a flood in Kentucky, those who had endured prior floods adapted better to a new flood than those who had not. Specifically, among flood victims who suffered losses in a prior flood, personal losses in the new flood and living in a community with high levels of community destruction did not affect their psychological functioning. Among victims with no prior flood experience, however, exposure to the new flood resulted in increased psychological symptoms.

Appraisal and Coping

Appraisal and coping are closely related processes that are linked to adaptation. Individuals who appraise a life crisis as a challenge that they can master may cope more actively with the problem and thus be more apt to grow from the experience. Cognitive coping strategies, such as focusing on positive aspects of the situation in order to minimize its psychological significance, may enable some people to emphasize the benefits of life crises. For example, the unpredictability and lack of control over a physical illness may lead individuals to use cognitive coping strategies to try to find meaning in their situation and gain some sense of control over it.

Germino, Fife, and Funk (1995) found that cancer patients and their partners searched for meaning in their illness in order to reduce its threat. Cancer patients may reflect on their relationships with others and review their lives as part of the coping process. These cognitive coping efforts can lead to greater appreciation of family members and friends and an enhanced sense of the meaning of the illness. Individuals who are able to find meaning tend to be more satisfied with their relationships and better adjusted.

How individuals appraise an event depends, in part, on their personal resources. Individuals with more personal and social resources are less likely to appraise a life crisis as a threat and more likely to rely on active coping strategies that are linked to successful adaptation and PTG. Taylor, Lichtman, and Wood (1984) found that cancer patients who believed that they could control their cancer, or that their physician could do so, adjusted better to the illness experience.

In a more recent study, Florian, Mikulincer, and Taubman (1995) found that Israeli recruits' control and commitment (hardiness) at the beginning of a grueling 4-month combat training period reduced their appraisal of its threat and thereby contributed to their well-being at the end of training. Likewise, commitment helped to reduce the recruits' psychological distress by inhibiting their use of avoidance coping responses such as distancing and emotion-focused coping. Control and commitment also influenced recruits' secondary appraisal, that is, they increased the recruits' estimates of their ability to cope with the training and enhanced their use of problem-solving and support-seeking coping strategies.

In general, people who react to stressors with approach coping strategies fare better than those who rely on avoidance coping (Moos & Schaefer, 1993). Friedman et al. (1988, 1990) noted that women with breast cancer who exhibited a fighting spirit (viewed as active coping) adjusted more positively to their illness, whereas women who used avoidance coping did not adjust as well. The women who coped more assertively showed better psychological and social adjustment and better attitudes, knowledge, and expectations about the illness and treatment.

Studies of men with HIV and AIDS provide more evidence for the efficacy of active cognitive and behavioral coping efforts. Grummon et al. (1994) found that men with AIDS who coped actively by seeking social support experienced more psychological well-being. Likewise, Leserman et al. (1992) noted that HIV-positive men who coped with the threat of AIDS by adopting active coping strategies, such as assertiveness and reframing stressors in a positive light, were more satisfied with their social support networks and more active participants in the AIDS community. In this vein, Schwartzberg (1994) found that involvement in support groups and community activities fostered a sense of kinship with other HIV-positive people and helped participants find meaning in their illness, transform their views of themselves, and foster their PTG.

A study by Holahan and Moos (1990) highlights the complex interplay between personal and social resources, coping, and improved functioning outcomes. As noted earlier, they tested predictive models of change in psychological functioning (depression) over a 1-year period in a community sample of adults. Overall, more than 30% of the participants reported better psychological functioning at follow-up than at baseline. Among the sub-group of these individuals who experienced low levels of stressors during the year, a combination of more personal (self-confidence and easygoingness) and social family support resources directly predicted better psychological functioning 1 year later. Among the subgroup of persons with high levels of stressors (2 or more negative events) during the year, those whose function-ing improved reported strengthened personal and social resources during the year, and more reliance on approach coping strategies. These individuals experienced growth despite the fact that they had confronted demanding life crises such as the death of family members or friends and severe financial problems. The findings exemplify the important interconnections between existing levels of personal and social resources, new life stressors, and reliance on approach coping in shaping the context that fosters an oppor-tunity for crisis growth.

PTG IN CONTEXT: FUTURE DIRECTIONS

This chapter highlighted findings from a growing body of research on life crises and PTG. We discussed these findings using a stress and coping framework to understand the process of adaptation to life crises. The past 10 years have been marked by expanding interest in personal growth as an important outcome of life crises, and one that is more frequent than initially expected. In the concluding section, we identify some promising directions for research in this area.

Psychological Distress and Growth

We do not yet understand the relationship between psychological distress and later personal growth. Intuitively, it seems reasonable to assume that psychological distress inhibits PTG in the short-term. Presumably, people need to at least partially resolve their depression and anger before the positive consequences of an event can develop or be recognized. But psychological distress is a catalyst for change; distress can arouse personal resilience and stimulate new coping efforts and more social resources. We need studies that will enable us to better understand the conditions under which psychological distress hinders or facilitates PTG.

Brown and Harris' (1989) finding that traumatic events sometimes jolt women out of depression points to other intriguing lines of research. Investigators might pursue the impact of PTG in one life domain on other life domains. For example, do improved family relationships following an illness lead to better relationships with coworkers? Do personal transformations that occur in the early phase of the adjustment process affect later phases of adaptation? Increased personal resources that enable individuals to cope more effectively with ongoing problems associated with a specific life crisis may also help them confront unrelated current problems and future problems.

Some intriguing evidence points to a link between PTG and subsequent physical health status. Affleck, Tennen, and Croog (1987) found that patients who experienced positive outcomes after a heart attack, such as changes in views of life, values, and family relationships, increased enjoyment of life, and insight into the need to avoid stress and the value of positive health behaviors were less likely to have another attack and had less morbidity 8 years later. Taken together with the work we reviewed earlier, such findings suggest that people with life-threatening illness and better physical health outcomes may more readily conceptualize their illness experience as having led to positive benefits. In turn, these benefits may contribute to better long-term physical health outcomes, perhaps through their influence on changes in lifestyle, coping responses, and interpersonal relationships that facilitate better health. In this respect, characteristics of social relationships, such as their stability and supportiveness, may be associated with patterns of neuroendocrine regulation that foreshadow better health and longevity (Seeman & McEwen, 1996).

Life Domains and the Postcrisis Environment

One key set of factors involved in eventual PTG is the postcrisis environment and the individual's overall pattern of life stressors and social resources. In a case example, we used the Life Stressors and Social Resources Inventory (LISRES; Moos & Moos, 1994) to describe the postcrisis environment of Dorothy M., a 38-year-old mother of two who had recently lost her husband in a car accident. As might be expected, immediately after her husband's sudden death, Dorothy experienced a high level of stressors, especially financial stressors and interpersonal problems with her children. In addition, she experienced excessive demands from her mother and in her job, which allowed for very little autonomy (Moos, 1995).

However, Dorothy had moderately supportive coworkers and close, long-standing friendships with two women, one of whom encouraged her to join a bereaved women's support group. Due in part to these resources, Dorothy developed a more supportive social environment, improved her relationship with her mother and her situation at work, and, at a 1-year follow-up, showed an increase in her self-confidence. This example illustrates the need to closely examine both stressors and social resources in each domain of a person's life in order to understand the determinants of PTG.

The Time Course of PTG

Longitudinal studies are imperative to understanding the process of PTG. Although some people undergo quantum change (Miller & C'de Baca, 1994), most often, PTG is the outcome of a developmental process that follows an initial stage of emotional distress and disorganization. Months or years of struggle may ensue before divorced or chronically ill people or disaster survivors find meaning in their plight and grow from their experiences. After many years, however, a life crisis experience may be fully integrated into an individual's current adaptation and both positive and negative effects may be attenuated.

According to Fromm et al. (1996), among individuals who had undergone a BMT, those who had the procedure more recently reported more positive outcomes. Patients who had survived more than 5 years reported the fewest positive effects. The tendency to report positive effects from a miraculous recovery, such as survival after BMT, may decrease with time. Over time, the experience becomes a less important aspect of the individual's current life. We posit that the positive concomitants of a crisis are likely to develop after the successful resolution of a crisis and then gradually decline. However, we also believe that most severe life crises leave an indelible imprint on an individual, for better or for worse.

The long-term trajectory of personal change may also be influenced by the postcrisis milieu and developmental tasks related to the initial crisis that individuals confront. For example, Wallerstein and Corbin (1989) found that younger, preschool girls typically have especially severe initial reactions to an impending parental divorce, but then seem to recover quickly and to be quite well-adjusted 10 years later. They suggest that these findings may reflect the continuing, close mother-daughter relationship and the fact that these girls, who were 13- to 15-years-old at follow-up, had not yet encountered the developmental tasks of late adolescence. However, a girl's close identification with a divorced mother who has been unsuccessful in love and marriage may jeopardize the girl's ability to meet the developmental tasks of dating and establishing meaningful relationships with young men that come with late adolescence and early adulthood. A life course perspective is needed to better understand the complex relationships between life crises, normal developmental transitions, and PTG.

Family and Community Coping and Growth

Although a traumatic event may strike one individual, it typically has a ripple effect on the individual's family members and friends, who may also benefit from coping successfully with the crisis. For example, when one family member is diagnosed with a life-threatening illness, other family members may experience enhanced relationships and a greater appreciation of life. Individuals may also develop increased self-confidence when they successfully cope with the demands that a family member's illness places upon them. Accordingly, studies should assess PTG not only among individuals who are directly affected by the crisis, but also among their family members and friends. As one step, researchers might identify the types and patterns of development families undergo as they cope with life crises.

When natural disasters or epidemics strike, whole communities become victims. People who share the same experiences and work cooperatively to resolve problems may develop an increased sense of community. A "shared emotional connection in time and space" between members of the community is one of the underlying dimensions of the psychological sense of community (Puddifoot, 1995). The shared experience of epidemics and disasters can lead to a stronger sense of cohesion that may serve as a resource to facilitate PTG among members of the community.

Future research might examine the types of growth that occur when a traumatic event strikes an entire community. A first step is to specify a typology of community-level growth. The gay community provides evidence for community-level growth in the wake of the AIDS epidemic. Community coping and growth are reflected in flourishing HIV and AIDS support groups and hotlines, and in the development of community organizations that have successfully lobbied for quicker access to experimental drugs, changed how new AIDS drugs are marketed, and obtained money for AIDS research. The massive AIDS quilt that has traveled throughout the country reflects not only individual efforts to cope with loss, but family and community coping as well. These examples suggest that one fruitful area for research is to determine the nature of reciprocal relationships between community-level coping and the PTG individual members of the community experience.

If we are to comprehend how, why, and when PTG occurs, we must develop integrated models that consider the complex interplay of personal and environmental resources, event-related factors, and appraisal and coping factors. As researchers strive to specify models that explain how PTG evolves, it is important to keep in mind that families and communities are the context within which life crises and growth occur. Thus, models of PTG that include family and community characteristics may help us to discern how life crises transform and enable us to grow as persons.

Understanding the long and often arduous journey toward healing and growth on which individuals, families, and communities embark after a crisis is a complicated endeavor, but one well worth the effort. For, as human beings, all of us face adversity and the challenge of personal metamorphosis.

ACKNOWLEDGMENTS

This work was supported by the Department of Veterans Affairs Health Services Research and Development Service and by NIAAA Grant AA06699. Connie Mah provided valuable assistance with the literature review for this chapter; she identified, retrieved, and organized a large number of articles.

REFERENCES

Affleck, G., Tennen, H., & Croog, S. (1987). Causal attribution, perceived benefits, and morbidity after a heart attack: An 8-year study. *Journal of Consulting and Clinical Psychology, 55*, 29–35.

Bromet, E., & Dew, M. A. (1995). Review of psychiatric epidemiologic research on disasters. *Epidemiologic Reviews, 17*, 113–119.

Brown, G. W., & Harris, T. O. (1989). Depression. In G. W. Brown & T. O. Harris (Eds.), *Life events and illness* (pp. 48–93). New York: Guilford.

Calhoun, L. G., & Tedeschi, R. G. (1989/1990). Positive aspects of critical life problems: Recollections of grief. *Omega, 20*, 265–272.

Carr, V. J., Lewin, T. J., Webster, R. A., Hazell, P. L., Kenardy, J. A., & Carter, G. L. (1995). Psychosocial sequelae of the 1989 Newcastle earthquake: I. Community disaster experiences and psychological morbidity 6 months post-disaster. *Psychological Medicine, 25*, 539–555.

Carver, C. S., Pozo-Kaderman, C., Harris, S. D., Noriega, V., Scheier, M. F., Robinson, D. S., Ketcham, A. S., Moffat, F. L., & Clark, K. C. (1994). Optimism versus pessimism predicts the quality of women's adjustment to early stage breast cancer. *Cancer, 73*, 1213–1220.

Coffman, S. (1994). Children describe life after Hurricane Andrew. *Pediatric Nursing, 20*, 363–375.

Curbow, B., Legro, M. W., Baker, F., Wingard, J. R., & Somerfield, M. R., (1993). Loss and recovery themes of long-term survivors of bone marrow transplants. *Journal of Psychosocial Oncology, 10*, 1–20.

Florian, V., Mikulincer, M., & Taubman, O. (1995). Does hardiness contribute to mental health during a stressful real-life situation: The roles of appraisal and coping. *Journal of Personality and Social Psychology, 68*, 687–695.

Friedman, L. C., Baer, P. E., Lewy, A., Lane, M., & Smith F. E. (1988). Predictors of psychosocial adjustment to breast cancer. *Journal of Psychosocial Oncology, 6*, 75–94.

Friedman, L. C., Nelson, D. V., Baer, P., Lane, M., & Smith, F. (1990). Adjustment to breast cancer: A replication study. *Journal of Psychosocial Oncology, 8*, 27–40.

Friedman, L. C., Nelson, D. V., Baer, P. E., Lane, M., Smith, F. E., & Dworkin, R. J. (1992). The relationship of dispositional optimism, daily life stress, and domestic environment to coping methods used by cancer patients. *Journal of Behavioral Medicine, 15*, 127–141.

Fromm, K., Andrykowski, M. A., & Hunt, J. (1996). Positive and negative psychosocial sequelae of bone marrow transplantation: Implications for quality of life assessment. *Journal of Behavioral Medicine, 19*, 221–240.

Gaskins, S., & Brown, K. (1992). Psychosocial responses among individuals with human immunodeficiency virus infection. *Applied Nursing Research, 5*, 111–121.

Germino, B. B., Fife, B. L., & Funk, S. G. (1995). Cancer and the partner relationship: What is its meaning? *Seminars in Oncology Nursing, 11*, 43–50.

Green, B. L., Korol, M., Grace, M. G., Vary, M. G., Leonard, A. C., Gleser, G. C., & Smitson-Cohen, S. (1991). Children and disaster: Age, gender, and parental effects on PTSD symptoms. *Journal of the American Academy of Child and Adolescent Psychiatry, 30*, 945–951.

Grummon, K., Rigby, E. D., Orr, D., & Procidano, M. (1994). Psychosocial variables that affect the psychological adjustment of IVDU patients with AIDS. *Journal of Clinical Psychology, 50*, 488–502.

Holahan, C. J., & Moos, R. H. (1987). Risk, resistance, and psychological distress: A longitudinal analysis with adults and children. *Journal of Abnormal Psychology, 96*, 3–13.

Holahan, C. J., & Moos, R. H. (1990). Life stressors, resistance factors, and improved psychological functioning: An extension of the stress resistance paradigm. *Journal of Personality and Social Psychology, 58*, 909–917.

Holahan, C. J., & Moos, R. H. (1991). Life stressors, personal and social resources, and depression: A 4–year structural model. *Journal of Abnormal Psychology, 100*, 31–38.

Holahan, C. J., & Moos, R. H. (1994). Life stressors and mental health: Advances in conceptualizing stress resistance. In W. R. Avison & I. H. Gotlib (Eds.), *Stress and mental health: Contemporary issues and prospects for the future* (pp. 213–238). New York: Plenum.

Holahan, C. J., Moos, R. H., Holahan, C. K., & Brennan, P. L. (1995). Social support, coping, and depressive symptoms in a late middle-aged sample of patients reporting cardiac illness. *Health Psychology, 14*, 152–163.

Holahan, C. J., Moos, R. H., Holahan, C. K., & Brennan, P. L. (1997). Social context, coping strategies, and depressive symptoms: An expanded model with cardiac patients. *Journal of Personality and Social Psychology, 72*, 918–928.

Kaniasty, K., & Norris, F. H. (1995). In search of altruistic community: Patterns of social support mobilization following Hurricane Hugo. *American Journal of Community Psychology, 23*, 447–477.

Kessler, B. G. (1987). Bereavement and personal growth. *Journal of Humanistic Psychology, 27*, 228–247.

Klohnen, E. C., Vandewater, E. A., & Young, A. (1996). Negotiating the middle years: Ego-resiliency and successful midlife adjustment in women. *Psychology and Aging, 11*, 431–442.

Kristjanson, L. J., & Ashcroft, T. (1994). The family's cancer journey: A literature review. *Cancer Nursing, 17*, 1–17.

Lauer, M. E., Mulhern, R. K., Bohne, J. B., & Camitta, B. M. (1985). Children's perceptions of their sibling's death at home or hospital: The precursors of differential adjustment. *Cancer Nursing, 8*, 21–27.

Leenstra, A. S., Ormel, J., & Giel, R. (1995). Positive life change and recovery from depression and anxiety: A three-stage longitudinal study of primary care attenders. *British Journal of Psychiatry, 166*, 333–343.

Leserman, J., Perkins, D. O., & Evans, D. L. (1992). Coping with the threat of AIDS: The role of social support. *American Journal of Psychiatry, 149*, 1514–1520.

Lonigan, C. J., Shannon, M. P., Taylor, C. M., Finch, A. J., Jr., & Sallee, F. R. (1994). Children exposed to disaster: II. Risk factors for the development of post-traumatic symptomatology. *Journal of the American Academy of Child and Adolescent Psychiatry, 33*, 94–105.

Manne, S. L., & Zautra, A. J. (1989). Spouse criticism and support: Their association with coping and psychological adjustment among women with rheumatoid arthritis. *Journal of Personality and Social Psychology, 56*, 608–617.

Miles, M. S., Demi, A. S., & Mostyn-Aker, P. (1984). Rescue workers' reactions following the Hyatt Hotel disaster. *Death Education, 8*, 315–331.

Miller, W. R., & C'de Baca, J. (1994). Quantum change: Toward a psychology of transformation. In T. Heatherton & J. Weinberger (Eds.), *Can personality change?* (pp. 253–280). Washington, DC: American Psychological Association.

Moos, R. (1995). Development and application of new measures of life stressors, social resources and coping responses. *European Journal of Psychological Assessment, 11*, 1–13.

Moos, R., & Moos, B. (1994). *Life Stressors and Social Resources Inventory Adult Form Manual.* Odessa, FL: Psychological Assessment Resources.

Moos, R. H., & Schaefer, J. A. (1993). Coping resources and processes: Current concepts and measures. In L. Goldberger & S. Breznits (Eds.), *Handbook of stress: Theoretical and clinical aspects* (2nd ed., pp. 234–257). New York: The Free Press.

Nader, K., Pynoos, R., Fairbanks, L., & Frederick, C. (1990). Children's PTSD reactions one year after a sniper attack at their school. *American Journal of Psychiatry, 147*, 1526–1530.

Nelson, G. (1989). Life strains, coping, and emotional well-being: A longitudinal study of recently separated and married women. *American Journal of Community Psychology, 17*, 459–483.

Nelson, G. (1994). Emotional well-being of separated and married women: Long-term follow-up study. *American Journal of Orthopsychiatry, 64*, 150–160.

Northouse, L. L. (1994). Breast cancer in younger women: Effects on interpersonal and family relations. *Journal of the National Cancer Institute Monographs, 16*, 183–190.

O'Connor, A. P., Wicker, C. A., & Germino, B. B. (1990). Understanding the cancer patient's search for meaning. *Cancer Nursing, 13*, 167–175.

Phifer, J. F., & Norris, F. H. (1989). Psychological symptoms in older adults following natural disaster: Nature, timing, duration, and course. *Journal of Gerontology: Social Sciences, 44*, S207–S217.

Price, R. (1994). *A whole new life: An illness and a healing.* New York: Atheneum.

Puddifoot, J. E. (1995). Dimensions of community identity. *Journal of Community and Applied Social Psychology, 5*, 357–370.

Pynoos, R. S., Goenjian, A., Tashjian, M., Karakashian, M., Manjikian, R., Manoukian, G., Steinberg, A. M., & Fairbanks, L. A. (1993). Post-traumatic stress reactions in children after the 1988 Armenian earthquake. *British Journal of Psychiatry, 163*, 239–247.

Rieker, P. P., Edbril, S. D., & Garnick, M. B. (1985). Curative testis cancer therapy: Psychological sequelae. *Journal of Clinical Oncology, 3*, 1117–1126.

Rosenthal, M. K., & Levy-Shiff, R. (1993). Threat of missile attacks in the gulf war: Mothers' perceptions of young children's reactions. *American Journal of Orthopsychiatry, 63*, 241–254.

Rubonis, A. V., & Bickman, L. (1991). Psychological impairment in the wake of disaster: The disaster–psychopathology relationship. *Psychological Bulletin, 109*, 384–399.

Rutter, M. (1987). Psychosocial resilience and protective mechanisms. *American Journal of Orthopsychiatry, 57*, 316–331.

Saylor, C. F., Swenson, C. C., & Powell, P. (1992). Hurricane Hugo blows down the broccoli: Preschoolers' post-disaster play and adjustment. *Child Psychiatry and Human Development, 22*, 139–149.

Scannell-Desch, E. A. (1996). The lived experience of women military nurses in Vietnam during the Vietnam War. *IMAGE: Journal of Nursing Scholarship, 28*, 119–124.

Schaefer, J. A., & Moos, R. H. (1992). Life crises and personal growth. In B. N. Carpenter (Ed.), *Personal coping, theory, research, and application* (pp. 149–170). Wesport, CT: Praeger.

Scheier, M. F., Matthews, K. A., Owens, J. F., Magovern, G. J., Sr., Lefebvre, R. C., Abbott, R. A., & Carver, C. S. (1989). Dispositional optimism and recovery from coronary artery bypass surgery: The beneficial effects on physical and psychological well-being. *Journal of Personality and Social Psychology, 57*, 1024–1040.

Schwartzberg, S. S. (1994). Vitality and growth in HIV-infected gay men. *Social Science and Medicine, 38*, 593–602.

Seeman, T. E., & McEwen, B. S. (1996). Impact of social environment characteristics on neuroendocrine regulation. *Psychosomatic Medicine, 58*, 459–471.

Swenson, C. C., Saylor, C. F., Powell, M. P., Stokes, S. J., Foster, K. Y. & Belter, R. W. (1996). Impact of a natural disaster on preschool children: Adjustment 14 months after a hurricane. *American Journal of Orthopsychiatry, 66*, 122–130.

Taylor, S. E., Lichtman, R. R., & Wood, J. V. (1984). Attributions, beliefs about control, and adjustment to breast cancer. *Journal of Personality and Social Psychology, 46*, 489–502.

Taylor, S. E., Lichtman, R. R., Wood, J. V., Bluming, A. Z., Dosik, G. M., & Leibowitz, R. L. (1985). Illness-related and treatment-related factors in psychological adjustment to breast cancer. *Cancer, 55*, 2506–2513.

Tempelaar, R., De Haes, J. C. J. M., De Ruiter, J. H., Bakker, D., Van Den Heuvel, W. J. A., & Van Nieuwenhuijzen, M. G. (1989). The social experiences of cancer patients under treatment: A comparative study. *Social Science and Medicine, 29*, 635–642.

Wallerstein, J. S. (1986). Women after divorce: Preliminary report from a 10-year follow-up. *American Journal of Orthopsychiatry, 56*, 65–77.

Wallerstein, J. S., & Corbin, S. B. (1989). Daughters of divorce: Report from a ten-year follow-up. *American Journal of Orthopsychiatry, 59*, 593–604.

Waltz, M., Badura, B., Pfaff, H., & Schott, T. (1988). Marriage and the psychological consequences of a heart attack: A longitudinal study of adaptation to chronic illness after 3 years. *Social Science and Medicine, 27*, 149–158.

Welch-McCaffrey, D., Hoffman, B., Leigh, S. S., Loescher, L. J., & Meyskens, F. L., Jr. (1989). Surviving adult cancers. Part 2: Psychosocial implications. *Annals of Internal Medicine, 111*, 517–524.

Yarom, N. (1983). Facing death in war: An existential crisis. In S. Breznitz (Ed.), *Stress in Israel* (pp. 3–38). New York: Van Nostrand Reinhold.

Zemore, R., Rinholm, J., Shepel, L. F., & Richards, M. (1989). Some social and emotional consequences of breast cancer and mastectomy: A content analysis of 87 interviews. *Journal of Psychosocial Oncology, 7*, 33–45.

Zemore, R., & Shepel, L. F. (1989). Effects of breast cancer and mastectomy on emotional support and adjustment. *Social Science and Medicine, 28*, 19–27.

6

Models of Life Change and Posttraumatic Growth

Virginia E. O'Leary
C. Sloan Alday
Auburn University
Jeannette R. Ickovics
Yale University

The field of psychology has widely acknowledged and clearly documented the negative impact of stressful events. Stress increases one's vulnerability to physical illness (Cohen, Tyrell, & Smith, 1993; Harris, 1991) and psychological difficulties (Avison & Gotlib, 1994; Frazier & Schauben, 1994; Vrana & Lauterbach, 1994). Posttraumatic stress disorder (PTSD), a syndrome originally intended to describe the symptoms of war veterans, first appeared in the *Diagnostic and Statistical Manual of Psychiatric Disorders* in 1980 (*DSM-III*), and has since been used to document symptoms and problematic behaviors of individuals following a variety of traumatic events: natural disaster, childhood sexual abuse, victimization, or witnessing a violent death (cf. Briere & Runtz, 1988; Browne & Finkelhor, 1986; Hodgkinson, Joseph, Yule, & Williams, 1995; Ursano, Fullerton, Kao, & Bhartiya, 1995).

In addition to regarding traumatic events as stressful, clinical psychology appears to view any change as stressful and potentially health damaging. The Social Readjustment Scale (Rahe & Arthur, 1978) quantifies stress in *life change units* (LCU), implying that it is the change inherent in certain events that produces stress. A wide variety of life events were assigned standardized weights based on judges' ratings of the degree of difficulty required to adjust to the event. Most possible life events, including those typically viewed as negative (e.g., job loss) as well as positive (e.g., job promotion), are considered stressful and assigned a value based on the relative magnitude of change. This instrument promoted a large body of research that documented the association between the stress associated with life changes and health outcomes. Stressful life events were associated with sudden cardiac death (Rahe & Lind, 1971) as well as susceptibility to illness such as heart disease and skin disease (Cohen, Kessler, & Gordon, 1995; Holmes & Masuda, 1974). Beyond the individual, rates of mental illness were highest in cities where social change is swift and extreme, such as communities facing natural disaster or racial unrest (Levy & Rowitz, 1974).

Ironically, despite clinical psychology's depiction of change as stressful, many would describe the goal of clinical psychology as change: change in cognition (Eargle, Guerra, & Tolan, 1994), behavior (Stoolmiller, 1994), or personality (Heatherton & Weinberger, 1994). A search of the general literature in psychology reveals that most fields in psychology are interested in change. Developmental psychologists focus on maturational changes across the life span (Aldwin, 1994; Siegler & Engle, 1994). The implementation of organizational change is central to the field of industrial/organizational psychology (Antonioni, 1994). Social psychologists investigate the mechanisms of attitude and behavior change (Bengtson, Schaie, & Burton, 1995). Neuropsychologists are interested in cognitive and behavioral changes resulting from injury or disease of the brain (Kim, Lee, Kim, & Suh, 1994; Ramsay & Lewis, 1994).

According to theories of evolution and adaptation, change is necessary for survival. The Roman philosopher, Lucretius, stated that "change is the only constant." Evolution teaches us that change is not only a common occurrence, but our only means of survival (Chance, 1988). Given the inevitability and adaptive necessity of change, psychologists in recent years have turned to focusing on how some individuals appear to avoid the negative consequences of traumatic events or sudden life changes.

Many investigators have documented the resilience of children able to overcome the adversity of harsh environmental, social, and familial conditions (Block & Block, 1980; Garmezy, 1983, 1991; Garmezy, Masten, & Tellegen, 1984; Masten, 1989; Rutter, 1981; Werner & Smith, 1982; Zigler & Trickett, 1978). Garmezy and Nuechterlein (1972) first used the term *resilience* to describe children from a poverty- and crime-stricken neighborhood who developed into relatively well-adjusted adolescents and young adults despite these harsh environmental challenges.

Research has also focused on resilient adults (Kahn, 1991; Rowe & Kahn, 1987). Styles of coping (Folkman & Lazarus, 1980; Lazarus & Folkman,

1984) and the phenomenon of stress resistance (Holahan & Moos, 1986, 1990, 1994) have received considerable attention. Some investigators refer to the personal growth that can occur following a life crisis (Hager, 1992; Schaefer & Moos, 1992), death of a loved one (Nerken, 1993), or a period of "psychological disequilibrium" (Mahoney, 1982). Others have gone beyond a focus on those who adapt to stress, to examine those who exceed previous levels of functioning following stressful or traumatic events. This experience of flourishing following a life crisis has been termed "thriving" (O'Leary & Ickovics, 1995), "transformational coping" (Aldwin, 1994), "quantum change" (Miller & C'deBaca, 1994), and "posttraumatic growth (PTG)" (Tedeschi & Calhoun, 1995). Although many investigators agree that one may benefit from a stressful or traumatic event, they vary in their depiction of the change process and the potential outcomes.

According to Schaefer and Moos (1992), new skills, improved relationships, and a changed perspective may result from a life crisis. Stories of cancer patients or accident victims describing their difficulty as "the best thing that ever happened" are not uncommon (Aldwin, 1994; O'Leary & Ickovics, 1995). Other benefits that follow a crisis may include greater empathy, increased self-understanding, finding more meaning or purpose in life, reordering priorities, accumulating wisdom, gaining a new appreciation for the helpfulness of others, and/or setting new life goals (Nerken, 1993; O'Leary & Ickovics, 1995; Tedeschi & Calhoun, 1995). Wolin and Wolin (1993) described seven categories of resiliency: insight, independence, relationships, initiative, creativity, humor, and morality. The physiological literature also supports the notion that stress can have positive effects; rats that are handled or receive mild electric shock as infants show better neuroendocrine and immunological functioning, and mature at a more rapid rate than those who do not (Gray, 1971).

Given that change is not only unavoidable, but may be essential for optimal adaptation, it is important for psychologists to understand the mechanisms of change. Through investigation of current models of change and growth, psychologists may learn how seemingly negative and stressful events may be beneficial for some individuals, resulting in higher levels of functioning and cognitive understanding. The purpose of this chapter is to describe a number of current theoretical models that contribute to our understanding of PTG and to identify the antecedents and correlates of positive change. Particular attention is paid to those models that describe positive changes resulting from negative events. It is important to note that this review is not exhaustive. Models of change that are exclusively behavioral such as that of Prochaska and DiClemente (1984) are not considered, as their model is only applicable to planned, intentional changes in health behaviors such as quitting smoking, increasing exercise and sunscreen use, participating in mammography screening, and reducing dietary fat intake. Stage-centered theories of reactions to critical life events such as Selye's (1946, 1956, 1976) General Adaptation Syndrome, Bowlby's (1980) work on attachment, Kuebler-Ross' (1969, 1982) five-stage description of reactions to confronting death are not covered nor is Klinger's (1977) more general Incentive–Disengagement Theory. Finally, cognitive theories such as Seligman's (1975) theory of learned helplessness, Wortman's work on coping with loss (Wortman & Brehm, 1975; Wortman & Silver, 1987), and Taylor's (1983) theory of cognitive adaptation to threatening events are not considered in detail.

MODELS OF CHANGE

To describe the models of change presented in this chapter, it is useful to examine specific dimensions of each. The models vary in their descriptions of the precursors of change, although there are some factors that are central to several of the models. Eight models are reviewed in this chapter. They are loosely considered in two categories: models describing intentional change and those describing unintentional change. Models that present change as intentional describe an evolutionary process of change. The change may be slow and incremental, perhaps requiring periods of seeming inaction or even "backsliding." This is a constant process, such as engaging in treatment for depression or substance abuse. Other models present change as sudden and unexpected. Typically, these models consider transformative experiences that may be the result of an unexpected crisis or tragedy (e.g., house destroyed by a hurricane or mudslide, diagnosis of a fatal disease). These experiences and the resultant change simultaneously affect multiple aspects of one's life. Discontinuous change is often more dramatic than incremental change, and less likely to be intentional.

As the models are reviewed, emphasis is placed on the common features among them. To facilitate the readers' understanding of the models described, each is accompanied by a figure presenting a graphic representation of its essential characteristics. All of the models have been described theoretically; however, not all have been tested empirically. The chapter concludes with a discussion of the methodological challenges associated with conducting this type of research and recommendations for the future.

Models Describing Intentional Change

Three of the models discussed explicitly describe intentional change. All three models address change during the course of psychotherapy, although these models are not restricted to therapeutically induced change.

Resolution and Growth in Grief. Nerken's (1993) model of growth following loss describes incremental change. This model, postulated as specific to the loss of a loved one, strictly describes change or growth during the grieving process (see Fig. 6.1). This model emphasizes the importance of the self in the process of change; it describes a dyadic model of the self, with a core and a reflective side. The *core self* consists of those individual or

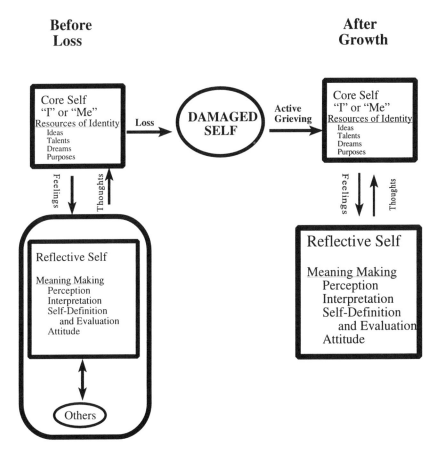

FIG. 6. 1. Resolution and growth in grief (Nerken, 1993).

personal resources often labeled as identity; this includes ideas, talents, dreams, and purposes. The *reflective self* is concerned with meaning and appraisal; this includes perception, interpretation, self-definition, evaluation, and attitudes.

According to Nerken (1993), the reflective side of the self is damaged when a loved one dies, because the reflective self is maintained through attachments to loved ones. For example, a great source of self-esteem may be caring for one's parent as an adult. The parent's death may trigger damage to the reflective self because of both the alteration in self-identity (i.e., loss of a role) and the loss of a source of confirmation of one's positive self-appraisal.

Confronting and attempting to understand the loss of a loved one can provide the impetus for personal growth. Such growth results in an enhanced reflective self; one capable of functioning independently, no longer tied to the attachment to the lost loved one. In Nerken's (1993) view, active grieving following the death of a loved one is necessary to experience growth. He suggests that change following a loss results from a focus on the self and a deepening of one's reflective side. If able to revise assumptions about the world and internalize the positive reflection obtained from the deceased, bereaved people are able to change their views of themselves and their prospects. They may develop the strengths and desirable attributes of the lost other. The personal growth that results from active grieving leads to an increase in self-functioning, capacity for self-perception, and empathy. Reflective abilities are enhanced by finding meaning in bereavement—an uncontrollable environmental event. When growth occurs following bereavement, a new self emerges that is more secure and stable (Nerken, 1993). Because the reflective self develops from relationships with attachment figures, it is assumed that previous positive experiences with attachment figures are necessary.

Human Change Processes in Psychotherapy. Mahoney's (1982) model of change centers on the psychotherapy process. However, this characterization of the process of psychotherapeutic change is virtually indistinguishable from more generic change processes (see Fig. 6.2). One begins with the status quo of an individual functioning at a particular level. Change is initiated by a psychological disequilibrium that either causes or signals reorganizing processes. Following disequilibrium, there may be a return to the status quo (no change) or restructuring may occur. Restructuring leads to a new synthesis. The goal of integration is to consolidate change into a new "dynamic directedness" that is not static, but remains open to future development (Mahoney, 1982).

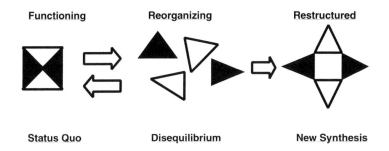

FIG. 6.2. Human change processes in psychotherapy (Mahoney, 1982).

Despite the complexities involved in the process of change, the primary emphasis in this model is on *constructing meaning*, a process similar to that described by Nerken (1993). Mahoney maintains that change results from the pursuit, construction, and alteration of meaning. Changes may occur in both cognitive processes and physical behaviors.

Mahoney (1982) suggested that meaning is constructed as a function of the nervous system. The nervous system organizes information by recognizing common patterns. The human urge to resist change originates from the nervous systems' efforts to maintain this order by adhering to the status quo. Patterns used by individuals in psychotherapy to order their experience must be understood by those who desire to help them change. The therapist assists the client to understand and integrate changes by helping to construct or attach meaning to these events. Mahoney and Craine (1991) indicated that the most important factors in change are associated with the therapeutic relationship, personal motivation and insight, social support, and self-esteem.

Chaos and Growth. Like Mahoney (1982), Hager's (1992) model of change refers primarily to psychotherapy-related change, and neither theorist considers the mechanisms responsible for change or growth to be under strict voluntary control. According to the model (Fig. 6.3), a client coping with an issue in psychotherapy first enters a period of chaos and disorganization. This disruption functions as a gestational period that allows the client to formulate a new construction of reality. Change occurs after this period of disorganization.

Although therapists often interpret periods of disorganization or confusion as negative indicators for the progress of treatment (i.e., resistance), Hager (1992) argued that they may be indicative of the beginning of change. Hager emphasized the importance of periods of chaos during psychotherapy as a necessary part of growth preceding change. During these periods of

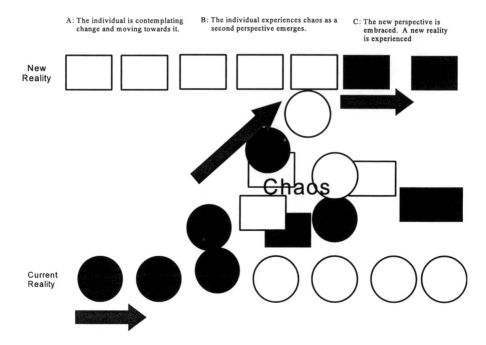

FIG. 6.3. Chaos and growth (Hager, 1992).

chaos, clients often describe feeling as if they are in transition or caught between alternatives. Of course, he acknowledged that some episodes of chaos may represent client resistance or regression. However, gestational periods of confusion differ from resistance or regression in that clients actively attempt to make sense of their disorientation. The goal of psychotherapy is to facilitate the reorganization in an adaptive way. These chaotic states represent developmental bridges between former constructions of reality and modified versions yet to be crystallized.

Models Describing Unintentional Change

The following five models describe unintentional change, and most depict change that is a byproduct of attempts to cope with an uncontrollable environmental event.

Life Crises and Personal Growth.   Schaefer and Moos' (1992) model of Life Crises and Personal Growth along with the Resources Model of Coping (Holahan & Moos, 1987, 1990, 1991) emphasized the role of life crises in promoting personal growth and enhancing adaptation (Fig. 6.4; see also chap. 5, this volume). Personal and environmental systems influence the type of life crisis or transition experienced. Factors related to the crisis event influence cognitive appraisal and coping responses, which in turn influence the outcome of the crisis or transition. All components of the model are linked by feedback loops, so that each stage influences and is influenced by all other stages. Primary personal systems include cognitive ability, health status, motivation, and self-efficacy. Additional personal resources include hardiness, temperament, self-reliance, self-control, and prior experience dealing with crises. Environmental systems include finances, life transitions, family and social support, and community assets.

Empirical support for this model is strong. Schaefer, Moos, and their colleagues provide support for the hypotheses that the combination of one's personal, environmental, and coping resources (prior to the event) determines the outcome following a life crisis or traumatic event. These investigators provide evidence that social support and active (i.e., problem-focused) coping responses are associated with the ability to manage stressful circumstances in studies of college students (Valentiner, Holahan, & Moos, 1994), patients with cardiac illness (Holahan, Moos, Holahan, & Brennan, 1995) and patients with depression (Fondacaro & Moos, 1989).

Active, problem-focused coping has been found to be more likely to lead

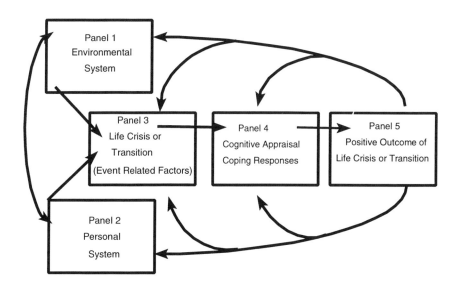

FIG. 6.4. Life crises and personal growth. From Schaefer and Moos (1992). Copyright 1992 by Greenwood Publishing Group. Reprinted by permission.

to personal growth following a crisis event than avoidance coping. Redefining a crisis event as a challenge or attributing meaning to it also is likely to
lead to a positive outcome (Schaefer & Moos, 1992). In a study of women's
adjustment to breast cancer, Ryan (1995) found that constructed meaning
was associated with positive reappraisal and the inhibition of avoidant
coping; collectively, these factors influenced adjustment to diagnosis and
emotional well-being. Similarly, both Nerken (1993) and Mahoney (1982)
suggested that growth occurs as a result of finding meaning in uncontrollable
environmental events. Several investigators have reported that more than
50% of all people who experience a traumatic event report some positive
outcome such as the development of new skills, improved relationships, and
a changed perspective (cf. Cleveland, 1980; Dhooper, 1983; Wallerstein,
1986; Yarom, 1983).

Quantum Change.   The theory of Quantum Change proposed by
Miller and C'deBaca (1994) describes sudden, unexpected deviations in the
lives of people that affect permanent and ubiquitous change. Their model
is distinct from the other models included in this section in that it focuses
more on the *process* than the outcome of change. In simplest terms, Miller
and C'deBaca (1994) suggested that individuals are functioning at some
normative level when they experience a sudden and transformational
change (see Fig. 6.5). This change may or may not be precipitated by an
environmental event, such as a trauma or a desire to change. The change
results in a new level of functioning that may be higher or lower than the
original (i.e., normative) level of functioning.

Miller and C'deBaca (1994) acknowledged that psychologists interested
in both learning (cf. Hunt & Matarazzo, 1970; Premack, 1970) and in
conversion experiences (cf. Barrett, 1989; Karoly, 1977; Orford, 1985) have
described sudden change. Researchers have attributed transformational
change to decision making (Hunt & Matarazzo, 1970), moral imperatives
(Karoly, 1977), and changes in attitudes (Orford, 1985). In studies of
recovery from alcohol abuse and other addictive behavior, Miller (1993)
suggested that the following factors are among the important determinants
of change: desire for help, motivation to change, personal distress, and the
establishment of personal goals.

Although transformational change has been acknowledged, such change
has proved difficult to describe, discuss, and measure. *Transformational,* or
quantum change, has received little empirical attention as it is an unexpected
or unsolicited private event amenable to study only through retrospective
reports. In an attempt to identify antecedents of such change, individuals

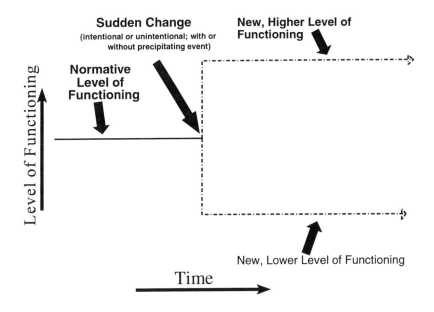

FIG. 6.5. Quantum change (Miller & C'deBaca, 1994).

who had experienced sudden and profound change were interviewed (Miller & C'deBaca, 1994). Interestingly, those who evidenced quantum change reported a higher than average number of negative life events and a lower than average number of positive life events prior to their transformation, as compared to published norms for the general population (Sarason, Johnson, & Siegel, 1978). Reasoning that such circumstances might enhance suscep-tibility to opportunities for change, Miller and C'deBaca (1994) asked whether those in their sample had been looking for such opportunities. Although approximately one third of the participants acknowledged that they had been hoping and praying for something life-altering to happen; almost 50% were taken by surprise.

All who experienced quantum change described it as conceptually and experientially different from incremental change because of its speed and magnitude. Such dramatic change generalized widely and was enduring. For example, in characterizing her experience with quantum change, one woman reported that during a 2-month recuperation period following surgery, she realized she was not living her life as she wanted. She quit her job, eliminated unwanted obligations, went back to school, and began spending more time with family and friends.

Four mechanisms may be involved in affecting quantum change: self-regulation, perceptual shift, value conflict, and transcendence (Miller & C'deBaca, 1994). *Self-regulation* refers to the process of conscious and effortful behavioral control. Although much of behavior is automatic, novel situations promote executive control and may initiate all-encompassing behavioral reorganization. Quantum change may occur when a previously held worldview conflicts with a newly established worldview with which it is incompatible. Confronting a health crisis often promotes reflections on mortality and thus may provide the impetus for re-examining, or shifting priorities. Similar notions are advanced in both Hager's (1992) model of chaos and growth and Mahoney's (1982) model of the human change process in psychotherapy. Quantum change also can be motivated by value conflict. Rokeach (1983) found that inducing value conflict in university students resulted in behavior change relative to controls; receiving feedback that one's values are incompatible with one's behavior apparently leads to efforts directed at supporting one's beliefs. The final mechanism for the process of quantum change is transcendence. Transcendence is used to explain the experiences of those who attribute their change to some external source, such as a higher power (i.e., God). No research has been done to date to explore individual differences in the processes used to stimulate profound change or in the circumstances in which one or another mechanism is effective or preferred.

Resilience and Thriving. Like Miller and C'deBaca (1994), O'Leary and Ickovics (1995) described discontinuous change. In their view, there are three possible outcomes following challenge: survival, recovery, or thriving (see Fig. 6.6). Those who merely survive never regain their previous level of functioning. Those who recover regain homeostasis and return to their previous level of functioning. Thriving, however, refers to the ability to go beyond the original level of psychosocial functioning, to grow vigorously, even flourish (O'Leary & Ickovics, 1995). Thriving may be behavioral, affective, or cognitive. O'Leary and Ickovics (1995) described thriving as transformative, much like Miller and C'deBaca's (1994) description of quantum change.

Thriving is a dramatic shift entailing a marked advance over recovery (return to baseline). Thriving is contingent on confronting adversity actively, although the confrontation may not be intentional or within awareness. According to O'Leary and Ickovics (1995), the availability of individual and social resources enhances the probability of thriving. Schaefer and Moos (1992) made a similar assumption regarding resources. The

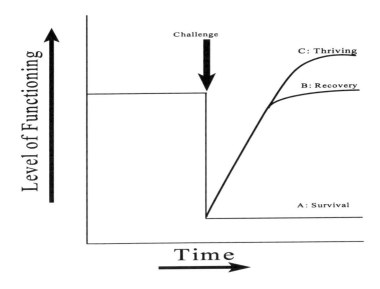

FIG. 6.6. Resilience and thriving. From O'Leary and Ickovics (1995). Copyright 1995 by Lawrence Erlbaum Associates. Reprinted by permission.

personal resources that increase the possibility of thriving include hardiness, active coping, sense of coherence, optimism, and a sense of humor (Antoni & Goodkin, 1988; Carver et al., 1993; Freidman, 1990, 1991). Cognitive coping methods, such as social comparison, compartmentalization, and finding meaning in negative events are also suggested to increase the likelihood that one will benefit from a traumatic event (Burgess & Holmstrom, 1979; Folkman, Chesney, & Christopher-Richards, 1994; Taylor, 1989). A reliance on faith to maintain a positive view of a meaningful life may also be important to some individuals.

The social resources include securing and using community and institutional resources, maintaining social support networks, and utilizing religious resources. Other social resources may increase the ability to thrive in the face of adversity, as well. For example, women of higher social class typically have more financial and social resources; not surprisingly, they are less likely to experience social stressors and are at less risk for morbidity and premature mortality (Adler et al., 1994).

Transformation.   In their book, *Trauma and Transformation*, Tedeschi and Calhoun (1995) discussed both the process and the outcome of change. They view change as the result of coping with some unexpected and uncontrollable trauma. Such change or growth appears to be incremental.

Tedeschi and Calhoun (1995) presented a model, depicted in Fig. 6.7, for the transition from trauma to triumph. It consists of feedback loops, much like the model of Schaefer and Moos (1992).

The initial response of the individual who experiences the trauma can be characterized in terms of affect, cognition, and behavior. The initial response is relatively ineffective, described in Panel 3 of the model, whereby distress is not manageable (affect), schemas are challenged or not comprehensible (cognition), and primary control of the situation fails (behavior). During the next stage of the process, a secondary response is triggered by failure to successfully manage the trauma. This secondary response requires some rumination—renewed consideration of how to handle the event and a revision of existing schema. Tedeschi and Calhoun (1995) suggested that the coping strategies employed during this period are primarily emotion-focused.

During the third phase of the process, emotional support and/or new ways of coping with the situation are offered by others (Panel 5). The influence of others supports the individual's passage from rumination to initial growth. As aspects of the trauma are accepted, goals are revised, new meaning is constructed, and cognitive schema are altered. During initial growth, the individual may begin trusting her or his personal strength or gain a new appreciation for the helpfulness of others. The final stage is labeled further growth and wisdom (Panel 7). In this stage, the positive effects of growth

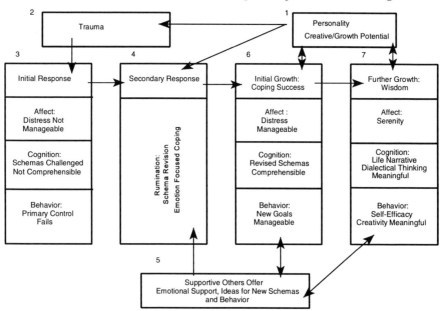

FIG. 6.7. Trauma and transformation. From Tedeschi and Calhoun (1995). Copyright 1995 by Sage. Reprinted by permission.

are stabilized and internalized. Affect has changed from "not manageable" in the initial response to a feeling of "serenity" in this final stage. Cognition is adapted to create new meaning and a new life narrative that encompasses the traumatic event, and behavior has evolved to be efficacious.

Like both O'Leary and Ickovics (1995) and Schaefer and Moos (1992), Tedeschi and Calhoun's (1995) model focuses on positive change, although they do acknowledge that not everyone triumphs over trauma and that transformation may be mixed with some continuing distress. In their view, the positive changes following a crisis represent more than reinterpretations of the event; they are the result of active attempts to cope. This is similar to O'Leary and Ickovics' (1995) recognition of the value of direct confrontation with challenge as a precursor to thriving and the process of active grieving described by Nerken (1993) in his model of resolution and growth following loss.

According to Tedeschi and Calhoun (1995), individual traits such as hardiness, optimism, extroversion, self-efficacy, and locus of control (LOC) are related to positive change following a stressful event. Furthermore, one's age, developmental stage, and gender may affect the perception of benefit following trauma. In their view, change does not occur until current coping resources are exhausted and new coping strategies emerge. According to Tedeschi and Calhoun (1995), new meaning is constructed during initial growth. Note that a revised version of this model is presented by Calhoun and Tedeschi (chap. 9, this volume).

Transformational Coping. Like most the models of change and growth described in this section, transformational coping postulated by Aldwin (1994) emphasizes the benefits of handling a stressful event. She suggested that coping may serve either a homeostatic function or it may be transformational, thereby resulting in change, either positive or negative. Homeostatic and transformational coping are represented diagrammatically in Fig. 6.8. Change resulting from transformational coping may be relatively minor, or the change may be major, such as rejecting a social network of friends in an attempt to remove oneself from situations that promote harmful behaviors such as heavy drinking and drug use. Aldwin (1994) proposed several mechanisms to explain the development of positive outcomes from stress or negative events.

The first such mechanism is the independence of positive and negative affect. Investigators have found that the experience of positive and negative affect are not inversely related, but orthogonal (Bradburn & Caplovitz, 1965; McGrath & Beehr, 1990; Watson & Clark, 1984). Therefore, one may experience both positive and negative affect simultaneously.

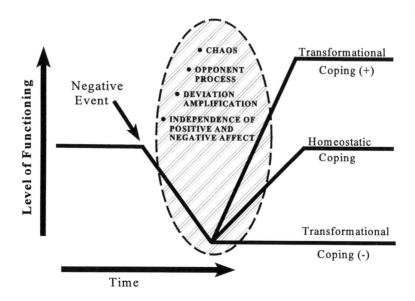

FIG. 6.8. Transformational coping (Aldwin, 1994).

Aldwin (1994) also described the opponent process model (Soloman, 1980). According to this model, a strong negative affective state is invariably followed by a strong positive affective state and vice versa. Therefore, the negative affect generated by trauma is followed by a positive affective swing. Change and growth may occur during the positive swing. For example, someone who has agonized over whether to end an unrewarding marriage may experience a great sense of relief and happiness after making the decision to divorce and, consequently, feel transformed.

Aldwin (1994) further characterized *deviation amplification theory*. According to this theory, a system with a feedback loop may function so that small changes in the system are amplified. As a result, traumatic stress may give rise to a magnitude of change sufficient to promote transformation (von Bertalanffy, 1969). To illustrate, a modest deviation in income may amplify into homelessness for someone living at the edge of poverty. Conversely, even a slight increment in income under such circumstances may lead to a significantly better quality of life. In addition, these effects may spiral such that greater financial resources lead to increased opportunities to benefit from social and community resources resulting in further benefits.

Aldwin (1994) suggested that intelligence, flexibility, determination, and willingness to take personal risks increase the likelihood that one will experience positive benefits from stress. Furthermore, Aldwin (1994) cited hardiness and sense of coherence as personality variables that predict growth following a life crisis. Optimists are likely to grow following a traumatic event and to use problem-focused coping, which may increase the probability that they will benefit from crisis (Aldwin, 1994).

METHODOLOGICAL IMPLICATIONS AND RECOMMENDATIONS FOR FUTURE RESEARCH

The theories presented in this chapter suggest a variety of personal and environmental resources as factors that may enhance the likelihood of positive outcomes following life-changing or traumatic events. Several of the constructs are regarded as central to the process of change following challenge by most theorists; others are model-specific, such as flexibility (Aldwin, 1994), humor (O'Leary & Ickovics, 1995), and self-esteem (Mahoney, 1982). The personal resources mentioned by most of the theorists reviewed are meaning-making (positive appraisal), self-efficacy, hardiness, coping style, and past experience (see Table 6.1). The most frequently cited social resource is social support. Sense of coherence, motivation, optimism, hardiness, coping style, social class, and community resources were also suggested. It is clear that although individual factors are presented, the determinants of outcome following a negative event are inextricably linked. Both the determinants and outcomes of change can be considered within the broad categories of affect, cognition, and behavior.

The postulated centrality of meaning-making in so many of the change theories reviewed suggests that further exploration of the role of cognition in promoting or inhibiting change following challenge may be fruitful. For example, in a recent study, Ryan (1995) obtained evidence that constructed meaning and self-esteem exerted a direct beneficial effect on women's adjustment to breast cancer. In addition, constructed meaning mediated well-being through the use of positive reappraisal and through the inhibition of avoidant coping. Recently, Fife (1994) suggested that constructed meaning is a particularly important determinant of the outcome of challenges

TABLE 6.1

Determinants of Outcome Suggested by Models of Change and Growth

	Nerken	Mahoney	Schaefer & Moos	Hager	Miller & C'deBaca	O'Leary & Ickovics	Tedeschi & Calhoun	Aldwin	Total
PERSONAL RESOURCES									
Self-efficacy			X				X	X	3
Sense of coherence (comprehensibility, manageability, meaningfulness)						X	X		2
Meaning making (appraisal)	X	X	X	X		X	X		6
Locus of control					X		X		2
Motivation		X	X						2
Optimism (self-esteem/ internal control/ active coping)						X	X	X	3
Cognitive status			X					X	2
Hardiness (control, challenge, commitment)			X			X	X	X	4
Past experience			X		X	X		X	4
Coping style			X			X	X	X	4
ENVIRONMENTAL RESOURCES									
Social support		X	X			X	X		4
SES			X			X			2
Community resources			X			X			2

The following are Personal and Environmental Determinants that are model specific:

Nerken	Mahoney	Schaefer & Moos	Miller & C'deBaca	O'Leary & Ickovics	Tedeschi & Calhoun	Aldwin
Reflective-self	Self-esteem Therapeutic relationship Insight	Self-reliance Self-control Health status Temperament Crisis environment Control over stressor	Inner-focused	Sense of humor Faith	Age Developmental stage Gender	Flexibility Risk taking

that disrupt and irrevocably change an individual's life, such as terminal illness.

Although there are many differences in the proposed antecedents of change, the processes described share some similarities. First, all of the theories presented refer to changes over time. For the theories referring to intentional change, the process is most often slow and incremental. In contrast, for the theories of unintentional change, there is typically an unexpected major event (sometimes traumatic), to which an individual must respond quickly. The initiation and early response to the event is often immediate, although the social and psychological resolution of the event is a continuous process that may not vary substantially from the intentional change models. Another similarity is that for all of the models, there is some period of decrement in (baseline) functioning (e.g., immediately following an event, chaos prior to reorganization). And finally, in each case, there is the possibility of enhanced outcome, or growth, following change.

Research designed to validate these models empirically has been scarce. In some cases, the models are based on expertise gleaned from clinical experience (e.g., Mahoney, 1982; Tedeschi & Calhoun, 1995), and in other cases, the theories are built upon a synthesis of literature in health, social and clinical psychology (e.g., O'Leary & Ickovics, 1995; Aldwin, 1994). Exploring positive outcomes of negative events presents many methodological challenges as described throughout this volume. As Table 6.1 attests, the overlap in postulated antecedents and correlates of change-producing reactions to challenge provides a starting place for empirical studies designed to establish which of these possible determinants effects change, directly or indirectly.

In the context of proposing a set of hypotheses, referred to as the generalized principle of cognitive consistency, to explain reactions to critical life events, Inglehart (1991) offered a set a questions that a good theory of such reactions should be able to answer. The questions which focus on explaining both the energizing and structuring components of these reactions, are (a) When will the tension arise?, (b) What determines the amount of tension arising?, (c) Which general kind of reaction will follow?, (d) Which specific kind of reaction (tension reduction or tension avoidance) will follow?, and (e) What long-term consequences will occur? These questions provide a set of evaluative criteria that can be employed to assess the adequacy of change theories to predict who will adapt or respond positively to challenge and who will not.

The measurement of successful adaptation will depend on the type of threat of challenge faced and will be influenced by the developmental stage of study participants. Both personal and social resources that have been suggested as influencing the outcomes of challenge can be measured in terms of type of resource, extent and frequency of use, and the value or usefulness of these resources. It may also be important to measure the perception of the availability of resources; this may play a role in the cognitive response to threat. For those with ample resources, knowing that they are there may be important even if they are not used. For those with limited resources, their lack of availability may heighten the threat.

Clearly the refinement of existing measures (see chap. 2, this volume) and the development of new measures are essential to promote research in this field. Measures must be carefully constructed and their psychometric properties evaluated. In addition to self-report measures on the benefits of challenge, it may be important to consider objective measures and observer ratings. For example, health and functional ability may be evaluated using data from medical records or ratings by health professionals.

The complex issues around positive outcomes to negative events lend themselves to an interdisciplinary approach. Scientists from different disciplines can provide important insight into the processes and dynamics of such outcomes. Depending on the domain under investigation, collaborators might include psychologists, sociologists, anthropologists, teachers, physicians, nurses, immunologists, and others.

The ideal design for a study of reactions to life challenges is longitudinal and prospective. Mobilization of resources as well as the short- and long-range consequences should be evaluated. This approach, although methodologically optimal, is time-consuming and expensive. It requires the identification of a cohort potentially at risk for challenge (e.g., women in their 70s at risk for widowhood, men at risk for prostate cancer or heart disease due to individual or family risk factors). A large sample would be essential to obtain adequate numbers of individuals who actually face a particular challenge. Alternatively, retrospective studies of individuals who have recently confronted a life change or trauma could be conducted (e.g., recent combat experience, victimization, new diagnosis of a chronic illness). Although research following the occurrence of a traumatic event is retrospective and one cannot accurately disentangle which resources were present before and/or after the event (or as a result of the event), exploratory research is necessary to begin understanding the phenomenon of markedly divergent outcomes following a traumatic event. The results of exploratory studies could guide the direction of more resource-intensive prospective studies. Also useful would be intensive case studies or studies of a smaller cohort of individuals designed to understand the depth and scope of responses.

Another methodological challenge for this field is the identification of appropriate comparison groups. One possibility is to observe either prospectively or retrospectively the mobilization of resources among a relatively large group of persons similarly challenged. Some of these individuals will have positive outcomes and some will not—providing a natural comparison cohort.

All of these methodological concerns deserve serious attention, and will need to be resolved before the field is able to move forward substantially. In the interim, incremental methodological advancement, measurement refinement and development, and the promotion of theoretically driven research must remain a priority. To date, empirical research investigating the integration of the constructs and processes reviewed has been extremely limited. An investigation of the personal and environmental resources of those who have experienced trauma is warranted within the context of testable theoretical propositions measured against clearly articulated evaluative criteria.

The values are numerous for understanding why and how some individuals grow in the aftermath of trauma, whereas others develop psychological and physical problems. Information regarding the role of social and environmental resources might lead to more effective clinical interventions. Life crises will never be eliminated, but identification of the most effective means of responding to life crises can contribute to limiting their negative impact.

REFERENCES

Adler, N. E., Boyce, T., Chesney, M. A., Cohen, S., Folkman, S., Kahn, R. L., & Syme, S. L. (1994). Socioeconomic status and health: The challenge of the gradient. *American Psychologist, 49*, 15–24.

Aldwin, C. M. (1994). Transformational coping. In C. M. Aldwin (Ed.), *Stress, coping, and development* (pp. 240–269). New York: Guilford.

Antoni, M. H., & Goodkin, K. (1988). Host moderator variables in the promotion of cervical neoplasia: I. Personality facets. *Journal of Psychosomatic Research, 32*, 327–338.

Antonioni, D. (1994). A new model for organizational change. *Organization Development Journal, 12*, 17–22.

Avison, W. R., & Gotlib, I. G. (1994). *Stress and mental health.* New York: Plenum.

Barrett, C. L. (1989). Presidential address and introduction to special issue: SPAB comes of age. *Psychology of Addictive Behaviors, 3*, 95–106.

Bengtson, V. L., Schaie, K. W., & Burton, L. M. (1995). *Adult intergenerational relations: Effects of societal change.* New York: Springer.

Block, J. H., & Block, J. (1980). The role of ego-control and ego-resiliency in the organization of behavior. In W. A. Collins (Ed.), *Development of cognition, affect, and social relations: The Minnesota Symposia on Child Psychology* (Vol. 13, pp. 39–101). Hillsdale, NJ: Lawrence Erlbaum Associates.

Bowlby, J. (1980) *Attachment and loss: Loss, sadness and depression* (Vol. 3). New York: Basic Books.

Bradburn, N. M., & Caplovitz, D. (1965). *Reports on happiness: A pilot study of behavior related to mental health.* Chicago: Aldine.

Briere J., & Runtz, M. (1988). Symptomatology associated with childhood sexual victimization in a non-clinical adult sample. *Child Abuse and Neglect, 12,* 51–59.

Browne, A., & Finkelhor, D. (1986). Impact of child sexual abuse: A review of the research. *Psychological Bulletin, 99,* 66–77.

Burgess, A. W., & Holmstrom, L. L. (1979). Adaptive strategies and recovery from rape. *American Journal of Psychiatry, 136,* 1278–1282.

Carver, C. S., Pozo, C., Harris, S. D., Noriega, V, Scheier, M. F., Robinson, D. S. Ketcham, A. S., Moffat, F. L., & Clark, K. C. (1993). How coping mediates the effect of optimism on distress: A study of women with early stage breast cancer. *Journal of Personality and Social Psychology, 65,* 375–390.

Chance, P. (1988). *Learning and behavior* (2nd ed.). Belmont, CA: Wadsworth.

Cleveland, M. (1980). Family adaptation to traumatic spinal cord injury: A response to crisis. *Family Relations, 29,* 558–565.

Cohen, S., Kessler, R. C., & Gordon, L. C. (1995). *Measuring stress: A guide for health and social scientists.* New York: Oxford University Press.

Cohen, S., Tyrell, D. A., & Smith, A. P. (1993). Negative life events, perceived stress, negative affect, and susceptibility to the common cold. *Journal of Personality and Social Psychology, 64,* 131–140.

Dhooper, S. S. (1983). Family coping with the crisis of heart attack. *Social Work in Health Care, 9,* 15–31.

Eargle, A. E., Guerra, N. G., & Tolan, P. H. (1994). Preventing aggression in inner-city children: Small group training to change cognitions, social skills and behavior. *Journal of Child and Adolescent Group Therapy, 4,* 229–242.

Fife, B. L. (1994). The conceptualization of meaning in illness. *Social Science and Medicine,* 38(2), 309–316.

Folkman, S., Chesney, M. A., & Christopher-Richards, A. (1994). Stress and coping in caregiving partners of men with AIDS. *Psychiatric Clinics of North America, 17,* 35–53.

Folkman, S., & Lazarus, R. S. (1980). An analysis of coping in a middle-aged community sample. *Journal of Health and Social Behavior, 21,* 219–239.

Fondacaro, M. R., & Moos, R. H. (1989). Life stressors and coping: A longitudinal analysis among depressed and nondepressed adults. *Journal of Community Psychology, 17,* 330–340.

Frazier, P. A., & Schauben, L. D. (1994). Stressful life events and psychological adjustment among female college students. *Measurement and Evaluations in Counseling and Development, 27,* 280–292.

Freidman, H. S. (Ed.). (1990). *Personality and disease.* New York: Wiley.

Freidman, H. S. (1991). *The self-healing personality: Why some people achieve health and others succumb to illness.* New York: Henry Holt.

Garmezy, N. (1983). Stressors of childhood. In N. Garmezy & M. Rutter (Eds.), *Stress, coping and the development in children* (pp. 43–84). New York: McGraw-Hill.

Garmezy, N. (1991). Resiliency and vulnerability to adverse developmental outcomes associated with poverty. *American Behavioral Scientist, 34,* 416–430.

Garmezy, N., Masten, A. S., & Tellegen, A. (1984). The study of stress and competence in children: A building block for developmental psychopathology. *Child Development, 55,* 97–111.

Garmezy, N., & Nuechterlein, K. (1972). Invulnerable children: The fact and fiction of competence and disadvantage. *American Journal of Orthopsychiatry, 42,* 328–329.

Gray, J. A. (1971). *The psychology of fear and stress.* New York: McGraw-Hill.

Hager, D. L. (1992). Chaos and growth. *Psychotherapy, 29,* 378–384.

Harris, T. O. (1991). Life stress and illness: The question of specificity. *Annals of Behavioral Medicine, 13,* 211–219.

Heatherton, T. F., & Weinberger, J. L. (1994). *Can personality change?* Washington, DC: American Psychological Association.

Hodgkinson, P. E., Joseph, S., Yule, W., & Williams, R. (1995). Measuring grief after sudden violent death: Zeebrugge bereaved at 30 months. *Personality and Individual Differences, 18,* 805–808.

Holahan, C., & Moos, R. H. (1986). Personality, coping and family resources in stress resistance: A longitudinal analysis. *Journal of Personality and Social Psychology, 51,* 389–395.

Holahan, C. J., & Moos, R. H. (1987). Personal and contextual determinants of coping strategies. *Journal of Personality & Social Psychology, 52,* 946–955.

Holahan, C. J., & Moos, R. H. (1990). Life stressors, resistance and improved psychological functioning: An extension of the stress resistance paradigm. *Journal of Personality and Social Psychology, 58,* 900–917.

Holohan, C. J., & Moos, R. H. (1991). Life stressors, personal and social resources, and depression: A 4 year structural model. *Journal of Abnormal Psychology, 100,* 31–38.

Holahan, C. J., & Moos, R. H. (1994). Life stressors and mental health: Advances in conceptualizing stress resistance. In W. R. Avison & I. H. Gotlib (Eds.), *Stress and mental health: Contemporary issues and prospects for the future.* New York: Plenum.

Holahan, C. J., Moos, R. H., Holahan, C. K., & Brennan, P. J. (1995). Social support, coping, and depressive symptoms in a late-middle-aged sample of patients reporting cardiac illness. *Health Psychology, 14,* 152–163.

Holmes, T. H., & Masuda, M. (1974). Life change and illness susceptibility. In B. S. Dohrenwend & B. P. Dohrenwend, *Stressful life events: Their nature and effects* (p. 340). New York: John Wiley & Sons.

Hunt, W. A., & Matarazzo, J. D. (1970). Habit mechanisms in smoking. In W. A. Hunt (Ed.), *Learning mechanisms in smoking* (pp. 65–90). Chicago: Aldine.

Ingelhart, M. R. (1991). *Reactions to critical life events: A social psychological analysis.* New York: Prager.

Kahn, R. L. (1991, May). *Retention, resilience, and enhancement: Components of vitality throughout the life course.* Course paper presented at the meeting of the MacArthur Foundation Successful Aging Program, San Francisco.

Karoly, P. (1977). Behavioral self-management in children: Concepts, methods, issues, and directions. In M. Hersen, R. M. Eisler, & P. M. Miller (Eds.), *Progress in behavior modification* (Vol. 5, pp. 197–262). San Diego, CA: Academic Press.

Kim, J. S., Lee, M. C., Kim H. G., & Suh, D. C. (1994). Isolated trigeminal sensory change due to pontine hemorrhage. *Clinical Neurology and Neurosurgery, 96,* 168–169.

Klinger, E. (1977). *Meaning and void: Inner experience and the incentives in people's lives.* Minneapolis: University of Minnesota Press.

Kuebler-Ross, E. (1969). *On death and dying.* New York: Macmillian.

Kuebler-Ross, E. (1982). *Working it through.* New York: Collier Books.

Lazarus, R. S., & Folkman, S. (1984). Stress, appraisal and coping. New York: Springer.
Levy, L., & Rowitz, L. (1973). The ecology of mental disorder. New York: Behavioral Publications.
Mahoney, M. J. (1982). Psychotherapy and human change processes. In J. H. Harvey & M. M. Parks (Eds.), Psychotherapy research and behavior change (pp. 77–122). Washington, DC: APA.
Mahoney, M. J., & Craine, M. H. (1991). The changing beliefs of psychotherapy experts. Journal of Psychotherapy Integration, 1, 207–221.
Masten, A. S. (1989). Resilience in development: Implications of the study of successful adaptation for developmental psychopathology. In D. Cicchetti (Ed), The emergence of a discipline: Vol. 1. Rochester Symposium on Developmental Psychopathology (pp. 261–294). Hillsdale, NJ: Lawrence Erlbaum Associates.
McGrath, J. E., & Beehr, T. A. (1990). Time and the stress process: Some temporal issues in the conceptualization and measurement of stress. Special Issue: Advances in measuring life stress. Stress Medicine, 6, 93–104.
Miller, W. R. (1993). What really drives change. Addiction, 88, 1479–1480.
Miller, W. R., & C'deBaca, J. (1994). Quantum change: Toward a psychology of transformation. In T. F. Heatherton & J. L. Weinberger (Eds.), Can personality change? (pp. 253–281). Washington, DC: American Psychological Association.
Nerken, I. R. (1993). Grief and the reflective self: Toward a clearer model of loss resolution and growth. Death Studies, 17, 1–26.
O'Leary, V. E., & Ickovics, J. R. (1995). Resilience and thriving in response to challenge: An opportunity for a paradigm shift in women's health. Women's Health: Research on Gender, Behavior, and Policy, 1, 121–142.
Orford, J. (1985). Excessive appetites: A psychological view of addictions. New York: Wiley.
Premack, D. (1970). A functional analysis of language. Journal of the Experimental Analysis of Behavior, 1970, 107–125.
Prochaska, J., & DiClemente, C. (1984). The transtheoretical approach: Crossing the individual boundaries of therapy. Homewood, IL: Dow Jones-Irwin.
Rahe, R. H., & Arthur, R. J. (1978). Life change and illness studies: Past history and future directions. Journal of Human Stress, 4, 3–15.
Rahe, R. H., & Lind, E. (1971). Psychological factors and sudden cardiac death: A pilot study. Journal of Psychosomatic Research, 15, 19–24.
Ramsay, D. S, & Lewis, M. (1994). Developmental change in infant cortisol and behavioral response to inoculation. Child Development, 65, 1491–1502.
Rokeach, M. (1983). Rokeach value survey. Palo Alto, CA: Consulting Psychologists Press.
Rowe, J. W., & Kahn, R. L. (1987). Human aging: Usual and successful. Science, 237, 143–149.
Rutter, M. (1981). Stress, coping, and development: Some issues and some questions. Journal of Child Psychology and Psychiatry, 22, 323–356.
Ryan, M. M. (1995). Modeling cognitive adaptation in women with cancer. Unpublished doctoral dissertation, Indiana State University, Terre Haute.
Sarason, I. G., Johnson, J. G., & Siegel, J. M. (1978). Assessing the impact of life changes: Development of the Life Experiences Survey. Journal of Consulting and Clinical Psychology, 46, 932–946.
Schaefer, J. A., & Moos, R. H. (1992). Life crisis and personal growth. In B. N. Carpenter (Ed.), Personal coping: Theory research and application (pp. 149–170). Westport, CT: Praeger.
Seligman, M. E. P. (1975). Helplessness: On development, depression, and death. San Francisco: Freeman Press.

Selye, H. (1946). The general adaptation syndrome and diseases of adaptation. *Journal of Clinical Endocrinology* 6: 117–230.

Selye, H. (1956). *The stress of life.* New York: McGraw-Hill.

Selye, H. (1976). *Stress in health and disease.* Reading, MA: Butterworths.

Siegler, R. S., & Engle, R. A. (1994). Studying change in developmental and neuropsychological contexts. *Current Psychology of Cognition, 13,* 321–349.

Solomon, R. L. (1980). The opponent process model of acquired motivation: The costs of pleasure and the benefits of pain. *American Psychologist, 35,* 155–184.

Stoolmiller, M. (1994). Antisocial behavior, delinquent peer association, and unsupervised wandering for boys: Growth and change from childhood to early adolescence. *Multivariate Behavioral Research, 29,* 263–288.

Taylor, S. E. (1983). Adjustment to threatening events: A theory of cognitive adaptation. *American Psychologist, 38,* 1161–1173.

Taylor, S. E. (1989). *Positive illusions: Creative self-deception and the healthy mind.* New York: Basic Books.

Tedeschi, R. G., & Calhoun, L. G. (1995). *Trauma and transformation: Growing in the aftermath of suffering.* Thousand Oaks, CA: Sage.

Ursano, R. J., Fullerton, C. S., Kao, T. C., & Bhartiya, V. (1995). Longitudinal assessment of posttraumatic stress disorder and depression after exposure to traumatic death. *Journal of Nervous and Mental Disease, 183,* 36–42.

Valentiner, D. P., Holahan, C. J., & Moos, R. H. (1994). Social support, appraisals of event controllability, and coping: An integrative model. *Journal of Personality & Social Psychology, 66,* 1094–1102.

von Bertalanffy, L. (1969). General systems theory: Foundations, development, applications. New York: Brazilier.

Vrana, S. & Lauterbach, D. (1994). Prevalence of traumatic events and post-traumatic psychological symptoms in a nonclinical sample of college students. *Journal of Traumatic Stress, 7,* 289–302.

Wallerstein, J. S. (1986). Women after divorce: Preliminary report from a ten-year follow-up. *American Journal of Orthopsychiatry, 56,* 65–77.

Watson, D., & Clark, L. A. (1984). Negative affectivity: The disposition to experience aversive emotional states. *Psychological Bulletin, 96,* 465–490.

Werner, E. E., & Smith, R.S. (1982). *Vulnerable but invincible: A study of resilient children.* New York: McGraw-Hill.

Wolin, S. J., & Wolin, S. (1993). *The resilient self: How survivors of troubled families rise above adversity.* New York: Ullard Books.

Wortman, C. B., & Brehm, J. W. (1975). Responses to uncontrollable outcomes: An integration of reactance theory and the learned helplessness model. In I. Berkowitz (Ed.), *Advances in experimental social psychology* (Vol. 8, pp. 278–336). New York: Academic Press.

Wortman, C. B., & Silver, R. (1987). Coping with irrevocable loss. In *Cataclysms, crises, and catastrophes: Psychology in action* (Master Lecture Series, Vol. 6, 189–235). Washington, DC: American Psychological Association.

Yarom, N. (1983). Facing death in war: An existential crisis. In S. Breznitz (Ed.), *Stress in Israel* (pp. 3–38). New York: Van Nostrand Reinhold.

Zigler, E., & Trickett, P. K. (1978). IQ, social competence, and evaluation of early childhood intervention programs. *American Psychologist,* 789–798.

7

Implications of Posttraumatic Growth for Individuals

Crystal L. Park
Miami University

Much of this book is devoted to describing what is known about how people may grow through traumatic events, the kinds of personal and situational factors that may be involved in determining who reports growth, when and how such growth is reported, and the kinds of growth people may experience. Given this information, an important question becomes, "So what? What does growth actually mean in the lives of the people who report experiencing it?" This chapter addresses the question of what self-reported growth following traumatic experiences means in people's lives in terms of their current and future functioning. Specifically, are they "better off" than people who do not experience such growth? If so, what mechanisms might account for this enhanced adjustment? And in what ways is this enhanced functioning exhibited? Are people who report growth happier, healthier, or less depressed that those who don't? Is self-reported growth related to better coping with current and future events? Like many other aspects of this field of study, both the theoretical and empirical literature regarding the consequences of growth for the individual are somewhat sparse and imprecise, although writers and researchers have recently begun to direct more sophisticated attention this way.

The focus of this chapter, then, is how posttraumatic growth (PTG) is related to various aspects of adjustment. Conceptual issues are discussed first; these include issues regarding the potential theoretical linkages between PTG and adjustment as well as some definitional issues. The relevant empirical literature addressing the links between PTG and adjustment is then reviewed within the proposed conceptual framework.

CONCEPTUAL ISSUES

The main conceptual issue in this chapter involves delineating the ways that PTG and adjustment may be related. This relationship can be conceptualized in several different ways, and these alternatives have important implications for how the empirical literature regarding the issue is approached. A second issue involves some thorny questions about definitions of growth and the roles that values play in this research.

Relationships Between PTG and Adjustment

Before examining relationships between PTG and adjustment, these terms need to be defined. For the purposes of this chapter, *adjustment* is used broadly to refer to the types of outcomes typically used as indicators of how well individuals have adjusted to their changed life circumstances. Adjustment, therefore, includes measures such as mood states and psychological and physical health and functioning. Defining growth is also complicated, and the relationships between PTG and adjustment can be understood in several different ways, depending on how growth is defined. For example, growth reported as a consequence of coping with a traumatic experience could be considered to be directly and accurately indicative of enhanced well-being. People may report feeling stronger or better prepared for the next time "something like this" happens, or they may feel a renewed sense of purpose or self-understanding. By definition, therefore, their well-being is enhanced. Alternately, growth can be defined as a construct that is conceptually independent from adjustment (as measured, for example, by depressive symptoms, physical health, or social functioning); this conceptualization promotes the examination of relationships between self-reported growth and measures of various adjustment constructs. Defining adjustment and growth is complicated; these issues are discussed later in this chapter.

Perceived Growth Is De Facto a Positive Outcome. Some authors (e.g., Taylor, 1983) have argued that perceptions of benefits or growth are worthy of study in their own right, that these "illusions" may be a positive outcome of coping transactions. Further, some researchers maintain that the objective nature of such perceptions of growth are impossible to determine, or, at best, irrelevant (e.g., Collins, Taylor, & Skokan, 1990). Many studies of growth or perceived benefits appear to be predicated on the assumption that reported growth is a reasonable outcome in and of itself.

From this perspective, there is no need to examine relationships between reported growth or positive changes and indices of adjustment. Instead, these studies focus on self-reports of perceptions that positive changes or benefits have occurred and suggest that these benefits are meaningful aspects or outcomes of coping processes (e.g., Taylor, 1983; Tedeschi & Calhoun, 1989–1990).

Perceived Growth Is a Construct Independent of Adjustment Outcomes. Taking the position that perceiving benefits or reporting growth is conceptually distinct from adjustment, on the other hand, argues for an examination of the relationship between these two sets of variables in order to determine whether perceived benefits or growth co-occur with or lead to better physical and psychological functioning. If associations are found, they may be understood or explained in a number of different ways: Growth may reflect actual changes in well-being or enhanced functioning, growth may enable enhanced functioning indirectly by promoting resolution and the making of meaning, or both growth and adjustment may be related to some other underlying adaptive variable related to personality functioning or coping.

Perceiving Growth May Accurately Reflect Enhanced Functioning. People who perceive benefits or report growth through coping with difficult life experiences may be accurately reporting on changes they have observed within themselves or in their interactions with others and the world (Affleck, Tennen, & Rowe, 1991). These changes may involve having learned new coping skills, having strengthened their social support network, or having reordered their priorities and goals (Schaefer & Moos, 1992). Such changes constitute increases in people's available psychosocial resources and coping repertoires, which would be expected to be associated with better current and future functioning.

Perceiving Growth May Enable Resolution and the Making of Meaning Leading to Enhanced Functioning. Over time, individuals may reevaluate the traumatic experiences by altering the perceived value and meaningfulness of the event itself. People may not have chosen to undergo stressful or traumatic experiences, but they often come to see them as ultimately powerful, even worthwhile, aspects of life (Janoff-Bulman, 1992). Events reframed favorably may lose their perceived harshness, resulting in decreased symptomatology (McMillen, Zuravin, & Rideout, 1995). When people who have experienced traumatic or highly stressful situations are able to perceive benefits or growth through their struggles and their coping, they may be better able to resolve or recover from these traumatic events, thus enhancing their functioning or adjustment. Perceiving benefits in difficult situations is one important way that individuals can reframe difficult experiences, find ways to assimilate them into their worldviews, and, perhaps, to accept and recover from them (Janoff-Bulman, 1992; Park & Folkman, in press; Tait & Silver, 1989). Thus, reported growth may enhance adjustment by enabling people to make or find meaning in their traumatic experiences.

Perceiving Growth May Be a Function of Broader Adaptive Traits and Coping Styles. Individuals may be more or less inclined to perceive growth from objectively similar traumatic experiences for a number of reasons (see Tennen & Affleck, chap. 4, this volume). Perhaps the proclivity to report PTG is part of a larger constellation of personality traits and coping strategies (Affleck et al., 1991; McMillen et al., 1995; Tedeschi & Calhoun, 1996). These broader traits and coping styles may be differentially associated with various adjustment outcomes as well, and may account for the relationships between perceived benefits or growth and adjustment. For example, both optimism and positive reinterpretation coping have been found in numerous studies to be related prospectively to better adjustment with a variety of stressors (e.g., Aspinwall & Taylor, 1992; Carver et al., 1993). Both optimism (Mendola, Tennen, Affleck, McCann, & Fitzgerald, 1990) and positive reinterpretation coping have been found to predict the amount of PTG individuals report (Park, Cohen, & Murch, 1996).

Issues of Definitions and Values

When attempting to study the phenomenon of PTG, difficult issues of definitions and values arise, issues with no easy answers. But in the process of conceptualizing their research and in operationalizing their constructs, researchers in the area are forced to make decisions. The issues are complex and wide-ranging. For example, when should increased religiousness be considered growth? Should greater emotional dependence, or increased autonomy—or both—be considered growth? Part of the answer, of course, may depend on a given individual's baseline levels of these characteristics, such that a person initially lacking close, trusting relationships, who develops these over the course of coping with a traumatic event, may be considered to "have grown," whereas an individual who has limited experience being on her or his own, who becomes more autonomous and self-reliant through coping with a traumatic situation, may also be considered to "have grown." Researchers in the area of PTG have only begun to grapple with such issues. One solution to this issue may lie in the use of methodologies that allow for individual variation in defining growth, such as qualitative research, or research using idiographic self-reports of growth, allowing people to define for themselves which changes constitute benefits or growth (Cohen, Hettler, & Pane, chap. 2, this volume). Of course, this approach complicates the forming of generalizable conclusions from research.

Defining Ideal Functioning. Perhaps an even more difficult issue involves that of the observers' views of ideal human functioning when determining what growth and adjustment are. Among researchers in personality, coping, and mental health, there is little consensus on these issues. For example, many psychologists consider religiosity a sign of immaturity or defensiveness (see Pargament & Park, 1995, for a review). On the other hand, people often report increased religiousness as a positive outcome of their coping with traumatic experiences (e.g., Curbow, Somerfield, Baker, Wingard, & Legro, 1993; Park et al., 1996; Tedeschi & Calhoun, 1995). Similarly, many individuals report as positive outcomes such existential changes as valuing life more as a result of recognizing its fragility, enjoyment of the present, or acceptance of their own mortality (Calhoun & Tedeschi, 1989–1990; Taylor, 1983). Although people often rate these changes as "positive" ones, psychologists and others involved in this research area must rely on their own views of human functioning when determining whether to accept these reports of "growth" or "perceived benefits" at face value.

A study of adult survivors of childhood sexual abuse (McMillen et al., 1995) illustrates this problem of values in defining what is positive. One hundred-fifty-four women were asked whether they felt they had benefited from the unwanted sexual contact in some ways. Forty-seven percent of the women reported perceiving some benefit from the child sexual abuse. These women were then asked to describe in what ways they felt they may have benefited from the unwanted sexual contact, and their answers were coded into four categories: Protecting children, self-protection, increased knowledge of childhood sexual abuse, and strength. Some of the verbatim responses McMillen et al. cite in their article beg the question of how to define benefits. For example, under the category "Protecting children" is this quote: "I won't let men around my daughters. I tell men I date that I will kill them if they touch my kids. I am very protective of my kids." Under the category "Self-protection" are these: " ... Makes you more cautious. More suspicious. Gives you a gut feeling about some people. Makes you more defensive ... " and "I don't trust men. That's good for me. I don't fall in love with people. I have never given myself wholly to anyone. As a result, I don't get hurt" (McMillen et al., 1995, pp. 1039–1040). These responses, considered *benefits* by the participants, were analyzed as positive outcomes by the researchers.

Can this issue be resolved by conducting research comparing reports of growth with adjustment outcomes that are independent of reported growth? Perhaps if these perceived benefits or reports of growth are viewed as distinct from outcomes, their relationship with outcomes can be assessed, thereby establishing validity of the reported positive changes (Cohen et al., chap. 2, this volume; and see Lehman et al., 1993, for an example of this approach). Problems remain with this strategy, however. For example, what constitutes adjustment or good mental health? Even an issue as seemingly simple as this is undecided and contended in the psychological arena (Shedler, Mayman, & Manis, 1993; Taylor & Brown, 1988).

"Negative" Growth. People new to the area of PTG research often ask whether negative growth can occur. The literature on adjustment to traumatic events is replete with measures of the negative changes that can occur in individuals who have undergone difficult life experiences; these include increases in negative mood, disruptions in relationships, and physical symptoms. It could be reasoned that if positive changes are reported to have occurred in domains such as relationships, coping abilities, sense of mastery, self-esteem, or sense of purpose in life, and these changes are considered growth, then negative changes reported in these areas would be negative growth. It is unclear, however, how the concept of negative growth would add to the literature regarding posttraumatic decrements in resources and functioning (cf. Joseph, Williams, & Yule, 1993). Although this may seem like mere wordplay, many critics of this area clamor for the inclusion of negative scoring on growth items.

Issue of Double Negative. A final semantic issue concerns positive changes that involve stopping a negative behavior or ameliorating a negative situation: Do these changes constitute growth (e.g., stop drinking, stop drinking and driving)? This semantic issue may be resolvable by thinking about the change in terms of its valence for the individual rather than whether the behavior or situation increases or decreases. In the example given, these changes could be relabeled "becoming abstinent" and "increasing the practice of safer driving techniques."

EMPIRICAL REVIEW

The preceding conceptualization of the ways that growth and perceived benefits may be related to adjustment serves as a useful framework in which to examine the empirical research regarding the consequences of perceived benefits or PTG in people's lives.

Perceived Growth as De Facto Evidence of Adjustment

If the position is taken that perceived growth is a favorable adjustment outcome in and of itself, then the empirical literature cited in previous chapters (e.g., Schaefer & Moos, chap.5, this volume) serves as a review of the many studies that have established that people do indeed report having experienced growth as a result of their coping with difficult life experiences in a variety of life domains, including relationships with others, personal coping resources and abilities, and changes in life values, goals, and philosophies. For example, Laerum, Johnsen, Smith, and Larsen (1987) found that one third of their sample of 88 men who were interviewed several months after acute myocardial infarction reported improved total life situations, including appreciable positive alterations in the domains of love and caring and in communication within their families. A study of bereaved elderly women (Lund, Caserta, & Dimond, 1993) found that many women who had filled very traditional "wife" roles prior to their husbands' deaths discovered latent abilities to handle many things that their husbands had reserved within their masculine roles as "husband." A significant number of cancer survivors studied by Collins et al. (1990) reported positive changes, such as reordering their priorities, appreciating each day, focusing on doing things *now* and enjoying life *now* instead of waiting, and making each day count. These types of studies focus on the respondents' self-reports of positive changes as de facto positive outcomes.

Perceived Growth and Adjustment as Conceptually Distinct Constructs

On the other hand, the position that perceived benefits or reports of growth are conceptually distinct from adjustment leads to a very different way of approaching the literature. This position advocates studying self-reported growth or perceived benefits as distinct from actual measured changes in a number of adjustment outcomes. The empirical literature that has taken this approach, while currently limited in quantity, may yield important insights into the influences that PTG can exert on various domains of adjustment, including mental and physical health, health behaviors and healthy lifestyles, changes in personality, changes in goals and purposes in life, and adaptation to current and subsequent stressors, including increases in important coping resources. Following is a review of the existing literature that approaches PTG from this perspective.

When examining this literature, it is important to keep in mind that associations between perceived benefits or PTG and adjustment may be due to enhanced functioning, meaning-making, or underlying third variables, as described earlier. These mechanisms are not mutually exclusive, but rather may describe different aspects of the same process of adaptation over time. It is also important to be aware of the research designs employed in these studies; nearly all of them have been conducted cross-sectionally rather than longitudinally. When PTG is found to be related to adjustment variables in cross-sectional research, the direction of the influence is unclear, and third variable problems are an ever-present issue. Longitudinal and especially prospective research designs are better at separating out issues of causality, at least on a temporal basis.

Another issue that arises when reviewing the empirical literature is that of null findings. That is, when studies fail to show a relationship between PTG and adjustment outcomes, does this mean that no relationships actually exist, or are there other likely explanations? This issue will be taken up following the empirical literature review.

Emotional Adjustment

Most of the research assessing relationships between PTG or perceived benefits and outcomes has considered as outcomes variables that are typically thought of as traditional indices of emotional adjustment. Research reviewed in this section includes studies that relate perceived benefits or PTG to indices of adjustment such as depression, anxiety, and life satisfaction. Most of the studies report some positive relationships between perceived benefits or growth and adjustment, although many of them report mixed results. Several studies failed to find any relationships between PTG and outcomes. This section first reviews those studies that provide clear support for a relationship between PTG and emotional adjustment, then describe those studies that found less support.

Studies That Support a PTG-Emotional Adjustment Link.   In the cross-sectional study of low-income women who were sexually abused as children (McMillen et al., 1995), discussed earlier, adjustment was measured by a self-esteem scale, a scale assessing the degree that one's views of others are benevolent, and a scale assessing three aspects of romantic relationship styles (degree of anxiety in relationships, comfort depending on others, and comfort being close to others). Degree of perceived benefit was associated to with three of the five adjustment indicators—self-esteem, relationship anxiety, and comfort depending on others. When compared with those who perceived no benefit, those who perceived a lot of benefit had higher self-esteem, more comfort depending on others, and less relationship anxiety, whereas there were no differences between those perceiving some benefit and those perceiving no benefit on those variables. Perceiving benefits was not related to views of others or comfort with closeness. In addition, those who perceived themselves as stronger had higher self-esteem, and those who perceived increased sexual abuse knowledge viewed others more favorably and were more comfortable getting close to others.

In a cross-sectional study of 78 women with breast cancer, Taylor and her colleagues (1983; Taylor, Lichtman, & Wood, 1984) asked the women about changes that had occurred since cancer in a number of life domains (e.g., stress management, work life, religious activities). Most women (70%) reported that cancer had made them think about their lives differently, and 60% said this change was positive. Perceived positive change was significantly related to adjustment, which was measured as a composite of several ratings and scale scores, including physician's and interviewer's rating of the women on a scale assessing adjustment to illness, the women's self-rated adjustment on a 5-point scale, their self-reports of psychological symptoms (e.g., anxiety, depression), and their scores on the Profile of Mood States (McNair, Lorr, & Droppleman, 1971) and Index of Well-Being questionnaires (Campbell, Converse, & Rogers, 1976; for details, see Taylor et al., 1984). In discussing the findings of this study, Taylor concluded, "When positive meaning can be construed from the cancer experience, it produces significantly better psychological adjustment. The cancer threat is perceived by many to have been the catalytic agent for restructuring their lives along more meaningful lines with an overall beneficial effect" (1983, p. 1163).

Two cross-sectional studies by Thompson found evidence for positive relationships between PTG and adjustment. The first (Thompson, 1985) studied 32 elderly people whose homes had been damaged or destroyed by a fire; this study, which surveyed the survivors immediately after the fire and 1 year later, actually provides two cross-sectional tests of the relationships between PTG and adjustment. Thompson assessed five ways that people focused on the positive aspects of the fire, two of which involved PTG (perceiving side benefits and redefining what one wants/changing goals), as well as making social comparisons, imagining worse situations, and forgetting the negative. Because these items were combined (with an alpha of .75 at Time 1 and .71 1 year later), this study provides, at best, a weak test of the relationship between PTG and adjustment. In this study, Thompson (1985) used four different measures of adjustment (one assessing how well respondents felt they were coping, one assessing negative feelings, one assessing the amount of pleasure derived from daily activities, and one assessing physical symptoms). At both times, focusing on the positive aspects was related to better self-rated coping and more positive emotions. At Time 1 only, focusing on the positive was related to experiencing more pleasure from daily activities.

In a second study of positive changes or benefits, 40 stroke patients, averaging about 9 months poststroke, and 40 primary caregivers were interviewed (Thompson, 1991). Thompson assessed what she termed "meaning" by an open-ended question: "Have you found any meaning in your experience with a stroke?" The answers to this question were essentially reports of perceived benefits (appreciate life more, learned to slow down, appreciate patient/caregiver more, appreciate family and friends, grow personally, become more compassionate, closer to God). Adjustment was a composite score including a depression scale (Geriatric Depression Scale; Brink, Yesavage, Lum, Heersema, Adey, & Rose, 1982) and a scale measuring meaningfulness in life (these scales were moderately inversely correlated). Fifty percent of patients and 45% of caregivers reported they had found meaning in their experience with stroke, and finding meaning was positively correlated with adjustment for both patients ($r = .50$) and caregivers ($r = .29$). In a regression controlling for severity of the stroke, and including measures of various types of attributions, finding meaning remained a fairly strong predictor of adjustment in the combined sample of stroke patients and caregivers ($b = .24$, Final $R = .70$).

Michela (1987) conducted a study of 40 married couples, in which the husband had had a heart attack (an average of 9 ½ months before the study). Results from the husbands are pertinent to this discussion. In this retrospective study, participants reported on three time periods: Time 0 (just prior to their myocardial infarction), Time 1 (shortly after their myocardial infarction), and Time 2 (at present). A questionnaire measuring effects of the heart attack included a subscale of perceived benefits (the sample item given is "being free of responsibilities from before the heart attack") and a subscale assessing reevaluation of life. Adjustment was measured by both depression (a composite of self-ratings of feeling sad, unhappy, and depressed) and marital satisfaction (measured by a questionnaire regarding different interpersonal domains of the respondent's marriage). Michela found that men were significantly more depressed at Time 1 compared to other times, and that scores on perceived gains were significantly negatively related to depression. Further, marital satisfaction increased from T0 to T1, and this increase was maintained at T2. Multiple regression results indicated that reevaluation of life (increased appreciation of life) was positively related to increased marital satisfaction.

In a study of 1,287 male veterans of World War II and the Korean War, Aldwin, Levenson, and Spiro (1994) found that, decades after the war, the extent of the veterans' combat exposure was modestly related to posttraumatic stress disorder (PTSD) symptoms (as assessed by the Mississippi Scale for Combat-Related PTSD; Keane, Caddell, & Taylor, 1988). Veterans' self-rated perceived benefits of military experiences (as measured by a 14-item scale assessing positive appraisals of military experiences), however, mediated this relationship, such that veterans who perceived benefits from their combat experiences were less likely to suffer from symptoms of posttraumatic stress disorder.

Zemore and Shepel (1989) examined the relationship between perceived emotional social support level and adjustment in a sample of 301 women who had undergone a mastectomy as treatment for breast cancer within the past 2 years, and a control group of 100 women diagnosed with benign breast lumps. Although they did not assess *change* in perceived social support, they did compare the cancer patients with the controls, inferring that any difference between groups would be due to their experiences coping with cancer. They assessed adjustment with a social adjustment scale, an emotional adjustment scale (measuring hopelessness, sensitivity/irritability, hostility, and life satisfaction), and a self-esteem scale. They found that cancer patients perceived more emotional social support than controls, and that perceived social support was related to better adjustment, providing some evidence that increases in perceptions of social support was related to better psychological adjustment.

The study of 36 widows and widowers (27 women, 9 men; Yalom & Lieberman, 1991), discussed earlier, involved in-depth interviews at Time 1 (4 to 11 months after spousal bereavement), and Time 2, 1 year later. Personal growth was assessed through judges' ratings of interview data (e.g., personally stretching, developing new interests, willing to explore new relationships, engaging in new or renewed forms of creative expression). Existential awareness was measured by judges' ratings of participants' increased awareness of their own death, sense of purpose, and regrets; depression and anxiety were measured with subscales derived from the Hopkin's Symptom Checklist (Derogatis, Lipman, Rickels, Uhlenhuth, & Covi, 1974). This research revealed a significant positive relationship between personal growth and existential awareness, and existential awareness was significantly related to depression (although no test of relationship between personal growth and depression was reported).

In a prospective study of families whose infants required placement in a Neonatal Intensive Care Unit (NICU), Affleck et al. (1991) found that mothers' perceptions of benefits from the crisis of their infant's hospitalization were not predictive of the mothers' adjustment 6 months later, but did predict more positive moods and less global distress 18 months later.

Studies That Provide Mixed Support for a PTG-Emotional Adjustment Link. The studies described previously are fairly consistent in their support for the existence of a relationship between PTG and perceived benefits and emotional adjustment. Other studies, however, provide less support for such a relationship. For example, Goodhart (1985) asked 173 psychology students about the outcomes (i.e., how the event turned out in the end, changes it brought about) of one traumatic event in each of three domains: personal, interpersonal, and achievement. Students rated how positive and negative the event turned out on 5-point rating scales, and scores were aggregated across the three events for an overall measure of positive outcomes. Adjustment included both negative measures (psychological symptoms of the Symptom Checklist and negative affect measured by a negative affect scale) and positive measures (positive affect, two measures of life satisfaction, and a measure of self-esteem). Cross-sectionally, perceived positive outcomes (which Goodhart termed "positive thinking") was associated with the measures of positive outcomes but not with negative ones. When positive outcomes were broken down into personal versus social changes, positive outcomes that were personal outcomes rather than social consequences had a stronger influence on positive adjustment, such that self-relevant positive thinking was related to Time 1 symptoms, positive affect, global satisfaction, and self-esteem. Following up 8 weeks later, Goodhart found that positive outcomes measured at Time 1 were significantly related to positive affect and self-esteem, but not to any other adjustment measures, at Time 2.

Mendola et al. (1990) studied perceived benefits and adjustment in a sample of 65 women with impaired fertility. They assessed perceived benefits by asking, "As difficult as this situation may be, do you believe that anything positive has come from this, some benefit or gain that has occurred that wouldn't have occurred if you were able to conceive?" (p. 83). Raters then coded responses into one of three categories: a strengthened marriage, personal growth, or greater appreciation of life. Results indicated that believing that infertility had strengthened their marriage was related to having fewer psychological symptoms as measured by global symptomatology on the SCL-90 (Derogatis, 1977; $r = -.32$). In multivariate analyses, controlling for medical problems, threat appraisal, and primary control, perceiving that infertility had the benefit of strengthening their marriage was still related to having fewer symptoms, providing fairly convincing support for a relationship between perceived benefits and psychological adjustment. On the other hand, the other two categories of perceived benefits, personal growth and greater appreciation of life, were unrelated to adjustment.

In a cross-sectional study of 113 rape victims, Burt and Katz (1987) asked the participants to rate the changes that had come from their efforts to recover from the rape. Perceived benefits/growth was measured by a 28-item questionnaire assessing their perceptions of how they are now compared to how they were before the rape. This measure was factor-analyzed into three subscales, self-value (e.g., "I value myself," "I'm able to choose a satisfying romantic partner"), positive actions (e.g., "I'm involved in social or political action," "I'm able to get my needs met"), and interpersonal skills (e.g., "I feel I know myself," "I choose supportive friends"). Results relating these three subscales of positive changes give mixed support to the idea of a relationship between PTG and adjustment. Only the self-value factor was associated with adjustment indices. This scale was positively related to self-rating of recovery and to self-esteem, was related favorably to all measured subscales of the Profile of Mood States (McNair et al., 1971; e.g., negatively to depression and anxiety, positively with vigor), and was negatively related to intrusion and avoidance (as measured by the Impact of Event Scale; Horowitz, Wilner, & Alvarez, 1979) and the Brief Symptom Inventory (Derogatis & Spencer, 1982). On the other hand, the other two positive change factors, positive actions and interpersonal skills, were essentially unrelated to measures of adjustment.

In a study of 35 survivors of an accident involving the sinking of a ship, Joseph et al. (1993) examined relationships 16 months after the accident between positive changes following the accident and a number of mental health outcomes, including symptomatology, self-esteem, just world beliefs, and the tendency to make internal attributions for negative outcomes. They assessed positive changes with a self-report scale designed to measure positive changes, and assessed psychological symptoms with the depression and anxiety/insomnia subscales from the General Health Questionnaire (Goldberg & Hillier, 1979) and the Impact of Event Scale (Horowitz et al., 1979). No significant associations were found between scores on the positive response scale and symptomatology measures. Higher scores on the positive response scale were positively associated with higher self-esteem but not with either just world beliefs or the tendency to take internal responsibility for negative outcomes.

In a study of 135 long-term survivors of bone marrow transplantation, primarily young men, 6 to 149 months posttransplant, Curbow et al. (1993) measured the positive (and negative) changes their participants reported having experienced related to their bone marrow transplant. Adjustment was assessed with an abbreviated form of the Profile of Mood States (Shacham, 1983) that measured negative mood, and by self-ratings of current and future life satisfaction. In bivariate analyses, positive changes were related to current and future life satisfaction, but not to depression. These effects disappeared in multivariate analyses, when marital status, gender, current illness, perceived health, and optimism were entered first. One interaction emerged, however, for future life satisfaction: For persons who had a high number of negative changes, a corresponding high number of positive changes was predictive of higher future life satisfaction. Conversely, persons with high negative changes and low positive changes reported the lowest levels of future life satisfaction.

Studies That Do Not Support a PTG-Emotional Adjustment Link.
Several studies have reported no relationships between PTG or perceived benefits and mental health outcomes. Videka-Sherman (1982) studied the effects of participation in a self-help group for bereaved parents called Compassionate Friends. In a sample of 194 bereaved parents who had become bereaved in the past 18 months, a self-report measure of experiencing a changed sense of self or sense of growth was unrelated to depression as measured by the Hopkin's Symptom Checklist (Derogatis et al., 1974).

In a longitudinal study of 54 people who had rheumatoid arthritis and were currently experiencing joint pain, Tennen, Affleck, Urrows, Higgins, and Mendola (1992) found that perceiving benefits from their pain as measured by a 5-item benefit appraisal scale (e.g., "Dealing with my pain has made me a stronger person") was unrelated to psychological adjustment in terms of daily mood (measured by a subset of items from the Profile of Mood States; Lorr & McNair, 1982).

Finally, no relationship was found between positive changes and psychological adjustment in a study of 94 people who had lost a spouse or child in a car accident 4 to 7 years previously (Lehman et al., 1993). Positive changes were assessed by coding open-ended questions about life changes, and adjustment was assessed by the SCL-90 (Derogatis, 1977) and the Bradburn Affects Balance Scale (Bradburn, 1969). No relationship between adjustment and positive changes, or the interaction of positive and negative changes, was found. However, the bereaved participants were worse off in terms of adjustment than a control group of nonbereaved people. This latter finding indicates that the bereaved participants may still be coping; their reports of positive changes may not only reflect accurate positive changes they have experienced, but also attempts to reappraise the situation positively. These very different meanings of endorsing positive changes weaken any potential relationships with adjustment measures (see the discussion of distinguishing coping from growth in Cohen et al., chap. 5, this volume).

Physical Health

Some researchers interested in the effects of perceived benefits or PTG have focused on physical health outcomes. A program of research carried out by Affleck, Tennen, and their colleagues has been accumulating convincing evidence that reports of growth and perceptions of benefits following traumatic events are related to positive changes in observable physical health indices.

In a study of men who had experienced an initial heart attack, Affleck, Tennen, Croog, and Levine (1987) interviewed 287 men 7 weeks after their heart attack and again 8 years later. In the first interview, the men were asked whether they saw any possible benefits, gains, or advantages in the experience. Men who construed gains from the initial attack not only were less likely to suffer a reinfarction, but they also experienced less morbidity when assessed at the followup 8 years later, even when taking into account social class and the severity of the first heart attack. Gains reported by the men included reconsidering their values, priorities, and interpersonal relationships; Affleck et al. (1987) noted that these perceived gains may have aided recovery directly, through their self-comforting quality, or indirectly, through their effects on social support networks or other lifestyle changes.

In the study of families whose infants required placement in a Neonatal Intensive Care Unit, Affleck et al. (1991) found that the infants had significantly better developmental gains (as measured by an infant development scale) 18 months later if their mothers had initially perceived benefits from the crisis of their infant's hospitalization.

In the study of people with rheumatoid arthritis, Tennen et al. (1992) found that appraisals of benefit from chronic rheumatoid arthritis pain predicted daily physical well-being (as measured by pain-limitations) prospectively over the course of the next 75 days. There were no main effects for perceiving benefits on either daily pain or daily activity limitation, but there was an interaction effect: Individuals with more severe arthritis pain reported fewer days in which their activities were limited by their pain when they initially reported perceiving more benefits associated with their pain.

Only a few other researchers have included measures of physical health in their studies of positive outcomes or PTG. In the study of people who had lost their homes in a fire, mentioned earlier, Thompson (1985) found that both shortly after the fire and 1 year later, focusing on the positive aspects of the fire was related to reports of fewer physical symptoms (as measured with a symptom checklist developed by the author).

Finally, in the study of 35 survivors of an accident involving the sinking of a ship, (described earlier), Joseph et al. (1993) found no significant relationships between positive changes and physical symptoms, as assessed by either the General Health Questionnaire (Goldberg & Hillier, 1979) overall score or somatic subscale score.

Healthy Lifestyles and Health Behaviors

Often, individuals' perceptions of benefits following traumatic or stressful experiences involve learning lessons about how to live and how to take care of themselves. These types of benefits may be particularly likely in situations involving health crises. Affleck et al. (1987) noted that making actual modifications in lifestyle and health habits may be easier when such changes are cast in the context of learning valued lessons about health promotion. In their study of men who had just experienced their first heart attack, the most frequently cited benefit after the first attack was that it underscored the advantages of preventive health behavior. Affleck et al. (1987) suggested that the observed physical health benefits over the 8-year period of their study may be due to the participants actually instituting positive health and lifestyle changes. Unfortunately, they did not include a measure of actual behavior changes following the first attack, so this explanation remains a conjecture.

In the study of women with breast cancer by Taylor and her colleagues (Taylor, 1983; Taylor et al., 1984), described earlier, the participants were asked about health-related behavioral changes they had made in their lives since being diagnosed with cancer. Twenty-two percent reported having made no changes, 55% had made a few changes, and 23% had made three or more changes. Reporting changes in diet and in handling stress were common, but were unassociated with psychological adjustment, whereas reported change in exercise patterns and taking increased time for leisure activities were also relatively common and were significantly positively related to adjustment, even with prognosis partialed out (Taylor et al., 1984).

Anecdotal evidence for changes that people sometimes make such changes abounds. For example, many reports of alcoholics who hit rock bottom and then were able to make necessary life changes including abstinence (e.g., Biernacki, 1986), and individuals who receive positive HIV serostatus tests and decide to change many health changes, as well as intra- and interpersonal changes, have been documented (e.g., Schwartzberg, 1993). However, few systematic studies of this issue have been conducted.

Changes in Personality

A transactional perspective on coping and adjustment posits bidirectional relationships between personality and coping. Although this perspective should engender research on the ways that events and coping shape person- ality as well as on how personality shapes events and coping, the impact of stress and coping processes on personality is rarely the focus of research (Aldwin, Sutton, & Lachman, 1996). In terms of research focusing on positive changes in personality that may result from perceived benefits, few studies have been conducted. In a study of 256 college students, Park et al. (1996) found that PTG (as measured by the Stress Related Growth Scale) prospectively predicted increases in optimism, positive affectivity, and both number of social support sources and satisfaction with social support 6 months later.

Changes in Life Goals and Purposes

Qualitative studies and anecdotal evidence indicate that many individuals become involved in causes larger than themselves as a result of their stressful or traumatic experiences. Two prominent examples of this are MADD (a group of women who banded together to work for tougher laws against drunk driving) and the phenomenon of ardent AIDS activists, many of whom are themselves HIV+ and have witnessed the deaths of friends and family members, organizing together to work for changes in policy and research regarding HIV and AIDS. In many cases, it may be that these individuals not only perceive this involvement as positive change, but that they actually actively create positive changes as attempts to cope with the aversive circumstances. Although these changes may initially be part of coping processes, over time, the creation of positive involvements and positive ways of being may become a part of the individual's life and identity. To date, empirical research on these issues is lacking.

Adaptation to Current and Subsequent Crises and Stressors

One of the most intriguing aspects of PTG is that it may allow more adaptive coping for individuals in the future. Such enhanced functioning may be the result of enhanced coping skills or bolstered resources. Although this idea is a primary assumption in many psychological theories of development, very little empirical research has actually put this idea to the test. Including the concept of growth in coping theory creates a truly transactional, cybernetic model. The components of the individual's resources, coping attempts, and outcomes are recursive; results of one coping transaction exert influences on coping with the next transaction. This model is certainly complex to study empirically, but more accurately captures the real-life nature of individuals dealing with life's adversities.

Aldwin (1994; Aldwin et al., 1996) proposed and began testing a deviation amplification model. In this model, taking instrumental action during stressful episodes may lead to perceiving positive long-term outcomes, which in turn should lead to higher mastery and lower depression levels. As coping transactions accumulate, positive spirals may occur, wherein coping with stress may result in the development of resources, which increases individuals' abilities to cope with stress. According to this theory, coping is a process that extends across situations by affecting changes in coping resources and skills. Aldwin et al. (in press) tested this model in a study of 941 individuals dealing with various stressors. The authors found that reports of positive changes from coping with a severe event earlier in their lives led to better adaptation to a future event (as measured by lower depression and higher mastery scores). This study illustrates how people can bolster their resources through coping transactions, which then enhances their coping with later stressors.

In a longitudinal study of 149 veterans, Elder and Clipp (1989) explored the retrospective accounts of positive and negative aspects of combat these veterans had experienced in WWII and the Korean War. When looking back over their lives and war experiences, the men who survived heavy combat claimed more often than others that they had learned to cope with adversity, which they perceived as a legacy that continued to empower them in difficult situations.

In a study of individuals coping with various stressors during a year-long period, Holahan and Moos (1990) identified a subgroup of people who actually experienced a high amount of stressors and showed improvement in their psychological functioning over the course of the year. Holahan and Moos noted that this subgroup was the only one where the resources composite score increased significantly during the year. The increase in resources for this group reflected increases on all three of the composite's underlying components: self-confidence, easygoingness, and family support. In other words, through their coping transactions, these individuals may have actually been able to develop or mobilize their coping resources, which was reflected in enhanced functioning.

The study of undergraduates' aggregated reports of positive changes over three stressful events just described (Goodhart, 1985) also looked at the effects of perceiving positive outcomes on later psychological vulnerability to stressors by looking at the influence of Time 1 self-rated positive outcomes as stress-buffers for adjustment to life stressors that occurred in the 8 week interim. There was no evidence of a stress-buffering effect on adjustment.

SUMMARY AND INTERPRETATION
OF EMPIRICAL FINDINGS

Given this diverse array of empirical studies, what kinds of conclusions can be drawn from this research? First, it is important to note that this literature is still in its infancy. As noted earlier, most of the studies are cross-sectional or retrospective; these designs cannot tease apart causal sequences or third-variable issues. The third variable issue, raised earlier, is an important consideration. The proclivity to perceive benefits or growth from traumatic coping transactions could be part of a broader adaptive coping style. Some research indicates that positive reappraisal coping is a stable coping style (e.g., Carver & Scheier, 1994; McCrae, 1989). More direct support for the idea that PTG may be part of a stable personality-like coping style comes from the study of college students by Park et al. (1996), mentioned earlier. Moderately high correlations of reported growth with different events over a 6-month time period were found within individuals, suggesting that the tendency to find growth may be a function of personality or other underlying tendencies.

This chapter began by asking several questions. First, what does growth actually mean in the lives of the people who report experiencing it? The studies reviewed give a mixed picture. Many report positive relations between PTG or perceived benefits and a wide variety of adjustment outcomes, whereas only a few found no relationship. Still, many of the studies report spotty and inconsistent findings. Certainly, the methodological differences among the studies and the crude conceptualization and measurement of PTG may account for some of these inconsistencies. On the other hand, the fact that so many studies using different populations, measures, and methodologies did find relationships between PTG and adjustment adds strength to the notion that a fundamental relationship between them exists. More sophisticated research in the future will help elucidate this complicated relationship.

Second, what mechanisms might account for the relationship (or lack of relationship) between reports of PTG and enhanced functioning? A number of possible mechanisms which might underlie associations between PTG and adjustment were proposed. These include the ideas that growth may reflect actual changes in well-being or enhanced functioning, growth may enable enhanced functioning indirectly by promoting resolution and the making of meaning, or both growth and adjustment may be related to some other underlying adaptive variable related to personality functioning or coping.

When studies find that perceived benefits and PTG are unrelated to traditional measures of adjustment and well-being, there are four possible alternative explanations:

1. Growth may encompass some shifts in values or beliefs that the individual experiences as favorable, as "growth," but these changes may, in fact be related to *more* rather than *fewer* symptoms of anxiety or depression (e.g., some existential beliefs, realization of vulnerability and need to take more precautions, wisdom; Yalom & Lieberman, 1991). This may mean that researchers need to include a broader range of outcome measures that encompass a wider range of potentially positive states.
2. It is possible that to the extent positive changes or growth occurs, it may be related to increased positive adjustment and affect, although not necessarily to decreased maladjustment. This is consistent with other research supporting the relative independence of positive and negative aspects of psychological adjustment (Aldwin et al., 1994; Goodhart, 1985; Warr, Barter, & Brownbridge, 1983).
3. It is also important to keep in mind that the domains in which growth occurs and domains of adjustment are conceptually distinct concepts. It is possible, then, that growth may occur in individuals' resources (picture a graph with an increasing slope of coping resources over time) that allows individuals to remain relatively stable in the face of future difficulties (picture a graph with a homeostatic or flat line across time or severity of life difficulties). The

growth or development of resources may lead to future adjustment, perhaps only having an effect when a major life stressor or crisis is encountered. For example, a person who is fairly well-adjusted in life may experience, through an encounter with a traumatic occurrence, increases in social support or self-efficacy in dealing with crises. These positive changes may not appear to boost this person's adjustment beyond "normal" pre-crisis levels. However, if this person encounters another traumatic experience, he or she may cope better because of the positive changes (e.g., a quicker return to pre-crisis adjustment levels). Sophisticated research designs are needed to capture such complicated effects.

4. Effects of reports of growth or perceptions of benefits on adjustment outcomes may also be obscured if studies do not distinguish between individuals who report only positive outcomes (who may be in denial) from those who report positive outcomes but also perceive and acknowledge negative changes as well. Many people who report positive changes also report negative changes (e.g., Curbow et al., 1993; McMillen et al., 1995), but positive and negative changes have been found to be unrelated (Aldwin et al., 1994; Joseph et al., 1993). Several authors have suggested the possibility that perceptions of growth or positive changes that are balanced with a recognition of negative changes as well may be the growth that is predictive of positive adjustment outcomes (Lehman et al., 1993; Taylor, Kemeny, Reed, & Aspinwall, 1991). For example, a study of 24 men living with AIDS found that positive life changes described by men who tested HIV+ were associated with better adjustment, but only among men who also reported some negative life changes, suggesting that denying the negative outcomes is problematic (Taylor et al., 1991).

FUTURE DIRECTIONS

The issues regarding the consequences of perceived benefits and growth for individuals are indeed complicated; the approaches for addressing these issues are many, whereas the number of conclusive empirical studies are few. It is encouraging, however, that psychologists interested in stress and coping are increasingly turning their attention to these issues and developing new, more inclusive paradigms that include wellness and thriving as well as illness and recovery (O'Leary & Ickovics, 1995; Tedeschi & Calhoun, 1995). As the field advances, future developments in theory and in empirical work promise to be exciting. For now, many questions await attention.

As the theoretical conceptualizations continue to develop in the area of posttraumatic growth, the debate regarding the utility of categorizing positive changes as important phenomena in their own right will likely continue. However, many theories are being proposed that incorporate perceived benefits and growth along with other independent measures of adjustment (see O'Leary, Ickovics, & Alday, chap. 6, this volume), and a number of researchers in the area of PTG now seem to be including independent measures of adjustment as well.

Does growth last? Certainly, abundant evidence indicates that negative effects of trauma can have lasting effects (Aldwin, 1994). Does the growth (i.e., the changes that people make in their beliefs, behaviors, and relationships) that people report remain? This question remains relatively unaddressed in the current literature, and awaits future study.

Finally, research in this area will be greatly advanced when theoretical conceptualizations more closely inform the design of PTG research. The numerous theories that are proposed (see O'Leary et al., chap. 6, this volume) offer many hypotheses that, when implemented in sophisticated empirical studies, will begin to paint a clearer picture of how and under what conditions PTG occurs, and will make great strides toward actually defining the very nature of PTG and the influences it exerts in the lives of individuals and their adjustment.

REFERENCES

Affleck, G., Tennen, H., Croog, S., & Levine, S. (1987). Causal attribution, perceived benefits, and morbidity after a heart attack: An 8-year study. *Journal of Consulting and Clinical Psychology, 55*, 29–35.

Affleck, G., Tennen, H., & Rowe, J. (1991). *Infants in crisis: How parents cope with newborn intensive care and its aftermath.* New York: Springer-Verlag.

Aldwin, C. M. (1994). *Stress, coping, and development: An integrative perspective.* New York: Guilford.

Aldwin, C. M., Levenson, M. R., & Spiro, A. (1994). Vulnerability and resilience to combat exposure: Can stress have lifelong effects? *Psychology and Aging, 9*, 34–44.

Aldwin, C. M., Sutton, K. J., & Lachman, M. (1996). The development of coping resources in adulthood. *Journal of Personality, 64*, 837–871.

Aspinwall, L. G., & Taylor, S. E. (1992). Modeling cognitive adaptation: A longitudinal investigation of the impact of individual differences and coping on college adjustment and performance. *Journal of Personality and Social Psychology, 63*, 989–1003.

Biernacki, P. (1986). *Pathways from heroin addiction: Recovery without treatment.* Philadelphia: Temple University Press.

Bradburn, N. (1969). *The structure of psychological well-being.* Chicago: Aldine.

Brink, T. L., Yesavage, J. A., Lum, O., Heersema, P., Adey, M., & Rose, T. L. (1982). Screening tests for geriatric depression. *Clinical Gerontologist, 1*, 37–43.

Burt, M. R., & Katz, B. L. (1987). Dimensions of recovery from rape: Focus on growth outcomes. *Journal of Interpersonal Violence, 2*, 57–81.

Calhoun, L. G., & Tedeschi, R. G. (1989–1990). Positive aspects of critical life problems: Recollections of grief. *Omega, 29*, 265–272.

Campbell, A., Converse, P. E., & Rodgers, W. L. (1976). *The quality of American life: Perceptions, evaluations, and satisfactions.* New York: Sage.

Carver, C. S., Pozo, C., Harris, S., Noriega, V., Scheier, M. F., Robinson, D. S., Ketcham, A. S., Moffat, F. L., Jr., & Clark, K. C. (1993). How coping mediates the effect of optimism on distress: A study of women with early stage breast cancer. *Journal of Personality and Social Psychology, 65,* 375–390.

Carver, C. S., & Scheier, M. F. (1994). Situational coping and coping dispositions in a stressful transaction. *Journal of Personality and Social Psychology, 66,* 184–195.

Collins, R. L., Taylor, S. E., & Skokan, L. A. (1990). A better world or a shattered vision? Changes in life perspectives following victimization. *Social Cognition, 8,* 263–285.

Curbow, B., Somerfield, M. R., Baker, F., Wingard, J. R., & Legro, M. W. (1993). Personal changes, dispositional optimism, and psychological adjustment to bone marrow transplantation. *Journal of Behavioral Medicine, 5,* 423–443.

Derogatis, L. R. (1977). *SCL-90: Administration, scoring and procedures manual for the revised version.* Baltimore: Clinical Psychometric Research.

Derogatis, L. R., Lipman, R. S., Rickels, K., Uhlenhuth, E. H., & Covi, L. (1974). The Hopkin's Symptom Checklist (HSCL): A self-report symptom inventory. *Behavioral Science, 19,* 1–15.

Derogatis, L. R., & Spencer, P. M. (1982). *The Brief Symptom Inventory administration, scoring, and procedures manual–I.* Baltimore: Clinical Psychometric Research.

Elder, G. H., Jr., & Clipp, E. C. (1989). Combat experience and emotional health: Impairment and resilience in later life. *Journal of Personality, 57,* 310–341.

Goldberg, D. P., & Hillier, V. F. (1979). A scaled version of the General Health Questionnaire. *Psychological Medicine, 9,* 139–145.

Goodhart, D. E. (1985). Some psychological effects associated with positive and negative thinking about stressful event outcomes: Was Pollyanna right? *Journal of Personality and Social Psychology, 48,* 216–232.

Holahan, C. J., & Moos, R. H. (1990). Life stressors, resistance factors, and improved psychological functioning: An extension of the stress resistance paradigm. *Journal of Personality and Social Psychology, 58,* 909–917.

Horowitz, M., Wilner, N., Alvarez, W. (1979). Impact of Event Scale: A measure of subjective stress. *Psychosomatic Medicine, 41,* 209–218.

Janoff-Bulman, R. (1992). *Shattered assumptions: Towards a new psychology of trauma.* New York: Free Press.

Joseph, S., Williams, R., & Yule, W. (1993). Changes in outlook following disaster: The preliminary development of a measure to assess positive and negative responses. *Journal of Traumatic Stress, 6,* 271–279.

Keane, T. M., Caddell, J. M., & Taylor, K. L. (1988). Mississippi Scale for Combat-Related Posttraumatic Stress Disorder: Three studies in reliability and validity. *Journal of Consulting and Clinical Psychology, 52,* 888–891.

Laerum, E., Johnsen, N., Smith, P., & Larsen, S. (1987). Can myocardial infarction induce positive changes in family relationships? *Family Practice, 4,* 302–305.

Lehman, D. R., Davis, C. G., Delongis, A., Wortman, C. B., Bluck, S., Mandel, D., & Ellard, J. H. (1993). Positive and negative life changes following bereavement and their relations to adjustment. *Journal of Social and Clinical Psychology, 12,* 90–112.

Lorr, M., & McNair, D. (1982). *Profile of Mood States-B.* San Diego: Educational Testing Service.

Lund, D. A., Caserta, M. S., & Dimond, M. F. (1993). The course of spousal bereavement in later life. In M. S. Stroebe, W. Stroebe, & R. O. Hansson (Eds.), *Handbook of bereavement: Theory, research, and intervention* (pp. 240–254). New York: Cambridge University Press.

McCrae, R. R. (1989). Age differences and changes in the use of coping mechanisms. *Journal of Gerontology: Psychological Sciences, 44*, 161–169.

McMillen, C., Zuravin, S., & Rideout, G. (1995). Perceived benefits from child sexual abuse. *Journal of Consulting and Clinical Psychology, 63*, 1037–1043.

McNair, D., Lorr, M., & Droppleman, L. (1971). *Profile of Mood States Scale manual*. San Diego: Educational Testing Service.

Mendola, R., Tennen, H., Affleck, G., McCann, L., & Fitzgerald, T. (1990). Appraisal and adaptation among women with impaired infertility. *Cognitive Therapy and Research, 14*, 79–93.

Michela, J. L. (1987). Interpersonal and individual impacts of a husband's heart attack. In A. Baum & J. E. Singer (Eds.), *Handbook of psychology and health: Stress* (Vol. 5, pp. 255–301). Hillsdale, NJ: Lawrence Erlbaum Associates.

O'Leary, V. E., & Ickovics, J. R. (1995). Resilience and thriving in response to challenge: An opportunity for a paradigm shift in women's health. *Women's Health: Research on Gender, Behavior, and Policy, 1*, 121–142.

Pargament, K. I., & Park, C. L. (1995). Merely a defense? The variety of religious means and ends. *Journal of Social Issues, 51*, 13–52.

Park, C. L., Cohen, L. H., & Murch, R. (1996). Assessment and prediction of stress-related growth. *Journal of Personality, 64*, 71–105.

Park, C. L., & Folkman, S. (in press). The role of meaning in the context of stress and coping. *General Review of Psychology*.

Schaefer, J. A., & Moos, R. H. (1992). Life crises and personal growth. In B. N. Carpenter (Ed.), *Personal coping: Theory, research, and application* (pp. 149–170). Westport, CT: Praeger.

Schwartzberg, S. S. (1993). Struggling for meaning: How HIV-positive gay men make sense of AIDS. *Professional Psychology: Research & Practice, 24*, 483–490.

Shacham, S. (1983). A shortened version of the Profile of Mood States. *Journal of Personality Assessment, 47*, 305–306.

Shedler, J., Mayman, M., & Manis, M. (1993). The illusion of mental health. *American Psychologist, 48*, 1117–1131.

Tait, R., & Silver, R. C. (1989). Coming to terms with major negative life events. In J. S. Uleman & J. A. Bargh (Eds.), *Unintended thought* (pp. 351–382). New York: Guilford.

Taylor, S. E. (1983). Adjustment to threatening events: A theory of cognitive adaption. *American Psychologist, 38*, 1161–1173.

Taylor, S. E., & Brown, J. D. (1988). Illusion and well-being: A social psychological perspective on mental health. *Psychological Bulletin, 103*, 193–210.

Taylor, S. E., Kemeny, M. E., Reed, G. M., & Aspinwall, L. G. (1991). Assault on the self: Positive illusions and adjustment to threatening events. In J. Strauss & G. R. Goethals (Eds.) *The self: Interdisciplinary approaches* (pp. 239–254). New York: Springer-Verlag.

Taylor, S. E., Lichtman, R., & Wood, J. (1984). Attributions, beliefs about control, and adjustment to breast cancer. *Journal of Personality and Social Psychology, 46*, 489–502.

Tedeschi, R. G., & Calhoun, L. G. (1995). *Trauma and transformation: Growth in the aftermath of suffering*. Thousand Oaks, CA: Sage.

Tedeschi, R. G., & Calhoun, L. G. (1996). The Post-Traumatic Growth Inventory: Measuring the positive legacy of trauma. *Journal of Traumatic Stress, 9*, 455–471.

Tennen, H., Affleck, G., Urrows, S., Higgins, P., & Mendola, R. (1992). Perceiving control, construing benefits, and daily processes in rheumatoid arthritis. *Canadian Journal of Behavioral Science, 24*, 186–203.

Thompson, S. C. (1985). Finding positive meaning in a stressful event and coping. *Basic and Applied Social Psychology*, 6, 279–295.

Thompson, S. C. (1991). The search for meaning following a stroke. *Basic and Applied Social Psychology*, 12, 81–96.

Videka-Sherman, L. (1982). Effects of participation in a self-help group for bereaved parents: Compassionate Friends. *Prevention in Human Services*, 1, 69–77.

Warr, P., Barter, J., & Brownbridge, G. (1983). On the independence of positive and negative affect. *Journal of Personality and Social Psychology*, 44, 644–651.

Yalom, I. D., & Lieberman, M. A. (1991). Bereavement and heightened existential awareness. *Psychiatry*, 54, 334–345.

Zemore, R., & Shepel, L. F. (1989). Effects of breast cancer and mastectomy on emotional support and adjustment. *Social Science and Medicine*, 28, 19–27.

8

By the Crowd They Have Been Broken, By the Crowd They Shall Be Healed: The Social Transformation of Trauma

Sandra L. Bloom
Friends Hospital, Philadelphia, PA

The social transformation of trauma is probably as old as the social nature of humankind. Our predisposition to gather in groups of mutual support and defense is an evolutionary response to the overwhelming stress, vulnerability, and helplessness of solitary primate existence. We are biologically programmed for attachment from "cradle to grave" and the natural human response to danger is to gather together, to seek out the safety of human companionship. The social transformation of trauma can be seen in its early form in the highly developed rituals of our ancestors. Rites of mourning, rites of healing, and rites of passage were all vital in helping us to resolve the traumas of the past and move ahead into the present and future (Lex, 1979). All important rites were accomplished in social settings, usually involving the entire group as participants. These rites provided a sense of group identity and cohesion and were essential to the life and well-being of each tribal group. In healing rites, the patient was frequently expected to become a member of a healing society after his or her own recovery (Van der Hart, 1983). The performative arts have their roots in these social rites and may have evolved, in part, as biopsychosocial mechanisms for resolving individual and group trauma (Bloom, 1995; Shay, 1995).

The subject of group transformation is a complex one and raises many questions about the relationship between the group and the individual. For the purposes of this discussion, I make several assumptions that I elaborate on elsewhere (Bloom, 1996). I assume that there is an intimate and interactive relationship between the individual and the group and that our individual identity is closely tied to our "group self" and that, in fact, our group self may be the core component of our sense of personal identity (Cohen, Fidler, & Ettin, 1995). Even more controversially, I assume that groupmind can exist as a meaningful concept. *Groupmind* is the word that has been used to describe a concept of the supra-individual nature and independence of the collective mind of a social group (Forsyth, 1990; Hewstone, Stroebe, Codol, & Stephenson, 1989; McDougall, 1920). *Group as a whole* refers to the behavior of a group as a social system with the assumption being that when a person behaves in such a group context, representing aspects of the group's unconscious mind, the individual is seen as a living vessel through which unconscious group life can be expressed and understood. In such a model, groups are seen as living systems and the individuals in the group are subsystems of which the group is comprised. From this perspective, a person speaks not only for him- or herself but also voices the unconscious sentiment of the group (Ettin, 1993; Wells, 1985). In such a model, leaders easily become delegates for both the conscious and, often more importantly, the unconscious wishes and desires of the group (DeMause, 1982).

Making these assumptions allows us to tentatively apply concepts rooted in individual dynamics to the psychology of the group. Because we now know that traumatic reenactment is a central dynamic in the development and adjustment of traumatized individuals, we must consider the possibility that traumatic reenactment is a strong possibility for traumatized groups as well. The author Tina Rosenberg has studied traumatized populations in Latin American and Eastern Europe (1995) and has stated that "Nations, like individuals, need to face up to and understand traumatic past events before they can put them aside and move on to normal life" (p. vxiii).

But how does a group overcome the powerful dynamic pull of traumatic reenactment in order to transform the trauma into something better for the group and the individuals within the group? There are several dimensions to such a topic. An individual's personal traumatic experience can serve as the basis for the creation and transformation of a group when the trauma-tized individual serves as the inspirational leader for the group. Alterna-tively, a group trauma occurs and must be transformed for the group as a whole, frequently through the mediation or inspiration of a leader who arises out of the group and becomes the delegate for the group, giving voice to the conscious and unconscious aspirations of the group. Additionally, the witnessed traumatization of others can cause a group response, even when the trauma has not been experienced directly by the group members. In the examples that follow, in most cases it is difficult to make such clear-cut distinctions. The interaction between the individual and the group, the leader and the led, is an interactive, dynamic one in which all of these elements are found.

TYPES OF SOCIAL TRANSFORMATION

Individuals and groups have searched throughout time for the means to turn adversity into strength. For the purposes of this discussion I divide the panoply of examples for social transformation into seven somewhat arbitrary categories. In reality, human motivations are usually quite complex and many of my examples could fall into several of the categories. Around the world, attempts are being made to begin to deal with these traumatic issues in a broader social context. The Nuremberg Trials are a post-war attempt to resolve the trauma of the Holocaust through the opportunity to bear witness and seek justice. In Chile, Argentina, El Salvador, South Africa, Bosnia-Herzegovina and other war-torn areas, similar engagements between witnesses, victims, and perpetrators are being explored, albeit tentatively. Live-Aid, Band-Aid and other organized and widely watched and attended performance events—including the highly ritualized parade of nations in the Olympics—are all indicative of our group attempts to share and transform suffering through the use of the arts. On television, we watch massive international rescue efforts to attenuate the effects of famine in Africa, save whales and dolphins off the coast of Japan, or minimize the effects of huge oil spills off of the Alaskan coast and in the North Sea. Self-help support groups have become a major part of the American therapy scene and for the last century various groups have contributed to preventing child exploitation, the abuse of animals and the environment, domestic violence, and virtually every other evil that man has invented, through education and through political action. And one unique human quality that provides a healing balm simultaneously for groups and individuals is humor. Perhaps we recognize that our salvation is at hand when we can begin to laugh together at the strange peculiarities of our species in the way that oppressed groups throughout time, have been able to find sustenance through laughter.

All of these categories of transformation appear to have at least one thing in common—a sense of moral commitment, a sense that personal and group trauma must be converted into a community asset, not just a personal asset or catastrophe. From such traumatic origins springs the co-construction or reconstruction of civilization. In this sense, there is a moral maturity about these transformations. Noam (1993) has said that "moral maturity needs to be judged by the relationship between the complexity of judgments and the capacity to transform judgments into positive adaptations" (p. 213). All of these transformations hinge on a moral position that is often implicit, but which is the guiding hand in such social transformations, and individuals who epitomize this moral position become the "moral exemplars" for the entire cultural system (Colby & Damon, 1993). This moral position hinges on a generalized sense of respect, compassion, and concern for all life and a willingness to risk one's self-interest for the sake of these values. Ultimately, all positive transformation is rooted in the attempt to make sense out of inherently senseless acts of violence. I do not separate out a religious or spiritual category of transformation because I believe that this search for higher meaning and higher connection is implicit in all transformative acts and is a fundamental striving of human nature. The transformation of trauma is not a possible option; it is a moral necessity and we cannot heal as individuals or as a group, without striving for something more whole, more loving, and more ethically coherent than our individual selves.

Transformation Through Education and Prevention

Felman (Felman & Laub, 1992) directly asked the question, "Is there a relation between crisis and the very enterprise of education? ... In a post-traumatic century, a century that has survived unthinkable historical catastrophes, is there anything that we have learned or that we should learn about education, that we did not know before?" (p. 1). For those of us who work with victims of trauma, individual progress often hinges on a process of reeducation, on a cognitive, emotional, and epistemological reordering and recategorizing of old information that occurs simultaneously with the integration of new, often contradictory information. Such education can stop the spiral of individual degradation and when placed in a group context, can prevent harm from occurring in the first place. As new knowledge spreads throughout a culture and is passed down through the generations, prevention replaces intervention. Two examples of this kind of transformation are illustrated through *Mothers Against Drunk Driving* (MADD), an extremely effective group that originated with the individual traumatic death of a child, and *Physicians for Social Responsibility* (PSR), which began when concerned American physicians became alarmed at the prospect of other Hiroshimas. Both groups have spent a great deal of effort in educating the public about their two fundamental concerns, and although both groups have also been involved in political action and witnessing, I was most impressed with how their educational and preventative methods have affected the larger social group.

Mothers Against Drunk Driving.   MADD was founded in 1980 by Candy Lightner following the death of her 13-year-old daughter, Cari, by a hit-and-run driver who was a repeat DWI offender. He was permitted to plea bargain to vehicular manslaughter and was sentenced to 2 years in prison, but was allowed to serve time in a work camp and later a halfway house. Candy Lightner was so enraged by lenient laws and a weak judicial response to drunk driving crimes that she decided to start a group that could educate the public, draw attention to the issue of drunk driving, and provide support for those victimized by drunk drivers. By 1985, MADD had 340 chapters in 47 states and 600,000 supporters, which grew to 1,100,000 by 1996.

Thanks in part to the efforts of this organization, more than 2,000 anti-drunk driving laws have been enacted nationwide and MADD has played a leading role in the enactment of the Age 21 Law, urging states to adopt age 21 as the standard legal drinking age. Two thirds of the states have passed Administrative License Revocation laws that allow the arresting officer to take the driver's license of those who fail or refuse to take a breath test. Judges in more than 200 counties across the United States are now assigning drunk driving offenders to attend MADD-operated Victim Impact Panels comprised of crash victims and survivors who tell offenders how drunk driving has affected their lives. MADD volunteers watch court cases involving drunk driving offenders and are reporting the outcome of cases to the media to ensure that drunk drivers are punished. They have produced an instructional video on Court Monitoring for all their chapters and Victim Advocacy Training is offered by MADD so that its chapters can provide a full range of victim support services in the community (Mothers Against Drunk Driving, 1996).

In their efforts to transform their own personal and private pain into social transformation, the volunteers of MADD have done much to educate the public about the profound effects of drunk driving and in impacting on the courts and legislation, they have been able to prevent an untold number of tragic deaths and disabilities.

Physicians for Social Responsibility.   Hiroshima is one of the defining events of the 20th century. Hiroshima and Nagasaki provided us with an irrevocable warning of a possible apocalyptic future, our last stop before the total annihilation prefigured in the Holocaust. The nuclear bomb and the death camps redefined the very meaning of trauma. For the United States, the detonations over Japan have left us with a sense of confused identity, an underlying and unresolved anxiety that unconsciously permeates postwar American society. As Lifton pointed out, "It has never been easy to reconcile dropping the bomb with a sense of ourselves as a decent people. Because this conflict remains unresolved it continues to provoke strong feelings. There is no historical event Americans are more sensitive about. Hiroshima remains a raw nerve" (Lifton & Mitchell, 1995, p. xi).

One of the group responses to the detonation of atomic bombs was the creation of PSR. The organization was founded in 1961 by Bernard Lown, a cardiologist and professor at Harvard's School of Public Health. The statement of purpose for PSR declared that "The physician ... must begin to explore a new area of preventative medicine, the prevention of thermo-nuclear war" (Lifton & Mitchells, 1995, p. 261). Lown organized a group of concerned physicians in his living room and then arranged for the publica-tion of a series of articles in the *New England Journal of Medicine* about the medical consequences of nuclear war. This work showed clearly that there was no adequate medical response possible and helped persuade the Ken-nedy administration of the futility of bomb shelters. PSR went into quies-cence after the 1963 signing of the Limited Test Ban Treaty until 1979 when the Reagan campaign's nuclear rhetoric revived old fears.

In 1980, Lown organized a 2-day meeting sponsored by Harvard and Tufts on "The Medical Consequences of Nuclear Weapons and Nuclear War." The meeting was carefully orchestrated to gain public attention and brought together the nation's leading arms-control advocates to address a large audience. Helen Caldicott, a pediatrician, became the president of the group and worked tirelessly, touring the United States and showing the film *The Last Epidemic*, which described how San Francisco would fare in an atomic attack. Caldicott saw her anti-nuclear campaigning as a simple extension of her medical work, "It is the ultimate form of preventive medicine. If you have a disease and there is no cure for it, you work on prevention" (Winkler, 1993, p. 198).

As a result of Caldicott's efforts, PSR attracted more than 300 new recruits per week and membership grew from 3,000 in 1981 to 16,000 in 1982. Speakers bureaus were set up in every chapter, slide shows were created, and materials were distributed so that physicians from every area of the country could go out and inform the public about the real conse-quences of nuclear war, thus serving as a useful counterpart to the dou-blespeak rhetoric about "limited nuclear warfare" that was being disseminated throughout the highest levels of government. PSR became part of an international group, International Physicians for the Prevention of Nuclear War in 1982. Among their many activities they provided a televised account of the dangers of nuclear war that was shown to Soviet viewers in June 1982 and to Americans in October of the same year. In an essay in the *Bulletin of Atomic Scientists*, George Kistiakowsky, former head of the Manhattan Project's explosives division, urged on the work before his death, "Forget the channels. There is simply not enough time left before the world explodes. Concentrate instead on organizing, with so many others who are of like mind, a mass movement for peace such as there has not been before" (Winkler, 1993, p. 199). In 1985, International Physicians for the Prevention of Nuclear War was awarded the Nobel Peace Prize. PSR continues to pursue its antinuclear goals and has expanded to include related concerns about interpersonal and environmental violence as well (Bloom & Reichert, in press). The educational efforts of this group and others like it have provided the entire international community with a more realistic appraisal of what nuclear disaster could hold in store for us, and so far, their efforts have been successful in helping to prevent a thermonuclear holocaust.

Transformation Through Mutual Self-Help

The title of this chapter is taken from a quotation by L. Cody Marsh, a minister and psychiatrist, and cousin to "Buffalo Bill" Cody. He served in World War I as a morale officer at an American hospital in Siberia and came back convinced that active, educational, and social approaches to treatment were necessary. Drawing on revivalist techniques, he related his approach to the "walking groups" of Pythagoras, Socrates, and Zoroaster. As early as 1931, Marsh was anticipating the modern milieu approach by holding community meetings at his hospital and providing a lecture series which involved testimonials from other patients (Ettin, 1992; Scheidlinger, 1993). Around the same time, Bill W. and Dr. Bob started Alcoholics Anonymous, the forerunner of all the Twelve-Step Programs.

Social Psychiatry and the Therapeutic Milieu.   After World War II, psychiatry was dominated by men and women who had served in the military. They had seen the effects of traumatic experience firsthand and they had seen the powerful healing influences that people were able to exert on each other in groups. These insights influenced the developing of a then-burgeoning approach to psychiatric problems known as "social psychiatry." One of the tenets of social psychiatry was that "the mentally ill person is seen as a member of an oppressed group, a group deprived of adequate social solutions to the problem of individual growth and development" (Ullman, 1969, p. 263). The result was the further development of group forms of treatment, most particularly the therapeutic milieu.

The therapeutic milieu—and its cousin, the therapeutic community—were based on the belief that an entire social system could exert powerful influences for positive change that surpassed the benefits of the sum of each separate component. But more than just a place for the treatment of individual patients, the hospital was seen as being a microcosm of the larger society, an experimental laboratory for social change (Tucker & Maxmen, 1973). Unlike many other settings, the values that formed the underpinnings for every milieu were clearly articulated—egalitarianism, permissiveness, honesty, openness, and trust (Almond, 1974; Leeman & Autio, 1978; Rapoport, 1960).

Like the Quakers who had originated Moral Treatment 200 years before them, the advocates of the therapeutic milieu discovered that the social milieu could provide a transformative experience within which the group and the individual interacted to bring about change which could allow the victim to transcend traumatic combat experiences (Jones, 1953; Wilmer, 1958) and then later, traumatic childhood experiences (Bloom, 1996, 1997). The therapeutic milieu was extremely effective and has died out—or been killed—largely because of an adverse political and economic climate and not because it was shown to be ineffective (Bloom, 1997). Nonetheless, the technology for managing groups of troubled and traumatized people in a nonviolent, democratic milieu within which all people learn and change in service of personal and group transformation is still available, and clearly, still needed (Bloom, 1994, 1997; Bills & Bloom, in press).

The Anonymous Groups. Alcoholics Anonymous, Narcotics Anonymous, Overeaters Anonymous, Sexual Compulsives Anonymous, and Adult Children of Alcoholics all have something in common besides their stated anonymity. They are community-based, self-supporting, and comprised of people who help themselves through helping others in overcoming some form of addictive, compulsive behavior that is damaging their lives. The Twelve Steps and Twelve Traditions of such groups are a structured and methodical way of transforming self-destructive and other-destructive behavior into an individually productive and socially constructive life. The Twelve-Step programs require that the individual connects with a larger whole in a meaningful way, recognizing that surrender of the addiction is necessary if progress is to be made. The individual must carefully review all the destructive things they have done to themselves and to others in taking a "fearless moral inventory." A fundamental part of progress in these groups involves revealing one's story to the group. In this way, a narrative forms as the individual conforms to the group norm of confession. But, the Twelve Steps insist on more than talking. The individual is instructed to "make amends" to all who have been harmed, and part of making amends and healing is to help others who have been seized by the addictive behavior (Alcoholics Anonymous, 1996; Narcotics Anonymous, 1996; Overeaters Anonymous, 1996; Sexual Compulsives Anonymous, 1996). The Twelve-Step process has much in common with ancient forms of healing rituals that can still be seen among native peoples. Sacrifice, trial, confession, making amends, and public testimony are all part of our ancient tribal heritage. As we are learning, a substantial proportion of addicted people have trauma as a contributing factor in the evolution of their disease process. The power of the group in helping to transform their primary and secondary pain into socially constructive lives lends convincing evidence to the idea that the group transformation of trauma is a potent, evolutionarily developed tool for healing.

Transformation Through Rescuing

Rescuing is a transformative act that powerfully impacts on the rescuer and those rescued. The notion of saving others—their bodies and their souls—has a long history and many of our cultural motifs and myths are related to the rescue of the innocent, the sick, the injured, the young, the helpless, the ignorant, or the alien. From *The Scarlet Pimpernel* to the *Helen Keller Story*, *Ole Yeller*, *ET*, and *Schindler's List*, watching and hearing the stories of great rescues makes us feel good, inspired, and sometimes even helps us to model future behavior. The examples of rescuers are so numerous that they could fill a book devoted to the topic. Many social action movements have originated in a fervid desire to rescue other living beings from some traumatic or degrading situation. From the Underground Railroad, to Clara Barton and the American Red Cross, to child labor laws, the ASPCA, rape crisis centers, domestic violence shelters, child abuse hotlines, and dozens of environmental protection groups, rescue efforts have played a dominant role in bringing the focus of public concern to endangered groups.

   To discuss rescuing as an act of transformation, we must look at the psychology of the bystander. What is it that turns a bystander into a rescuer, oftentimes at great risk to life and limb? Helpers are not born, they are raised. In studies of rescuers, many have come from families in which strong moral concerns are transmitted by the parents to the children along with a fundamental sense of empathy without regard to social, ethnic, or religious background. Rescuers often have been marginalized or victimized themselves, and yet despite this they have—for a variety of different reasons—placed a high premium on maintaining human connection. And helping behavior is learned. As children see their parents acting as rescuers, there is an increased likelihood that they will follow in the same pattern. As in the case of Oskar Schindler, it has often been noted that helping behavior is reinforced and modeled at all ages, that the more one engages in helping others, the more likely it is that the same behavior will be tried again, often with an increasing sense of commitment (Fogelman, 1994; Staub, 1989). Two examples, one historical and one current, serve to illustrate the involvement in rescuing as group normative behavior.

The Huguenots and the Danes in World War II. The genocidal behavior of the Nazis also provided opportunities for individuals and groups to react against this slaughter, and some did react with inspiring displays of courage. Le Chambon-sur-Lignon in France was one place where an entire town colluded in rescuing persecuted Jews, and the behavior of the citizens of Le Chambon raises the question of the transformative influence of group traumatic memory.

Protestantism was brought to France in the 16th century by the Lutherans, or, as they were known in France, the Huguenots. For 300 years, French Protestants were persecuted. They had their property seized, they were imprisoned, and sometimes they were killed. In the 18th century, the King of France manned great galleys by men enslaved because of the crime of Protestantism. In a tower near Marseilles, Protestant women were imprisoned and left to die of starvation, cold, heat, and despair.

Protestantism came to Le Chambon in the first half of the 16th century. In 1685, with the virtual destruction of Protestant rights in France under the revocation of the Edict of Nantes, 1,000 refugees fled to Le Chambon for protection where they stayed with their religious brethren and became a part of the community. Even by the time of World War II, the Huguenot history was still alive and vivid in the mind of the villagers of Le Chambon. Solidarity and resistance in the face of persecution, combined with an intense loyalty to their pastors, were fundamental characteristics of the people of Le Chambon.

So when their pastors, André Trocmé and Édouard Theis began doing more than talking about the love of Jesus and the practice of nonviolence by defying the Nazis through providing safe passage and safe houses for fleeing Jews, the people of Le Chambon followed suit. In Le Chambon, even many of the Vichy police were "converted" to helping Jews. In doing this work, the ministers felt that they were filling two moral dictates: They were rescuing the innocent from harm and they were preventing those in authority from violating the commandment against killing. As Pastor Theis explained to the author who later told the story of Le Chambon, they believed that "if they failed to protect those in Le Chambon, they, the ministers, would share the guilt of the evil ones who actually perpetrated the harm-doing" (Hallie, 1994, p. 283). By the end of the war, this small village of 3,000 impoverished people had saved the lives of about 5,000 refugees, most of them children.

The Danes also rescued Danish Jews and they did it as an entire nation. At the time, Denmark had a population of 4½ million and only 8,000 of them were Jewish. There was no history of anti-Semitism in Denmark (Goldberger, 1987). As far back as 1690 a Danish police commissioner had been removed for having suggested the establishment of a Jewish ghetto in Copenhagen (Abrahamsen, 1987). Although there was cultural pressure for the Jews to fit into a society as homogenous as the Danes, the Jews had survived as a distinct religious entity.

Churchill called Denmark "the sadistic murderer's canary." Denmark had done little to protect itself from the Nazis from the beginning, seemingly determined to retain the neutrality they had established in World War I. The Nazis occupied Denmark in early 1940 and the government of King Christian X conceded to their demands. Many Danes felt embarrassed and humiliated by this lack of resistance, but in reality, Denmark was geographi-cally indefensible against the overwhelming power of the Nazi panzer divisions. The Nazis responded to the Danish politeness with an unusually high degree of consideration. They wanted Danish cooperation to provide them with products, especially food. Hitler also saw the tall, blond Danes as true Aryans, as brothers in the cause. In exchange for their nonviolent cooperation, the Danes insisted on retaining absolute control of their own domestic affairs and, in doing so, they retained the civil rights of their citizens, including the Jews. As far as the Danes were concerned, there was no "Jewish problem" in Denmark. The Nazis going into Denmark recog-nized early on that the Danes were different from other occupied coun-tries—they would oppose the imprisonment of Jews (Flender, 1963).

As the Nazi plan for extermination of the Jews enlarged and encompassed much of Europe, the Danes held firm in their resistance to genocide. At first, the protection of their Bill of Rights kept them safe. But as Nazi intentions became more clear, the Danish citizenry quietly began developing "study groups," "sewing circles," and "book circles" throughout Denmark. Organi-zations were formed along professional lines as well. By the time the Nazis gave the order to exterminate the Danish Jews in September 1943—an order that was leaked out to Danish officials ahead of time by a Nazi official—the nation of Denmark rose, almost as a single wave, in a coordi-nated rescue mission of physicians, clergymen, fishermen, farmers, businessmen, taxi drivers, homemakers, students, professors, engineers, civil servants, union members, nurses, and ambulance drivers. The Danish physicians became known as the "White Brigade" and assisted more than 2,000 Jews, believing that in doing so they were fighting the "disease" of anti-Semitism. Out of a total population of 7,800 (including 1,300 half Jews) about 7,200 were transported to safety in Sweden across treacherous seas. Known as "Little Dunkirk" this rescue was a totally spontaneous action of the Danish people. About 90% of the church membership participated and close to 100% of the university. Why was Denmark so different from other countries? There were many factors but Abrahamsen has pointed out what may have been the most important factor:

> This nation had developed over the centuries what the Danes call *livskunst* (the art of living). It was a society where people *cared* about one another, where respect for individual and religious differences, self-reliance, cooperation, and good humor had become hallmarks of a civilized nation. These moral, intellectual, and ethical attitudes made the Danes say: "The Jews are our fellow citizens and fellow human beings; we shall not given them up for slaughter." And they did not. That's why the Danes became the *real* victors in Europe. They did not lose their souls. (Abrahamsen, 1987, p. 8).

International Rescue Committee.   The model for transforming trauma can be conveyed from one generation to another. The International Rescue Committee (IRC) was founded in 1933 at the behest of Albert Einstein to assist anti-Nazis fleeing Hitler's programs of terror. It remains today the leading nonsectarian, voluntary organization still providing relief, protection, and resettlement services for refugees and victims of oppression or violent conflict around the world. The Board of Directors is entirely voluntary and includes Henry Kissinger, Daniel Patrick Moynihan, Liv Ullman, and Elie Weisel among its members. In the past 6 years the IRC has tripled in size, helping victims of racial, religious, ethnic, or political persecution as well as people uprooted by war and violence. Support for the IRC comes from individuals, foundations, unions, and the business community as well as civic, education, and human rights groups in the United States and abroad. Since 1980, nearly 94 cents of every dollar contributed has gone directly for lifesaving assistance to refugees; *U.S. News and World Report* called IRC one of only five "Standout Good Guys" in 1995, the only international charity to make the list.

Recruits to the IRC come from a wide range of specialties. President DeVecchi commented on recruitment in a recent issue of the Harvard Business School Bulletin (internet), "Our line of work demands extraordinarily resourceful and dedicated people," he said. "We offer impossible hours, plenty of physical danger and discomfort, a miserable salary, and no clear career path."

Nonetheless, recruitment is working. The IRC now maintains aid programs in more than 20 different nations. In the former Yugoslavia they are repairing water and gas lines, renovating schools, hospitals, factories, and homes, and reviving agricultural production. They are organizing psychological help for the traumatized population with special services for rape victims. They have started a medical program serving war-injured children. In Rwanda the IRC is concentrating on reestablishing basic infrastructure, relief services, and economic activities. In Azerbaijan and Tajikistan the IRC's work focuses on improving the water supply and sanitation facilities, winterizing buildings and housing, and initiating income-generating projects to promote self-sufficiency. The list goes on and on. Currently the IRC maintains operations in Ghana/Ivory Coast, Guinea, Mozambique, Sudan, Southern Sudan/Kenya, Somalia, Tanzania, Rwanda, Cambodia, Thailand, Pakistan, Former Yugoslavia, Azerbaijan, Georgia, and Tajikistan (International Rescue Committee, 1996). Einstein would be proud of the fruit of his suggestion.

Transformation Through Witnessing and Seeking Justice

The verb "to witness" has several related meanings. It means to see, hear, or know by personal presence and perception; to be present at an occurrence as a formal witness, spectator, or bystander; and to bear witness to, testify to, give or afford evidence of something that has happened, usually something unfair, unjust, or in some way problematic. In this century of genocide, totalitarian control, mass oppression, and torture, bearing witness has become one of the most potent and nonviolent methods for transforming experienced and witnessed traumatic experience. Witnessing the perpetration of an unjust act elicits a desire for justice. As Herman (1992) has put it, "To study psychological trauma means bearing witness to horrible events ... when the traumatic events are of human design, those who bear witness are caught in the conflict between victim and perpetrator. It is morally impossible to remain neutral in this conflict. The bystander is forced to take sides" (p. 7).

In many parts of the world, through written, videotaped, and artistically derived creations, victims have been urged to use their traumatic experiences as a way of bearing witness to their losses, giving the dead a voice, serving as a warning to perpetrators and bystanders of the future. The

United States Holocaust Memorial Museum in Washington, the Simon Wiesenthal Center in Los Angeles, Yad Vashem in Jerusalem, the Vietnam Memorial, the video archive for Holocaust Testimonies at Yale University, the digital archives of Cambodian Holocaust survivors—these and countless other memorials serve as visual reminders of the trauma of this century. Created by groups of survivors and other witnesses, their shared motto is "never forget." Two current examples are available to us from two very different parts of the globe.

Mothers—and Grandmothers—of the Plaza de Mayo. Between 1976 and 1981, Argentina's military seized and murdered thousands of innocent young people. They are the *desaparecidos,* the "disappeared." Taken from their homes, their jobs, or off the streets, they just disappeared, never to be seen or heard from again. On a day in 1977, 14 mothers met in the Plaza de Mayo in central Buenos Aires to present a petition to the man who was then President of Argentina, General Videla. The petition was a demand to know what happened to their children at the hands of the "Triple A," a paramilitary force schooled in torture, whose particular favorite "victims" were pregnant woman from whom they would tear out their unborn babies—those who lived were often given to military families as "war prizes." The instigator of this movement of mothers, Azucena Villaflor de Vicenti, was arrested and never seen again, but the movement she started continues today. When first prodded to move by the soldiers in the Plaza, the Mothers took the order seriously and began walking in a circle; they have been circling ever since. "How else should the Mothers march?," explains Hebe Bonafini, the movement's guiding spirit, "than round—like their bellies and the world through which their protest echoes" (Ortiz, 1995, p. 23). The Mothers march around the Plaza de Mayo, not seeking compensation but instead, silently protesting the silent death of their children. They call themselves "living apparitions." For them "calling off their protest would mean that death had won ... Once each mother marched with the photo of her own child. Now they carry any picket sign, irrespective of the photo on it. They are universal mothers" (p. 24).

Mothers become grandmothers and so there are also the "Grandmothers of the Plaza de Mayo." The Grandmothers, led by Estella de Carlotto, seek out the children of their children who were kidnapped by the military. They are using a genetic fingerprinting system set up jointly by two women physicians—one from Argentina and the other from the United States—to establish the actual family links of children who are investigated. Of 500 children known to have disappeared they have found about 56 through this method. The Mothers and the Grandmothers bear witness to all the disappeared children of the world and continue to seek justice for those who were illegally detained, tortured, and killed. Their silent and moving testimony has been heard around the world. Since winning the Sakharov Prize, their example has been followed by mothers in many other countries: by Sicilian mothers fighting against the mafia, by Spanish mothers fighting against drugs, the CoMadres of El Salvador and the Conavigua Widows of Guatemala seeking justice for their lost loved ones killed by military dictatorships, by Ukrainian victims of Chenobyl, and by Palestinian, Israeli, Turkish, and Yugoslav mothers who reject war (Ortiz, 1995; Radcliffe & Westwood, 1993; The grandchildren of Argentina, 1985).

Truth and Reconciliation Commission of South Africa. When apartheid ended, South Africa remained a deeply divided and traumatized society with a long history of violent and unjust acts perpetrated against its citizens, many of whom began to assume positions of power in the new government. Some voices were raised calling for a general amnesty, but it was recognized that such a measure could not provide a sound basis for the healing that the country must go through if progress without violence is to be made. As the Minister of Justice Dullah Omar (1996) has said, "We recognized that we could not forgive perpetrators unless we attempt also to restore the honor and dignity of the victims and give effect to reparation … we need to heal our country if we are to build a nation which will guarantee peace and stability."

Under the inspired leadership of President Mandela, the Interim Constitution established the basis for the development of the Truth and Reconciliation Commission. Archbishop Desmond Tutu was appointed as the Chairperson of the Commission and 17 people from diverse backgrounds were appointed to sit on the Commission. Conferences were held to explore how other countries were engaged in dealing with the past and included representatives from Eastern Europe, Argentina, and Chile. The South Africans recognized from this international experience that "if we are to achieve unity and morally acceptable reconciliation, it is necessary that the truth about gross violations of human rights must be: established by an official investigation unit using fair procedures; fully and unreservedly acknowledged by the perpetrators; made known to the public, together with the identity of the planners, perpetrators and victims" ("What International Experience Shows," 1996).

The Commission recognized that it must deal with three major questions that bear a striking resemblance to the fundamental questions of individual survivors: (a) How do emerging democracies deal with past violations of human rights? (b) how do new democratic governments deal with leaders and individuals who were responsible for disappearances, death squads, psychological and physical torture and other violations of human rights? and (c) how does a new democracy deal with the fact that some of the perpetrators remain part of the new government and/or security forces or hold important positions in public life? (Boraine, 1996). Three separate committees were established to deal with three critical areas surrounding the problem: a Human Rights Violations Committee, which conducts public hearings for victims/survivors, a Reparation and Rehabilitation Committee, which works on policies and recommendations arising from those hearings, and an Amnesty Committee, which hears applications for amnesty. The objective of the Commission is not so much to punish as to investigate, record, and make known the crimes against human rights that were committed in the name of the State. The commitment and reason for this effort is to "break from the past, to heal the wounds of the past, to forgive but not to forget and to build a future based on respect for human rights" (Omar, 1996).

The Commissioners travel throughout South Africa and take the reports of victims of atrocities and torture, which are all carefully recorded. The hearings are open to the public and have open media coverage. The names of the victims and the perpetrators are published. The Commissioners have the right of subpoena as well as search and seizure. Alleged perpetrators are invited to testify at the hearings, but if they decline, they may be subpoenaed and evidence will be gathered against them.

South Africa has been struggling with the thorny issue of amnesty and has been trying to benefit from the experience of other countries. Too often, a general amnesty has been offered by the very regimes responsible for the human rights violations and therefore the amnesty has been looked upon as just another betrayal of trust by human rights organizations and attorneys. As Vice Chairperson Boraine (1996) has pointed out,

> There are many implications flowing from general amnesty which really amounts to impunity … impunity threatens belief in a democratic society, … confuses and creates ambiguous social, moral, and psychological limits, … tempts people to take the law into their own hands, … invalidates and denies what has happened and thereby limits the possibility of effective communication between fellow citizens, … strengthens powerlessness, guilt and shame, … affects belief in the future and may leave people in a historical "no-man's land," … and reduces the scope for collective mourning and a collective working through of the suffering.

The Commissioners decided to institute a different kind of amnesty program which would include accountability and disclosure. There is no blanket amnesty—amnesty must be applied for on an individual basis. Applicants for amnesty must fill out a prescribed form that details information relating to specific human rights violations. Applicants must make a full disclosure of their human rights violations in order to qualify for amnesty and, in most instances, these applicants will be required to appear before the Amnesty Committee at public hearings. The time period covered for granting amnesty is between 1960 and 1993 and the applicants only had a 12-month period within which they could seek amnesty, from December 1995 to December 1996. Under the terms of the Commission, amnesty is not to be granted if the human rights violations were for personal gain, out of personal malice, ill will, or spite.

The hearings have not always gone smoothly. There is a sentiment on the part of some victims that the perpetrators should be more harshly punished, and that only then can justice be served. This has been a difficult issue to resolve in all attempts to do so thus far, just as it remains a difficult issue in the cases of individual survivors of violent acts (Friedman, 1996). The architects of the Truth and Reconciliation Commission are well aware of the compromise that is involved. "South Africa has decided to say no to amnesia and yes to remembrance; to say no to full-scale prosecutions and yes to forgiveness" explains Boraine (1996). This tension has been described as a central conflict between the politics of compromise and the radical notion of justice, or as one commentator drawing on Greek tragedy has put it, between the "logic of mourning/remembrance and political logic" (Boraine, 1996).

Seeking justice is a uniquely human act, a form of traumatic transformation that is as old as civilization. At the end of the 20th century, there are similar transformative movements for justice going on in several different parts of the globe—in Eastern Europe, in South America, and in South Africa—all seeking justice for acts of state oppression. There have been 19 truth commissions operating in 16 countries over the last 20 years (Boraine, 1996). These movements have a great deal in common and could be used as a metaphorical description of the tasks that exist in recovery for the individual victims of overwhelming interpersonal trauma. As the Vice Chairperson of South African's Truth and Reconciliation Commission described in a recent speech:

A shift from totalitarianism to a form of democracy;
A negotiated settlement—not a revolutionary process;
A legacy of oppression and serious violations of human rights;

A fragile democracy and a precarious unity;
A commitment to the attainment of a culture of human rights and a respect
for the rule of law;
A determination that the work of the Commission will help to make it
impossible for the gross violations of human rights of the past to happen again
(Boraine, 1996).

Although there is controversy over the effectiveness and fairness of these
various commissions, perhaps the most important aspect of them is that they
have existed. In our global, species consciousness, we appear to be at least
wrestling with the issues of justice, accountability, forgiveness, and transformation. For South Africa, amnesty is the price they are paying for peace
and stability, for a national life that learns from the past but moves ahead
into a new future. It is a grand, global experiment and it is too soon to know
the outcome. But the experiment continues to grow—nearby Namibia has
recently asked for help in establishing a similar group. The outcome without
such an experiment, however, is easier to predict. As Roberto Canas of El
Salvador has put it, "Unless a society exposes itself to the truth it can harbour
no possibility of reconciliation, reunification and trust" (Boraine, 1996).

Transformation Through Political Action

In *The Soul of Politics*, Jim Wallis (1994) offers the opinion that "We need a
politics that offers us something we haven't had in a long time: a vision of
transformation" (p. viii). Certainly, the study of victims of trauma provides
us with an opportunity to once again realize the long-standing feminist
notion that the personal is political and that perhaps personal transformation has something to teach us about political transformation just as political
transformation can inspire personal change. The interpersonal traumas that
so many of our patients sustain occur in a sociopolitical context in which
the abuse of power is encouraged and sustained. Whether we talk about the
sexual and physical abuse of women and children, the abuse of the inmates
of asylums and prisons, the imprisonment and torture of people of conscience, or the abuses of the totalitarian state, all violence focuses on the
unfair distribution of power and the abuse of this power by the powerful
against the helpless. The solutions to these problems are not individual
solutions; they require political solutions. It is not surprising, therefore, that
many traumatized individuals turn to political action as a way of transforming their own individual and group pain. A 19th century determined woman
and a 20th century playwright provide examples of social activism and
political change.

Asylum Reform.   At the end of the 18th century, the care of the mentally ill was often harsh, brutal, and inhumane. One of those who suffered poorly at the hands of her keepers was a Quaker girl from York, England, who died in suspicious circumstances in 1791, a few weeks after being admitted to a local asylum. Her social group, The Society of Friends, were so traumatized by this event that they responded to the tragedy by creating a new kind of asylum, "in which a milder and more appropriate system of treatment than that usually practiced, might be adopted" (Busfield, 1986, p. 212). In doing so, the Quakers opened up a new chapter in the history of psychological treatment and they called their approach *Moral Treatment.* Moral Treatment was based on respect for the individual and the belief that just as the environment was an important cause of mental illness, so too could an environment be designed that would promote healing. The social milieu was considered to be the most important factor in promoting recovery (Bockoven, 1963).

But by the mid-18th century, the asylums for Moral Treatment, which had been created in almost every state in the country, had severely deteriorated. Underfunding and a flood of chronically mentally ill and neurologically impaired patients made the practice of Moral Treatment impossible based as it was on small, socially, and physically healthy environments (Dwyer, 1987; McGovern, 1985; Rothman, 1980). Mrs. E. P. W. Packard was one traumatized woman who responded by transforming her pain and suffering into direct political action, thereby influencing her entire social group.

In 1860, Mrs. Packard, married to a minister and mother of six children, was hospitalized against her will in the Illinois State Hospital for the Insane at Jacksonville. Her husband had taken issue with her more liberal religious beliefs and, according to state law, a husband could commit his wife, even without any evidence of insanity. There she remained for 3 years. While in the asylum she was physically abused by other inmates and by members of the staff. But worse than the violence directed at herself was the violence she witnessed, particularly the cruel and sadistic treatment of the inmates by their keepers. She witnessed many episodes of violence, including attempted murder. Her defense of other patients led to punishment by the superintendent and his aides, often by deliberately forcing her to stay in wards with seriously violent patients. While imprisoned, she spent much of her time writing a book that would later be titled, *The Prisoners' Hidden Life* or *Insane Asylums Unveiled* (Packard ,1868). After release, her husband locked her in a room to prevent her from seeing her children, while he planned for a commitment that would keep her locked away for life. She escaped only by secreting out a note to a neighbor who helped to have her case brought to trial. In a sensational trial that achieved national attention, she was declared sane, and on the night the verdict was given, her husband absconded with all the marital property and the children, leaving her alone and destitute. She provided for herself by obtaining a loan to get her book published and then by selling her book and lecturing throughout the country. Her experience of being a married woman with no rights had left a deep impression on her and she dedicated herself to righting the wrongs she had suffered. She spent the next 20 years successfully campaigning for personal liberty laws that would protect individuals and particularly married women from wrongful commitment to and retention in asylums. Among her many accomplishments she saw to it that the superintendent who had so wronged her was relieved of duty and that the personal liberty laws in Illinois, Massachusetts, and Connecticut were changed. By the time of her death in 1897, she was a nationally and internationally recognized activist for the rights of women and the mentally ill (Grob, 1994; Packard, 1868, 1882; Sapinsley, 1991)

Vacláv Havel and the Czech Republic.   The Czech Republic, ancient Bohemia and Moravia, has a long history of trying times and provides us with a meaningful example of the national transformation of trauma through political action. Geographically trapped between the east and the west, bordered by Poland, Germany, Austria, and Slovakia, Czechoslovakia was formed after the strife of World War I and declared an independent republic with a liberal democratic constitution. Thomas Masaryk was a philosophy professor at the University of Prague who led the Czech independence movement from 1907 and became the first president of the new republic after World War I until 1935. An ardent liberal and democrat, he was revered by the Czech people, although he was always faced with strong opposition from extremist groups. The west, faced with Hitler's demands, handed Czechoslovakia over to the Nazis in 1939 in a futile gesture of appeasement (Polišenský, 1991). The Nazi oppression was severe. After liberation the country once again had a brief period of independence until the Soviet takeover of 1949. Except for the brief flurry of liberation known as the Prague Spring, that succumbed when the Soviet tanks rolled into Prague in 1968, Soviet totalitarianism ruled supreme until 1989.

Into this stormy world, Vacláv Havel and many of his literary and artistic compatriots were born in 1936. They grew up under the watchful and malevolent eyes, first of the Nazis and then of the Communists. This was the generation of intellectuals and artists who would end up using their talents, skills, and moral commitment to give birth to the Velvet Revolution of 1989. For the 20 years between 1968 and 1989, it was the artist who gave life to what would become a nonviolent revolution. For each artist or intellectual figure who was imprisoned or persecuted, thousands silently and secretly lent their support and were inspired by their example, for future acts of rebellion. In briefly tracing the course of this progression we can get a look at how individual trauma and sacrifice interacts with the group to produce long-term, massive results (Whipple, 1991).

In 1976, a rock group, *Plastic People of the Universe,* were arrested and imprisoned, giving rise to the first petition drives and dissident groups. Charter 77 was formed in 1977 as a way of putting group pressure on the government to adhere to its own laws and human rights obligations. The first three signatories to the charter were the philosopher Jan Patočka, the Prague Spring foreign minister Jiri Hájek, and the playwright Vacláv Havel. In March, Patočka died after police interrogation. In 1978, the Committee for the Defense of the Unjustly Prosecuted (VONS) was formed to focus on individual cases of unjust persecution by providing legal advice and the next year, large-scale police action against VONS signatories climaxed in the sentencing of six founding members to long prison terms. Throughout these years, *samizdat* (illegal) journals, novels, poetry, plays, articles, and essays circulated freely among the population, fueling the growing dissident movement. For most of these artists and authors, publication was not permitted and only through *samizdat,* could their works achieve an audience. Books were smuggled in from abroad; conspirator librarians would keep a special secret cache of forbidden books. As Kriseová (1993) has said, "Almost everything we in Havel's and my generation learned and studied in the fifties was against the will of the regime and in resistance to it. They were always forcing something on us, commanding us, shoving our noses into one thing, so that we would not see something else" (p.19).

Because of his political activities, Havel was publicly vilified, and there were fewer and fewer friends he could turn to as the years passed. Some immigrated, some were imprisoned, others were afraid. His plays were being produced abroad, but he could not have them produced at home. But he continued to write—letters, essays, and plays—through which he became arguably the most vocal moral voice of his generation. He was constantly under surveillance and even his friends and neighbors were watched. On one occasion, two teenage girls, the daughters of friends, were kidnapped by the police and interrogated about the Havels. Kriseová describes the constant state of terror that prevailed throughout this period: "the days of Stalinist terror were still vivid in people's memories. The irrational fear that someone could disappear and never be seen again, or could be executed without any crime ever having been proved against him, is buried some-where deep in our unconscious minds—the fear that anything could hap-pen, that those in power cannot be controlled" (p. 127). Dissidents instructed people in how to behave when their houses were searched and during interrogations. The State Security were more likely to physically abuse people who were young and less well-known and people from the underground were treated with particular cruelty.

Havel endured his first imprisonment in 1977 for 6 weeks. But it backfired when Charter 77, VONS, his captors' attempts to discredit him, and his imprisonment all served to fuel the resolve on the part of the public. "People straightened their backs; they were no longer so weighed down; they ceased to be tired; and they had the feeling that life was worth the effort and that it was possible to do something, even if it involved a known risk. Citizens recognized that they were not as powerless and the government not as all-powerful as they had assumed" (Kriseová, 1991, p. 137). Professors who had been purged from the institutions of higher learning began secretly teaching well-attended classes in apartments. In 1978, Havel wrote "The Power of the Powerless," which he dedicated to Jan Patočka, and sub-sequently he was put under house arrest (Havel, 1985). Neighbors were warned not to have any contact with him or with his family. In 1979 he was imprisoned again along with many of his colleagues. His letters to his wife became the basis of a book of letters from prison published as *Letters to Olga* (Havel, 1983). While in prison, Joe Papp, the New York director, had his plays produced in the United States, bringing increased awareness of the Czechoslovakian situation to the West. After a quick trial, Havel was sentenced to 4½ years of prison, charged with subversion of the republic. He consistently refused any opportunity to travel, although he knew he could get away, because the government would have used it as a way of getting rid of him and therefore silencing his message to the people. He knew he was much more a danger to the government in prison because in prison he was more conspicuous and more famous than before. They even offered to let him move to the United States but he refused.

In 1983, he was released from prison and suffered for a while with what has been called *postprison psychosis*, finding it difficult to adjust to life outside. But once again he threw himself into politics, although he knew he could easily wind up imprisoned again. He wrote several new plays, *Largo Desolato* and *Temptation.* He continued to write, to teach, to make public appear-ances, and to participate in the growing number of dissident activities. Once again, in 1989, he was imprisoned and sentenced to 9 months, but when 1,000 intellectuals signed a letter demanding his release, his sentence was reduced to 1 month. The people were beginning to reclaim their country; the Soviet era was drawing to an end and the nonviolent Velvet Revolution began. On November 21, 2 million people gathered on Wenceslas Square where Havel addressed them for the first time, threatening a general strike unless their demands for the release of political prisoners and freedom of the press were met. Demonstrations increased around the country and on November 27, four fifths of the total labor force stopped work in support of the people's groups, Civic Forum and Public Against Violence, insisting on full political pluralism and representation in a new government. By the end of December, Vacláv Havel was unanimously elected—after being released from prison only 2 months before—as the first President of the new republic.

Vacláv Havel and the Czech republic provide a convincing example of how an entire nation can transform trauma into freedom through the consistent exercise of strong, personal, moral authority. Havel (1990, 1997) is most notable as a leader for the unfortunately rare qualities of linking politics, art, spirituality, tolerance, compassion, humility, and morality.

Transformation Through Humor

It has been said that all great comedy is rooted in tragedy. According to the well-known drama critic, Walter Kerr (1967), "Comedy, it seems, is never the gaiety of things; it is the groan made gay. Laughter is not man's first impulse; he cries first. Comedy always comes second, late, after the fact and in spite of it or because of it … It seems likely that comedy comes *from* tragedy" (p. 19). Laughter is, of course, one of the most potent antidotes to fear. A combat soldier, recalling a night of running and laughing on the rooftops of Casablanca as German bombs exploded around him, explained, "We knew we might get killed any second but we didn't want to let that scare us, so we just laughed" (Jenkins, 1994, p. 49). For the adult victims of childhood trauma who we treat on our unit, a sense of humor has been one important prognostic feature that makes transformation more likely to occur.

Laughter is so potent because it is a complex biopsychosocial behavior that has diverse effects. It has powerful physical effects, increasing blood circulation, working the abdominal muscles, raising heart rate, and dropping blood pressure. It lowers stress hormones like cortisol and epinephrine and heightens the activity of the body's T-cells, antibodies, and natural killer cells (Angier, 1996a, 1996b). Nathanson's work on the mechanism of shame helps us understand why laughter is so vital for healing because the effect of comedy is deeply related to the way both individuals and groups manage shame. Traumatic experience is overwhelmingly accompanied by the arousal of every conceivable negative effect or emotion. The flashbacks that follow closely on the heels of the trauma, then trigger once again these powerful negative emotional memories, locking the survivor into cycles of terror, despair, and shame (Van der Kolk, McFarlane, & Welsaeth, 1996). It is humor, enjoyment, and joy that serve to diminish these chronic negative feelings. Nathanson (1992), quotes Buddy Hackett: "There are two kinds of pain. Physical and psychological. Any time I do something that releases you from that pain, I create laughter. The laughter is a feeling of relief, of release and relief … And that's the whole story of laughter. Release from pain. And that's the whole story of what I do" (p. 392).

But perhaps more importantly for our topic, laughter is an infectious social experience. As researcher Robert R. Provine, professor of neurobiology and psychology at the University of Maryland puts it, "Laughter is above all, a social act" (Angier, 1996a). Through shared laughter a group is able to synchronize its moods, increasing the possibility of synchronous actions. Noting the value of humor, Nathanson (1992) has said that "if love is the balm that heals the pain of individuals, comedy is solace, consolation and relief for entire tribes" (p. 379). Even when we laugh in moments of solitude we are interacting with an author of a book, watching a comedian on the screen, or remembering a shared experience of humor with another person.

Comic Clowns of the Native Americans. In traditional cultures, humor has always played an important group role in increasing group cohesion, reducing group tensions, and resolving intra- and intergroup conflict. In studies of Native American culture, humor is considered integral for existence. Complex customs utilizing humor as a central element can be seen in most cultures, as in the vital role of the clowns in the ritual behavior of the Hopi tsuklalwa and the Contraries or Heyhokas of the Plains Indians (Brown, 1985; Loftin, 1991). "The place of sacred clowns in Native American cultures has been well documented. These clowns and masked dancers are often closely connected to healing and to the most awesome power of the universe, even though their antics are the source of a great deal of laughter" (Bruchac, 1987, p. 28). Among the Iroquois, the strike-pole dance afforded an opportunity for members of the tribe to say things to each other through jokes and teasing, that could otherwise be perceived as hurtful or aggressive. When a man would rise, he would strike the pole, then relate a story about one of his fellow clansmen. When everyone was done laughing, he would give a small present to the butt of the joke to soothe over any bad feelings.

Laughter in Lithuania. The use of humor among oppressed and traumatized groups is well established. Jewish humor, African-American humor, and feminist humor are all rooted in a willful desire to overcome the powerlessness of their respective positions. As Ron Jenkins (1994) put it, in his marvelous book *Subversive Laughter,* "In a world fraught with danger and despair, comedy is a survival tactic, and laughter is an act of faith" (p. 1). From Aristophanes' comedies mocking the corrupt dictators of his time, to Richard Pryor's attacks on racism, humor has always played an important role in the wider sociopolitical context. Likewise, the powerful fear and often try to control the comedians—during the Nazi era, comedians were kept on the Gestapo's shortest leash (Angier, 1996a).

Eastern Europeans, while still engaged in the struggle against Soviet rule, provided excellent examples of the group use of humor to transform trauma into freedom. Landisberger was the president of the republic of Lithuania during these critical years. He saw that nonviolent resistance to military power required the use of symbolic weapons like art, music, and theatrical representations. Where the leader went, the people followed. Ridiculing their enemy, the Soviet state, became a group effort through jokes, comedic performances, and public performance art. Drawing on a long history of political satire that dated back at least a century, the Lithuanian people declared their independence through laughter, inspiring a subversive attitude toward Soviet authority:

> Humor provided Lithuanians with a psychological weapon for reversing the terror tactics employed for decades by the KGB. People who had been paralyzed by the fear of unspecified reprisals were liberated by the exhilarating force of their own laughter. The tyranny of the totalitarian state was subverted by the teasing suggestion of its comical vulnerability … The public's belief in the fallibility of the once invincible Communist monolith was nurtured by years of laughing at its flaws. (Jenkins, 1994, p. 75)

On noticing this same comic sense among his countrymen, Vaclav Havel, playwright, jailed dissident, and then President of the Czech Republic said, "It seems that in our central European context what is most earnest has a way of blending in a particularly tense manner with what is most comic. It seems that it is precisely the dimension of distance, of rising above oneself and making light of oneself, which lends to our concerns and actions precisely the right amount of shattering seriousness" (Vladislav, 1986, p. 181).

Transformation Through Artistic Creation

I suspect a reasonably strong case can be made that our uniquely human capacity to create works of literature, art, drama, and dance is an evolutionary adaptation to help a verbal, curious, and remembering primate transform overwhelming experience into a form of expression that can be simultaneously verbal and nonverbal, private and shared (Bloom, 1995). Art is fundamentally transformative in its very essence. Out of simple materials, meaning is born.

The examples of artistic creativity inspired by both individual and group traumatic circumstances are seemingly endless. Fragments of *The Plague* by Camus were published as an underground testimony for the French Resistance in Occupied France (Felman, 1992). Dostoevsky was arrested and condemned to death, and his sentence was commuted only during the middle of an execution ceremony as he stood before a firing squad—*Notes From the House of the Dead* and *Notes From the Underground* follow as "testimony to a trauma" (Felman, 1992). In 1985, in Poet's Corner, Westminster Abbey, a memorial was unveiled to the 16 poets of World War I, among them Rupert Brooks, Robert Graves, Wilfred Owen, and Siegfried Sassoon. Inscribed on the memorial are the words of Owen, "My subject is War, and the pity of War. The Poetry is in the pity" (Balcon, 1985, p. x). Magritte's mother committed suicide by drowning in 1912 when the artist was only 14. As the story goes, Magritte and his brother had gone to look for their mother and found her body practically naked but for a wet night-dress that was over her head and sticking to her skin (Meuris,1994). He left us a legacy of haunting pictures, many of them containing mysterious figures some of whose heads are covered in diaphonous cloth, others in which feminine objects stand before a storm-tossed sea, another of a woman's lower torso with a fish's head. Picasso painted Guernica in 1937 and named it after the small Basque town that had been destroyed by Hitler's bombers. In doing so he said, "One does not paint in order to decorate apartments. Painting is an instrument of offensive and defensive war against the enemy" (Picasso, 1976). Beethoven, even in his deafness, gave us the musical expression of transformation as in the *Fifth Symphony* and the *Ninth Symphony* which take us musically from storm and stress to triumph. Joan Baez moved us in song through the pain of Tiananmen Square to the triumph of the lone man standing before the tanks and leads us to a hope for the future in her song, *China*. Samuel Beckett served in the French Resistance until his group was arrested by the Gestapo and he was forced to go into hiding. Later he served in the Irish Red Cross at a military hospital in France. Out of all this came some of the most important works of 20th century drama, including the

unforgettable *Waiting For Godot* (Beckett, 1976). Judy Chicago used painting, photography, tapestry, stained glass, and words, and continues the
attempt of many artists for the last half century to make some sense, some
transformation out of the Holocaust (Chicago, 1993). *Shoah, Schindler's List,*
and *Apocalypse Now* are all examples of the power of film to bear witness to
traumatic events, a witness in which we as the audience all participate. Here
are two examples of art in action, creativity waged against the forces of
oppression, destitution, and loss.

Philadelphia, the Painted City.   In 1983, 26 teenage graffiti artists
were paid $3.25 an hour to paint the North Philadelphia Amtrak station as
part of an experimental program to turn ugly urban buildings and walls into
artwork and to turn law-breaking wall-writers into artists (Sutton, 1983).
This project, founded by Tim Spencer, who was 26 years old at the time,
became known as the Anti-Graffiti Network, a nonprofit civic organization.
Spencer had become involved in the idea when he saw a neighbor almost
use a gun against a neighborhood youngster caught writing graffiti (Kaufman, 1984). Beginning in one area of the city, the project gained the support
of the Mayor and City Council and became a city-wide agency. Support
came as well from businesses who donated materials and the media who
gave the Network wide coverage.

Huge, colorful, and sometime inspired murals began to emerge around
the city, many of them in major public areas. The Reading Terminal financed
murals on their buildings (Cooke, 1984). Pictures appeared on bridge
abutments, subway cars, schoolyard walls, and vacant buildings. Between
1983 and 1986, the Anti-Graffitti Network produced 375 murals around
the city, turning graffiti buffs into practiced artists, mentored by trained
professionals, some of whom had been to art school and others who had
taught art (Sutton, 1987). By 1987, the program had become a $2.2 million
city program and was hiring 700 inner-city youths each summer to paint
murals, remove graffiti, and clean vacant lots (Cooke, 1987). Large volunteer efforts were started to clean graffiti from existing walls. In 1988 the
program enlisted 132 graffiti writers into its amnesty program for those who
admitted they had defaced a property and pledged not to do it again. They
recruited 1,156 youths to volunteer for cleanups of 4,227 residences, 700
businesses, 17 public schools, and 335 vacant lots, while painting 144 murals
on buildings around the city (King, 1989). By 1989, over 400 cleanup drives
had been organized and more than 7,000 buildings were cleaned (Wood,
1989). Teens arrested for writing graffiti were assigned to the program for
community service, given 50 to 300 hours of "scrub time" (Pavlik, 1989).
The Anti-Graffiti Network sponsored art auctions of works done by the

youths. In 1990, a mural was done in one of the high-violence areas of the city to commemorate the violent deaths of 34 children in the previous 18 months (Colimore, 1990). In 1991, the Anti-Graffiti Network received 1 of 10 Innovation Awards presented by the Ford Foundation and Harvard University. By that time, the program had painted 1,093 murals and removed graffiti from about 3,500 properties a year, and 9,000 youths had volunteered in the program (Copeland, 1991). In 1992, the Network painted another memorial dedicated to 35 more children who died of violence and began planning another for 42 other children. These memorials served as opportunities for bereaved parents to gather together and mourn the deaths of their children (Rosenberg, 1992). During the 1980s, the homicide rate for Black teenagers more than doubled in Philadelphia. These memorial murals became a symbol of resistance in this undeclared domestic war (McCoy, 1993).

At this point, the future of the Anti-Graffiti Network is very much in doubt. Funding has been cut and in 1996, the founder, Timothy Spencer died after a prolonged illness. Graffiti remains a problem for the city of Philadelphia. Nonetheless, for the 13 years that the program existed, thousands of children were encouraged to transform the trauma of their violent urban experience into artistic creativity. Thousands of volunteers became involved in community action around this creative effort and the lives of all Philadelphians have been enriched by the explosion of public art that still surrounds the city.

Theatre of the Oppressed.   The year 1994 marked the 20th anniversary of the publication of Augusto Boal's *Theatre of the Oppressed.* Boal is a Brazilian theater artist who understands, from first-hand experience, the vital importance of the role drama plays in transforming trauma. In his work, Boal has sought ways of combining theater, therapy, politics and art in the service of this transformation. From 1956–1971, Boal directed the Arena Theatre in São Paolo where he and his collaborators created a theater founded on local experience. Brazil was taken over by a military coup in 1964 and an even more repressive regime began in 1968. Boal was widely known and politically active, developing "Forum Theatre" among the peasants and workers, a format that gave spectators the chance to discover their own solutions to collective problems. Working in direct opposition to the military regime, Boal was arrested in 1971, jailed, and tortured. After 3 months he was released and told that he would be killed if he continued with his theater activities. He fled to Argentina where he lived until 1976. There he developed "Image Theatre" in which physical expression is favored over the spoken word and the human body is used as a tool to transform physical sensation into communicable language.

Argentina, however, became increasingly repressive, so he devised "Invisible Theatre" as a way to continue stimulating debate on current political issues. Staged in public spaces and acting as if it were real life, actors uncovered politically hot issues of social injustice and encouraged impassioned discussions on the street. In 1976, Boal escaped to Europe where, in Paris, he developed "Theatre of the Oppressed" (Boal, 1985; Schutzman & Cohen-Cruz, 1994). In Europe he encountered other forms of oppression besides political oppression, and began to see that all forms of oppression have similar roots. His work has been related to the psychodrama and sociodrama of Moreno (1953) and his colleagues. Both worked to help people overcome oppression and liberate themselves as individuals and as a group (Feldhendler, 1994). Their vision of the role of artistic creativity in bringing about change is similar, what Boal (1995) calls "the superposition of fields: the theatrical and the therapeutic" (p. 38).

In 1986, Boal was invited to return to Brazil after a change in government and there he founded a Rio de Janeiro Center of Theatre of the Oppressed. He remains in Brazil, is President of the Centre of Theatre of the Oppressed in Rio de Janeiro and Paris, travels extensively giving workshops, and furthers development of his ideas. He is now a Member of Parliament for Rio de Janeiro and was awarded the UNESCO Pablo Picasso Medal in 1994.

The Theatre of the Oppressed has two fundamental and linked goals: to help the spectator/actor (spect–actor) transform himself or herself into a protagonist of the dramatic action and rehearse alternatives for any situation so that he or she is then able to extrapolate into his real life the changed actions practiced in the theater (Boal, 1995). He believes that "every oppressed person is a subjugated subversive" (p. 42) and that the transformation that occurs to the spect-actor on stage also can transform the audience through what he calls the process of "osmosis." The stage can try to transform the audience and the audience can also transform anything. "If the oppressed artist is able to create an autonomous world of images of his own reality, and to enact his liberation in the reality of these images, he will then extrapolate into his own life all that he has accomplished in the fiction. The scene, the stage, becomes the rehearsal space for real life (p. 44).

CONCLUSION

Herman (1992) has spoken eloquently about recovery from traumatic experiences, pointing out that "While there is no way to compensate for an atrocity, there is a way to transcend it, by making it a gift to others. The trauma is redeemed only when it becomes the source of a survivor mission"

(p. 38). This chapter has illustrated the many ways that trauma can be transformed in a manner that goes far beyond the individual, serving as a source of major dynamic change within a group and within an entire society. But such a transformation can only occur within a political climate that permits such a discourse. Herman has demonstrated the intimate relationship between the political climate and the recognition of abuse. McFarlane (1995) has discussed how trauma in warfare could not even be recognized until Vietnam because of torn allegiances between military and medical objectives. Summerfield (1995) has pointed out the criticism of the medical models of PSTD arising in oppressive societies, notably in Latin America, where working with victims of trauma is inevitably human rights work as well. As he has noted, symptoms of trauma are an indictment of the social contexts in which they occurred.

One of the dangers of writing about the "transformation" of trauma is that the reader can be led to believe that experiencing trauma is actually of positive benefit because it brings about such positive change. It must be said that the examples that illustrate this chapter are points of light in an otherwise dismal landscape of terror and horror. However, this is an exciting and largely unexplored area. In this chapter I have only touched on various ideas and examples, hopefully opening up a wider discourse on the subject. I say "hopefully" because these are all vital questions at the present historical moment. We know that unmetabolized, untransformed trauma interferes with healthy adaptation at an individual level. The individual adapts to a hostile environment and then proceeds to recreate a similar environment in order to make the best use of these adaptations. If groups—communities and even nations—respond in a similar way, then we are dealing with a dangerous and volatile situation (Gamboa-Eastman, 1993). The 20th century, the century of "megadeath," has produced and continues to produce an extraordinarily high level of traumatic experience for a vast proportion of the world's population (Brzezinski, 1993). As we are seeing in our own inner cities, individual forms of intervention and treatment cannot turn back the tide of post traumatic destruction. As long as we still had the luxury of believing that psychopathology originated in individual dysfunction, our models of intervention were justified. But now, as we see whole populations traumatized by war, famine, plague, disaster, and political oppression, our individualistic arguments are no longer persuasive. We must find larger scale, group forms of intervention to escalate the rate of transformation or the balance may very well shift further in the direction of global self-destruction.

It is vital that we learn from these group forms of social transformation in the service of prevention. As I write these words, the political climate of my own country appears to be moving further away from, not toward, an atmosphere that promotes such transformation. We must follow the example of the political leaders, artists, physicians, clergymen, scientists, survivors, and just plain common folk who people the pages of this chapter and this book, and listen closely to the lessons they have learned. Each of our lives is the stage on which we strut, for good or for ill, but even on the stage, life is never a monologue. We are all, in some way, survivors, and we all have a social responsibility to the whole. Boal (1995) may have the closing words:

> Thus, within the limits of the scene and the moment, the free exercise of all asocial tendencies, unacceptable desires, forbidden behaviors and unhealthy feelings is allowed. On stage, all is permissible, nothing is forbidden. The demons and saints which inhabit the person of the actor are completely free to blossom, to experience the orgasm of the show, to pass from potential into act. In a mimetic and emphatic fashion, the same thing happens with the analogous demons and saints which are awakened in the hearts of the spectators. Always in the hope that, after it is all over, they will be tired out and will go back to sleep. In the hope that, in this holy and diabolic ball, the saints and demons of the actors and audience will return, exhausted, to the unconscious darkness of the person, restoring the health and equilibrium of the personalities, which will then be able, without fear, to reintegrate their lives into society. (p. 38)

REFERENCES

Abrahamsen, S. (1987). The rescue of Denmark's Jews. In L. Goldberger (Ed), *The rescue of the Danish Jews: Moral courage under stress* (pp. 3–12). New York: New York University Press.

Alcoholics Anonymous. (1996). http://www.alcoholics-anonymous.org/enghp.html

Almond, R. (1974). *The healing community*. New York: Jason Aronson.

Angier, N. (1996a, February 27). Laughs are rhythmic bursts of social glue. *New York Times*, p. C1.

Angier, N. (1996b, February 27). Laughter has a myriad of benefits. *New York Times*, p. C1.

Balcon, J. (Ed.). (1985). *The pity of war: Poems of the first world war*. London: Shepheard-Walwyn.

Beckett, S. (1976). *Encyclopedia Britannica Macropaedia*, (Vol. 2, pp. 788–790). Chicago: Encyclopedia Britannica.

Bills, L. J., & Bloom, S. L. (in press). From chaos to sanctuary: Trauma-based treatment for women in a state hospital system. In B. L. Levin, A. K. Blanch, & A. Jennings, (Eds.). *Women's mental health services: A public health perspective*. Thousand Oaks, CA: Sage.

Bloom, S. L. (1994). The sanctuary model: Developing generic inpatient programs for the treatment of psychological trauma. In M. B. Williams & J. F. Sommer (Eds.), *Handbook of post-traumatic therapy: A practical guide to intervention, treatment, and research* (pp. 474–491). New York: Greenwood Publishing.

Bloom, S. L. (1995). *Bridging the black hole of trauma: Victims, artists, and society.* Unpublished manuscript.

Bloom, S. L. (1996). Every time history repeats itself the price goes up: The social reenactment of trauma. *Journal of Sexual Addiction and Compulsivity,* 3(3), 161–194.

Bloom, S. L. (1997). *Creating sanctuary: Toward the evolution of sane societies.* New York: Routledge.

Bloom, S. L., & Reichert, M. (in press). *Bearing witness: Trauma and social responsibility.* Binghamton, NY: Haworth Press.

Boal, A. (1985). *Theatre of the oppressed.* New York: Theatre Communications Group.

Boal, A. (1995). *The rainbow of desire. The Boal method of theatre and therapy.* New York: Routledge.

Bockoven, J. S. (1963). *Moral treatment in American psychiatry.* New York: Springer.

Boraine, A. (1996, July). *Alternatives and adjuncts to criminal prosecutions.* Speech presented at Justice in Cataclysm: Criminal Tribunals in the Wake of Mass Violence, Brussels, Belgium. http://www.truth.org.za/speech01.htm

Brown, J. E. (1985). The wisdom of the contrary: A conversation with Joseph Epes Brown. *Parabola,* 4(1), 54–65.

Bruchac, J. (1987). Striking the pole: American Indian humor. *Parabola,* 12(4), 22–29.

Brzezinski, Z. (1993). *Out of control: Global turmoil on the eve of the 21st century.* New York: Scribner's.

Busfield, J. (1986) *Managing madness: Changing ideas and practice.* London: Unwin Hyman

Chicago, J. (1993). *Holocaust project: From darkness into light.* New York: Viking.

Cohen, B. D., Fidler, J. W., & Etting, M. F. (1995). Introduction: From group process to political dynamics. In M. F. Ettin, J. W. Fidler, & B. D. Cohen (Eds.), *Group process and political dynamics* (pp. 1–22). Madison, CT: International Universities Press.

Colby A., & Damon, W. (1993). The uniting of self and morality in the development of extraordinary moral commitment. In G. C. Noam & T. E. Wren (Eds.), *The moral self* (pp. 149–174). Cambridge, MA: The MIT Press.

Colimore, E. (1990, August 15). In S. Phila., a mural born of many young victims. *Philadelphia Inquirer,* p. B05.

Cooke, R. (1984, March 6). A new medium—ex-graffiti writers turn to mural painting. *Philadelphia Inquirer,* p. B01.

Cooke, R. (1987, November 5). Audit finds improvement in anti-graffiti agency. *Philadelphia Inquirer,* p. B07.

Copeland, L. (1991, September 26). Anti-graffiti network wins grant. *Philadelphia Inquirer,* p. B04.

DeMause, L. (1982). *Foundations of psychohistory.* New York: Creative Roots.

Dwyer, E. (1987). *Homes for the mad.* New Brunswick, NJ: Rutgers University Press.

Ettin, M. F. (1992). *Foundations and applications of group psychotherapy: A sphere of influence.* Boston: Allyn & Bacon.

Ettin, M. R. (1993). Links between group process and social, political, and cultural issues. In H. I. Kaplan & B. J. Sadock (Eds.), *Comprehensive group psychotherapy* (pp. 699–716). Baltimore: Williams & Wilkins.

Feldhendler, D. (1994). Augusto Boal and Jacob L. Moreno: Theatre and therapy. In M. Schutzman & J. Cohen-Cruz (Eds.), *Playing Boal: Theatre, therapy, activism* (pp. 87–109). New York: Routledge.

Felman, S. (1992). Education and crisis, or the vicissitudes of teaching. In S. Felman & D. Laub (Eds.), *Testimony: Crises of witnessing in literature, psychoanalysis and history*. New York: Routledge.

Flender, H. (1963). *Rescue in Denmark*. New York: Holocaust Library.

Fogelman, E. (1994). *Conscience and courage: Rescuers of Jews during the Holocaust*. New York: Anchor Books.

Forsyth, D. R. (1990). *Group dynamics, second edition*. Pacific Grove: CA: Brooks/Cole.

Friedman, M. (1996, March). *Truth and memory in South Africa*. Presented at Psychological Trauma Conference, Harvard University School of Medicine, Boston.

Gamboa-Eastman, S. (1993). *After Chernobyl: Community trauma and community healing*. San Francisco, CA: Stephen Gamboa-Eastman.

Goldberger, L. (1987). Explaining the rescue of the Danish Jews. In L. Goldberger (Ed.), *The rescue of the Danish Jews: Moral courage under stress* (pp. 197–214). New York: New York University Press.

The grandchildren of Argentina. (1985, November). *Discover*, p. 12.

Grob, G. N. (1994). *The mad among us: A history of the care of America's mentally ill*. New York: The Free Press.

Hallie, P. (1994). *Lest innocent blood be shed: The story of the village of Le Chambon and how goodness happened there*. New York: Harper Perennial.

Havel, V. (1983). *Letters to Olga: June 1979–September 1982*. New York: Henry Holt & Company.

Havel, V. (1985). The power of the powerless. In J. Keane (Ed.), The power of the powerless: Citizens against the state in central-eastern Europe (pp. 23–96). Armonk, NY: M. E. Sharpe.

Havel, V. (1990). *Disturbing the peace: Conversations with Karel Hvizdala*. New York: Alfred A. Knopf.

Havel, V. (1997). The art of the impossible: Politics as morality in practice. New York: Alfred A. Knopf.

Herman, J. L. (1992). *Trauma and recovery*. New York: Basic Books.

Hewstone, M., Stroebe, W., Codol, J., & Stephenson, G. M. (1989). *Introduction to social psychology*. Oxford, England: Basil Blackwell LTD.

International Rescue Committee. (1996). www.intrescom.org.

Jenkins, R. (1994). *Subversive laughter: The liberating power of comedy*. New York: The Free Press.

Jones, M. (1953). *The therapeutic community: A new treatment method in psychiatry*. New York: Basic Books.

Kaufman, M. (1984, January 2). Cleaning up the writing on the wall. *Philadelphia Inquirer*, p. B1.

Kerr, W. (1967). *Tragedy and comedy*. New York: Simon & Schuster.

King, L. (1989, September 20). The scrawls on city walls. *Philadelphia Inquirer*, p. N04.

Kriseová, E. (1993). *Vacláv Havel: The authorized biography*. New York: St. Martin's Press.

Leeman, C. P., & Autio, S. (1978). Milieu therapy: The need for individualization. *Psychotherapy and Psychosomatics, 29*, 84–92.

Lex, B. (1979). The neurobiology of ritual traunce. In E. G. D'Aquili, C. D. Laughlin, Jr., & J. McManus (Eds.), *The spectrum of ritual: A biogenetic structural analysis* (pp. 117–151). New York: Columbia University Press.

Lifton, R. J., & Mitchell, G. (1995). *Hiroshima in America: Fifty years of denial*. New York: Grosset/Putnam.

Loftin, J. D. (1991). *Religion and Hopi life in the twentieth century*. Bloomington: Indiana University Press.

McCoy, C. (1993, July 1). Recalling victims of violence: They were children who died on the streets. *Philadelphia Inquirer*, p. B01.

McDougall, W. (1920). *The group mind*. London: Cambridge University Press.

McFarlane, A. C. (1995). The severity of the trauma: Issues about its role in posttraumatic stress disorder. In R. K. Kleber, C. R. Figley, & B. P. R. Gersons (Eds.), *Beyond trauma: Cultural and societal dynamics* (pp. 31–54). New York: Plenum.

McGovern, C. M. (1985). *The masters of madness: Social origins of the American psychiatric profession*. Hanover, NH: University Press of New England.

Meuris, J. (1994). *René Magritte*. Germany: Benedikt Taschen.

Moreno, J. L. (1953). *Who shall survive?: Foundations of sociometry, group psychotherapy and sociodrama*. Beacon, NY: Beacon House.

Mothers Against Drunk Driving. (1996). MADD HomePage. www.lifetimetv.com/parenting/MADD.

Narcotics Anonymous. (1996). http://www.netwizards.net/recovery/na/

Nathanson, D. (1992). *Shame and pride*. New York: Norton Books.

Noam, G. C. (1993). "Normative vulnerabilities" of self and their transformations in moral action. In G. C. Noam & T. E. Wren (Eds.), *The moral self* (pp. 209–238). Cambridge, MA: MIT Press.

Omar, D. (1996). *Introduction by the Minister of Justice, Mr. Dullah Omar*. Truth Commission Web Site.www.truth.org.za.

Ortiz, A. D. (1995, September). The Mothers of the Plaza de Mayo. *UNESCO Courier*, p. 22–24.

Overeaters Anonymous. (1996). www.netwizards.net/recovery/oa.html

Packard, E. P. W. (1882). *Modern persecution or married woman's liabilities*. Hartford: Case, Lockwood & Brainard.

Packard, E. P. W. (1868). *The prisoner's hidden life or insane asylums unveiled*. Chicago: A. B. Case.

Pavlik, P. (1989, June 21). Graffiti writers get lesson in completing sentences. *Philadelphia Inquirer*, p. N14.

Picasso, P. (1976). *Encyclopedia Brittanica, Macropaedia*, (Vol. 14, pp. 440–444). Chicago: Encyclopedia Brittanica.

Polišenský, J. V. (1991). *History of Czechoslovakia in outline*. Prague: Bohemia International.

Radcliffe, S. A., & Westwood, S. (Eds.). (1993). *Viva: Women and popular protest in Latin America*. New York: Routledge.

Rapoport, R. N. (1960). *Community as doctor*. Springfield, IL: Thomas.

Rosenberg, A. (1992, October 30). A mural to 35 killed in their youth. *Philadelphia Inquirer*, p. B01.

Rosenberg, T. (1995). *The haunted land: Facing Europe's ghosts after communism*. New York: Vintage Books.

Rothman, D. J. (1980). *Conscience and convenience*. Glenview, IL: Scott, Foresman & Company.

Sapinsley, B. (1991). *The private war of Mrs. Packard*. New York: Paragon House.

Scheidlinger, S. (1993). History of group psychotherapy. In H. I. Kaplan & B. J. Sadock, (Eds.), *Comprehensive group psychotherapy* (pp. 2–9). Baltimore: Williams & Wilkins.

Schutzman, M., & Cohen-Cruz, J. (1994). Introduction. In M. Schutzman & J. Cohen-Cruz (Eds.), *Playing Boal: Theatre, therapy, activism* (pp. 1–16). New York: Routledge.

Sexual Compulsives Anonymous. (1996). www.sca-recovery.org/

Shay, J. (1995, November). *The Greek tragic theater and a contemporary theater of witness*. Presentation at the XI Annual Meeting of The Treatment of Trauma: Advances and Challenges, International Society for Traumatic Stress Studies. Boston, MA.

Staub, E. (1989). *The roots of evil: The origins of genocide and other group violence.* Cambridge, MA: Cambridge University Press.

Summerfield, D. (1995). Addressing human response to war and atrocity: Major challenges in research and practices and the limitations of western psychiatric models. In R. K. Kleber, C. R. Figley, & B. P. R. Gersons (Eds.), *Beyond trauma: Cultural and societal dynamics* (pp. 17–30). New York: Plenum.

Sutton, W. (1983, July 24). Turning "graffitists" into artists. *Philadelphia Inquirer*, p. B01.

Sutton, W. (1987, August 4). Murals soar from squad's creative wing. *Philadelphia Inquirer*, p. B01.

Tucker, G., & Maxmen, J. (1973). The practice of hospital psychiatry: A formulation. *American Journal of Psychiatry, 130,* 887–891.

Ullman, M. (1969). A unifying concept linking therapeutic and community process. In W. Gray, F. J. Duhl, & N. D. Rizzo (Eds.), *General systems theory and psychiatry (pp. 253–266).* Boston: Little Brown.

Van der Hart, O. (1983). *Rituals in psychotherapy: Transition and continuity.* New York: Irvington Publishers.

Van der Kolk, B. A., McFarlane, A. C., & Weisaeth, L. (Eds.). (1996). *Traumatic stress: The effects of overwhelming experience on mind, body, and society.* New York: Guilford.

Vladislav, J. (1986). An anatomy of reticence. In *Vaclav Havel: Living in truth* (pp. 164–195). London: Faber & Faber.

Wallis, J. (1994). *The soul of politics.* New York: The New Press.

Wells, L., Jr. (1985). The group-as-a-whole perspective and its theoretical roots. In A. D. Colman & M. H. Geller (Eds.), *Group relations reader 2* (pp. 109–126). Washington, DC: The A. K. Rice Institute.

What international experience shows. (1996). At Truth and Reconciliation web site. http://www.truth.org.za/back/bill.htm.

Whipple, T. D. (Ed). (1991). *After the Velvet Revolution: Vaclav Havel and the new leaders of Czechoslovakia speak out.* New York: Freedom House.

Wilmer, H. A. (1958). *Social psychiatry in action: A therapeutic community.* Springfield, IL: Thomas.

Winkler, A. M. (1993). *Life under a cloud: American anxiety about the atom.* New York: Oxford University Press.

Wood, S. (1989, February 26). Wall-to-wall combat over graffiti gears up. *Philadelphia Inquirer*, p. N06.

9

Posttraumatic Growth: Future Directions

Lawrence G. Calhoun
Richard G. Tedeschi
University of North Carolina at Charlotte

To paraphrase the ancient sage, the more we know about posttraumatic growth (PTG), the more we know that we do not know very much. This volume demonstrates, however, that there are a variety of aspects about which we have some reliable data. It is clear that individuals who have faced a wide array of negative life challenges report that their struggle with those difficulties have, paradoxically, had positive effects on their lives. It is the personal struggle precipitated by the environmental demands, rather than the events themselves, that sets into motion the cluster of changes that we call posttraumatic growth.

There is consistent evidence, from earlier anecdotal sources, from studies investigating other processes, and more recent investigations of the phenomenon itself, that individuals claim a variety of positive changes resulting from their encounter with difficult situations. Avenues for measuring PTG in systematic and quantitative ways have and are being developed, making possible the identification of variables that may be related to PTG. Although the greater proportion of the work in this area has been with adults, an equivalent process may also occur at earlier stages of development. In the individual differences domain a variety of possible correlates have been identified, although the sparseness of the literature, and occasional contradictory findings, make generalizations about most variables difficult to surmise. The phenomenon is not confined to specific events and it is possible that similar kinds of outcomes may occur with social units well beyond the individual level. And, the findings on positive changes coming from the kinds of negative events that can cause high levels of psychological distress have significant implications for the practicing clinician. In this chapter, we integrate what has been covered by other contributors to this volume into an evolving model of PTG, and describe the many issues that remain open for further inquiry.

UNRESOLVED ISSUES AND FUTURE DIRECTIONS FOR RESEARCH

Characteristics of Events

A key issue for this area of inquiry is the delineation of the characteristics of events or situations that make them "traumatic." Although there is extensive literature on the delineation of the qualities of events that make them a threat to psychological adjustment and well-being, a similar identification still remains to be done in the area of PTG. Events that are sudden, unexpected, perceived as undesirable and uncontrollable, out of the ordinary, and threatening to one's life and general well-being can be regarded as traumatic (McCann & Pearlman, 1990; Tennen & Affleck, 1990).

In the context of highly stressful events that lay the groundwork for the possibility of subsequent growth, a key element may be the event's ability successfully to "shake the foundations" of the individual's assumptive world. The events must be *seismic*, like an earthquake, in their ability to produce in the individual a severe shaking of the foundations of his or her understanding of the world, and in some instances the shattering (Janoff-Bulman, 1992) of the elemental components of the individual's worldview. A minimum threshold may need to be catastrophically crossed before events can have sufficient seismic power to produce the level of subjective disruption that is required for PTG to be possible. Does the amount of PTG increase proportionally with the stressfulness of an event, or is growth set in motion when a catastrophic change in the individual's worldview is precipitated when the seismic power of the event reaches a certain threshold? It may also be the case that the possibility for growth requires the crossing of a minimal threshold of disruption, but that once the event has reached the minimal seismic threshold, subsequent growth may covary with the degree of stressfulness of the event.

PTG and Mental Health

A closely connected issue is the degree to which PTG is related to psychological well-being on the one hand, and psychological distress on the other. The evidence so far is both limited and inconsistent (Edmonds & Hooker, 1992; Joseph, Williams, & Yule, 1993; McMillen, Zuravin, & Rideout, 1995; Park, chap. 7, this volume). It may be possible that PTG is independent of psychological well-being or adjustment. Or if not independent, then growth may be differentially related to well-being, a positive constellation of elements (feeling good), and to psychological distress, a negative constellation of elements (feeling bad). For example, whereas self-esteem has been found to be positively correlated with growth (McMillen et al., 1995), distress also has been found to be positively correlated with growth (Edmonds & Hooker, 1992).

A clear indication from the available data (Park, chap. 7, this volume), however, is that the occurrence of growth may not necessarily covary with a reduction of psychological distress or with an increase in psychological well-being. Growth may well be more likely to occur as a result of a process that begins with the shaking of the foundations of the individual's assumptive world, and a concomitant increase in psychological pain and distress. There is some evidence in the clinical literature, for example, (Edmonds & Hooker, 1992; Yalom & Lieberman, 1991), that some degree of distress may be necessary, or at least reliably predictive of higher levels of growth. A useful avenue for further work in this area, then, is the investigation of the ways in which growth is related to "mental health." What the data currently seem to suggest is that growth will not necessarily decrease pain or increase happiness, but on the contrary, significant growth may only occur when it is preceded by, or when it occurs together with significant amounts of subjective distress. The timing as well as the level of distress may be an important variable. For example, early extreme distress, together with significant relief and enduring lower levels of distress, may promote PTG.

Another important consideration in identifying the relationships between growth and mental health may be the multidimensional character of PTG. Both the content analysis of the types of changes reported, and some of the factor analytic evidence (Cohen, Hettler, & Pane, chap. 2, this volume; Tedeschi & Calhoun, 1995, 1996) indicate that the growth individuals report in their struggle with trauma occurs in more than a single domain. As discussed previously in this volume (Tedeschi, Park, & Calhoun, chap. 1) and elsewhere (Tedeschi & Calhoun, 1995), three possible areas of growth have been identified: changes in self, changes in philosophy of life and spiritual/existential beliefs, and changes in relationships with others.

The distinction of different types of growth may be particularly relevant to the examination of the relationship between growth on the one hand, and mental health variables on the other.

It is possible that an individual can experience growth in some areas, negative changes in others, and that different dimensions of growth may be differentially related to well-being and distress. Potential variations in these relationships can raise conceptual and theoretical issues about what constitutes "adjustment," "well-being," and "mental health." How should we conceptualize the state of an individual, for example, who is terminally ill, who is deeply saddened and distressed by his imminent "departure" from his friends and family, but who has recently experienced a surge of spiritual enlightenment and a sense of closure in interpersonal relationships, and whose family reports he has never been "so close" to them? Or consider an even more ambiguous set of circumstances, where a person whose companion has recently died, who reports extreme yearning, sadness, fatigue, and depression, but who also indicates that she has never seen so clearly the purpose and meaning of her life?

PTG in Spiritual and Religious Life

It is not coincidental that these illustrations involve clear existential and spiritual themes. The available data clearly indicate that a significant element of PTG can involve, for many persons, an increase in the importance of existential, spiritual, and religious matters. Although there has presumably been a recent surge in the interest and importance behavioral scientists and practicing clinicians have regarding the role of religion and spirituality in human behavior (Shafranske & Malony, 1996), this is an arena in which scientists, scholars, and to some degree clinicians, are distinctly uncomfortable. Given the inherently subjective nature of some of the domains of PTG, an important area of additional work is the determination of what types of measures of growth are to be considered valid indicants of all facets of the construct.

Validity Issues in PTG

The typical, and not unreasonable, expectation of scientific psychology has been to require that constructs be validated with empirically observable referents. This has traditionally meant that variations in quantities of the hypothesized construct must be observed to "produce" measurable variations in behavior. Given the psychometrically and anecdotally identified dimensions of PTG, it may be a difficult, if not impossible, challenge to identify satisfactory external referents at least for some of the proposed dimensions. Although for some aspects of PTG, such as changes in relationships, clear external referents and validational criteria can be identified, for other aspects such external criteria are not readily identifiable.

A significant element in the positive change that individuals experience in the wake of trauma, is a transformation of their understanding of themselves, of their understanding of the priorities of life, and of their place in the universe. These are areas that are viewed by some persons as religious, and more generally as existential issues. For some persons, the experience of growth amounts to what might described as a conversion experience, whether religious or secular in nature, in which one's understanding of the meaning of life undergoes a radical transformation, at least from the perspective of the individual who is experiencing it.

How can such experiences be validated by external criteria? And, if we are to attempt to "validate" those perceptions and experiences, by what methods should that be done? Others have raised the issues surrounding the proper methodological procedures to use in studying PTG (Cohen et al., chap. 2, this volume; Tedeschi & Calhoun, 1995). For some aspects of PTG, traditional quantitative and "objective" approaches can be useful, and may well be the general method of choice. However, for other aspects of growth, reliance must be placed on qualitative approaches that encourage and allow an exploration of the individual's own understanding of his or her experience, but within a set of procedures that permits some evaluation of the validity or "trustworthiness" of the data (Guba & Lincoln, 1989).

Although to some investigators we may be suggesting a scandalous acceptance of paradigms that can logically contradict each other, at this stage of investigation it seems desirable to encourage the use of both the best of quantitative, "scientific" approaches and the best of qualitative "postmodern, new paradigm" approaches as well. Domains for which external criteria are neither readily available nor appropriate, such as one's experience of changed philosophy of life, are more appropriately approached with qualitative methods, whereas those domains of growth for which external criteria are appropriate, such as reported changes in behavior (e.g., "I am less likely to become angry at the little things"), are more appropriately approached with quantitative methods that employ clearly identifiable criteria of validity.

An analogous issue is whether PTG is best regarded as an outcome, as a coping skill, or as a subset of the more general concept of adjustment or adaptation. To some degree, the choice will be a direct consequence of the perspective within which the investigator is already working. From the point of view of the individuals who experience it, PTG tends to be viewed as an outcome, rather than as a process in the service of some other goal, such as reduction of distress. It has been established that something called PTG does happen rather frequently, and we have some general understanding of what it looks like. A major focus of the next phase of the work should focus on growth as an outcome, in an attempt to identify its antecedents and correlates, and the processes through which it occurs.

A promising area of such work has begun in the area of individual differences. A variety of personality antecedents, or at least correlates have begun to stand out from the list of "the usual suspects" (Tennen & Affleck, chap. 4, this volume). Individual differences may also provide some clues about the kind of "processing" of trauma that tends to produce PTG. Although data are not consistent, our interpretation of the available findings is that there tend to be gender differences in the likelihood of PTG, with women tending to report more growth than men (Park, Cohen, & Murch, 1996; Tedeschi & Calhoun, 1996). If available data are predictive of what tends to be the case generally, then an important issue will be to try to understand the particular factors related to this difference between men and women. At least under some circumstances women appear to be more capable than men of experiencing growth in the aftermath of tragedy, but the reasons for this gender difference remain to be investigated.

As O'Leary, Alday, and Ickovics described in chapter 6 of this volume, there have been initial attempts to develop models of PTG. Taking into consideration developments in this field in the past 2 years since the publication of our model (Tedeschi & Calhoun, 1995), and as an attempt to integrate themes that resonate through the various chapters in this volume, we elaborate on our previous effort. In doing so, there will appear some connections with the conceptualizations of PTG offered by Aldwin and Sutton (chap. 3, this volume) and Schaefer and Moos (chap. 5, this volume).

A FUNCTIONAL-DESCRIPTIVE MODEL OF POSTTRAUMATIC GROWTH

We have chosen the name "functional-descriptive," in order to convey the inductive quality of the model we are proposing as a way of looking at PTG. In our previous discussion of this model (Tedeschi & Calhoun, 1995) we have left open some of the detail of the process of growth, discussing the general principles involved and speculating on the relationships among several apparently significant variables. We fill in more of this detail, referring to many of the issues raised in previous chapters. A general outline of the model is given in Fig. 9.1.

Growth Outcomes

It is clear that PTG can be multidimensional (Tedeschi & Calhoun, 1996). Persons may report growth experiences of one sort, say improved relationships, while not experiencing growth of another sort, for example, spiritual

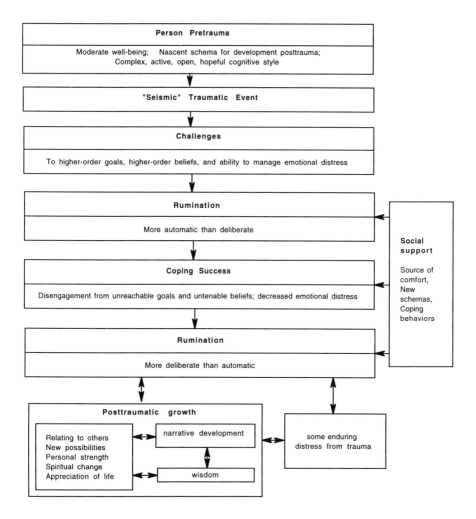

FIG. 9.1. A model of posttraumatic growth.

change. Different aspects of PTG may be affected most strongly by certain aspects of personality (see Tennen & Affleck, chap. 4, this volume), and perhaps be initiated by somewhat different kinds of traumas or social support contexts (see Schafer & Moos, chap. 5, this volume). The routes to PTG may involve somewhat different processes for the different domains of PTG. For example, each of the factors of the PTG Inventory (PTGI; Tedeschi & Calhoun, 1996), represents a somewhat different domain of change: Relating to Others appears to be primarily an interpersonal behavior domain; New Possibilities represents a shift in goals; Personal Strength involves a change in identity; Spiritual Change and Appreciation of Life seem to primarily involve aspects of the belief system.

In understanding the processes by which these different changes occur, it would be important to refer to theories that focus on the different domains involved. To account for PTG, then, it is important to be able to account for how beliefs, goals, identity, and interpersonal behavior change as the result of stiff challenges to preexisting patterns in these areas. Janoff-Bulman (1992) described the processes of posttraumatic changes in fundamental beliefs. Changes in major life goals have been described by Rothbaum, Weisz, and Snyder (1982), McIntosh (1996), and Carver and Scheier (in press). Changes in identity seem to be the focus of McCann and Pearlman (1990). Changes in interpersonal relationships and behavior are of course the domain of many theories of psychotherapeutic change.

In each of these domains, however, there are common elements that need to be highlighted: the recognition that the usual way of doing the business of living, including beliefs, goals, and behavior, do not work very well after the trauma has changed things; a process of sorting through what among these things should be retained, further developed, or jettisoned; what new belief, goal, or behavior needs to be incorporated; a reflective narrative is developed that ties the whole story together—the life before the trauma, the struggle with the ensuing changes, and the new way of living, that results in a changed identity. Of course, the process is not particularly orderly, but is combined with efforts to cope with great emotional distress, so that PTG coexists with many of the symptoms of posttraumatic psychological disorder. The distress also provides motivation to comprehend and manage the aftermath of trauma, fueling some of the processes that lead to PTG. A process that we consider central to PTG is rumination, because it has been generally implicated in changes in beliefs, goals, behaviors, and identity (Epstein, 1990; Martin, Tesser, & McIntosh, 1993). How well people utilize this period of rumination is influenced by certain individual difference factors that had evolved during life before the trauma.

Pretrauma Factors That Influence Growth

We previously described some of the preexisting personality characteristics that may allow people to more easily move in the direction of PTG (Tedeschi & Calhoun, 1995). In chapter 4 of this volume, Tennen and Affleck mention that consideration of different aspects, or "levels" of personality may be useful in understanding how individual differences interact with traumatic events to produce growth or not. It appears that what may be most important among individual difference variables, when it comes to likelihood of experiencing PTG, is the way people process information and develop creative solutions to problems. Some of the variables suggested by us (Tedeschi & Calhoun, 1995, 1996), Tennen and Affleck (chap. 4, this volume), and Schaefer & Moos (chap. 5, this volume) include hope, optimism, extraversion, openness to experience, and creativity.

Hope and Optimism. Although optimism is moderately correlated with scores on the PTGI (Tedeschi & Calhoun, 1996), it may be that the Life Orientation Test that measures this construct (Scheier & Carver, 1985) combines elements of optimism with tendencies toward growth or benefit-finding, as Tennen and Affleck point out in chapter 4. They suggest that hope may be a more powerful predictor of growth. Farran, Herth, and Popovich (1995) distinguished hope from optimism, giving us a rationale for why hope is a more useful construct in understanding why people might be prepared to experience PTG: "One rarely, if ever, would feel optimistic about something that is not good. Hope, on the other hand, is affectively expressed in more open terms—the situation may be difficult and painful, but the person remains open to the pain and to its eventual possibilities" (pp. 12–13). Optimism involves expectations of positive outcomes, and has a logical quality. When positive outcomes are blocked, the more "flexible" outcome of hope is necessary. Farren et al. describe this beautifully using an example of couples in infertility treatment:

> Their initial and primary goal may look most like wishing and optimism in that it is very specific: They want to become pregnant and have a child ... Behaviorally, the couples explore multiple options or procedures to achieve a goal that may be blocked by physiological or unknown limitations beyond their control. When the positive outcome of having a viable pregnancy and a healthy child is not attained over time, they must deal with their feelings of loss, grief, and disappointment and call forth the difficult but comforting and healing aspects of hope: experiencing the pain of this experience; rethinking and assuming a nonspecific goal of somehow dealing with this difficult

experience; developing a way of thinking that imagines other possibilities; and behaving in a way that may call forth an "active surrendering." (p. 13)

Hope, then, is seen as characterized by flexibility, activity, and openness, allowing an open response to the distress of the trauma while revising goals, perspectives, and behaviors.

Open, Complex Cognitive Style. Given that trauma demands adaptations to unexpected and highly distressing events, people who have a cognitive style of being able to actively try new things, or new perspectives (extraversion, openness to experience), and an ability to be open to and tolerant of feelings (openness to experience) are in a better position to derive most benefit from the experience. Rumination is a crucial part of moving from distress to growth (Tedeschi & Calhoun, 1995), and certain people appear to be best suited for using rumination in a constructive fashion, and as Tennen and Affleck suggest in chapter 4, ruminating in a deliberate, effortful fashion. We have suggested (Tedeschi & Calhoun, 1995) that people experiencing growth are "creative copers." They have a way of processing the distressing information, of accepting major changes to their way of understanding and anticipating life, that yields new levels of understanding and appreciation for life—wisdom, if you will.

There are several researchers and theorists who have recently discussed this kind of creative approach. For example, we mention in chapter 1 that hardiness is characterized by a "challenge" perspective in the face of difficulty, and that a "sense of coherence" may be related to health and growth. Additional concepts, more closely related to creative problem solving or perspective taking, that may be important for growth are chaotic cognition and creativity.

Chaotic cognition has been described by Finke and Bettle (1996) as a cognitive style contrasted with ordered thinking. Although ordered thinking is most useful in times of stability, chaotic cognition has advantages in times of uncertainty and crisis. It encourages the emergence of order and structure in chaotic situations, allowing the unpredictable or bizarre to yield meaningful insights and discoveries. It encourages creativity by the embracing of a difficult situation, viewing it from multiple perspectives, and quickly seeing ways to respond to the difficulty. However, chaotic thinkers do not value establishing order over the chaos. In fact, they understand life to be inherently chaotic, tolerate it, and can thrive in it. They understand that life is unpredictable, and tend to live in the present more than the past, which is over and done with, or the future, which has so many possibilities that to plan for it approaches futility. Chaotic thinkers also cultivate complexity, seeing the connections and tangents in situations, rather than trying to order or simplify. While emphasizing how chaotic thinkers often respond impulsively, Finke and Bettle also describe chaotic thinkers as comfortable with incubation periods that allow the structure of situations to emerge, as opposed to imposing order through premature foreclosure. Chaotic thinkers have little use for pride or justification of their behavior or past mistakes. This allows them to move on to new ideas and situations more comfortably. Ordered thinking can be thought of as the antithesis of the characteristics that define chaotic thinking, and ultimately, the most effective cognitive approach is a balance between the ordered and chaotic styles.

Creative persons have been described as inquisitive, imaginative, able to suspend judgment, and able to let go of the conventional ways of viewing the world (Sternberg, 1985). Strickland (1989) linked creativity with individual difference variables found primarily in social learning theories and self-regulation theories, including internal locus of control, constructive thinking, and mindfulness. For example, Strickland points out that persons with an internal locus of control demonstrate attributes related to creativity: autonomy, information-seeking, willingness to take reasonable risks, and self-confidence. Mindfulness involves active processing of both cognitive and affectively derived information in flexible ways that promote perspective taking. Constructive thinkers are able to integrate affective and intellectual states in a holistic approach to stress and problems. These approaches are essentially constructivist, that is, they assume that people are active construers of their environments and life events (Kelly, 1955). But *how* do people go about construing? Strickland points out that it is useful to embrace the affective and artistic aspects of people as well as Kelly's individual "as scientist" metaphor of human functioning. Here we seem to have another way of describing the duality of chaotic versus ordered thinking. Yet Strickland's notion of creative adaptation seems to involve both the chaotic and the orderly, because she states that "creativity means change, escaping contingencies, and finding connections between seemingly unrelated issues—sometimes bringing order out of chaos" (1989, p. 7). These creative people appear to be cognitively complex, and when trauma strikes, this complexity applied to positive self-representations is related to thinking constructively and minimizing distress (Morgan & Janoff-Bulman, 1994). Our research has shown (Tedeschi & Calhoun, 1996) that the facet of openness to experience that is most closely tied to PTG is openness to *feelings*, demonstrating a comfort with the complex affective aspects of the self.

It appears, then, that people who process distress in a way that incorporates the affective as well as the intellectual, tolerating ambiguity and uncertainty, and perceiving new connections and perspectives, creatively cope with trauma and are more likely to experience PTG.

Tendencies Toward Action.   The "active surrendering" referred to by Farran et al. (1995) represents one of the paradoxes of dealing with trauma successfully. Giving in is linked with taking action. People who experience psychological growth appear to be action-oriented people. The relationship between extraversion and PTG is primarily due to the extraversion facets of activity and positive emotions (Tedeschi & Calhoun, 1996). But the action taken posttrauma is not conventional action, or that dictated by previous plans. These do not apply very well in the face of trauma. Instead, it appears that people who experience PTG may be willing to experiment with new approaches. They combine hope and creativity, giving in to the reality of the changed life situation, but not becoming resigned to it. Instead, the new situation is somehow embraced, and something is made of it. The old idea of crisis as opportunity seems to apply here, with the recognition that there is an opportunity to understand life more profoundly, challenge oneself more completely, give oneself to others, and to take risks to try things that one has feared would produce failure, shame, or loss.

Pretrauma Mental Health.   Finally, we should note the relationship between PTG and the general level of mental health of the survivor before the trauma. We have found no relationship between neuroticism and any aspect of PTG (Tedeschi & Calhoun, 1996). But as Tennen and Affleck pointed out in chapter 4, there is evidence that persons who experienced a modest degree of control over their lives are more likely to have transformative experiences (Miller & C'deBaca, 1994). This modest level of perceived personal control fits with our prior theorizing (Tedeschi & Calhoun, 1995) that persons who experience PTG need to have had room to grow, but be healthy enough to cope relatively successfully with their emotional distress. There may be a curvilinear relationship between psychological health or adjustment and tendency to experience growth. Persons who have particularly poor coping skills may be more likely to be overwhelmed by trauma rather than derive benefit from it. Persons who already have developed an approach to life that is consistent with PTG may experience a ceiling effect or diminishing returns, where the growth is relatively consistent with already existing patterns of living. Those persons who have some of the characteristics just described, that is, hopeful, creative, and active, but whose lives were to some degree unsatisfactory may be most likely to experience significant distress in the face of trauma, yet not be overwhelmed by it, and find that their lives have been transformed.

The Trauma

As has been noted, a wide variety of events have been reported to be springboards to PTG. It is unclear the degree to which certain events are more likely to produce growth than others. A key element, however, that initiates the process that may produce the kinds of changes that are summarized by the word "growth," is the occurrence of an event of seismic proportions. The event severely shakes or destroys some of the key elements of the individual's important goals and worldview, setting in motion a process of great emotional distress, high levels of rumination, and attempts to engage in behavior that is designed to reduce distress and discomfort. Change in sense of identity may follow as people produce personal accounts of what has happened to them. Again, it is important to understand that it is not the event per se, but the *struggle* with the negative event and the changes it has wrought that is viewed as the source of subsequent positive change. This struggle takes place to a great extent internally, in the process of rumination.

Rumination

Rumination involves a process of frequently returning to thoughts of the trauma and related issues, characterized by a sense of intrusion of these thoughts during daily activities. Although rumination appears to be a necessary element in coping with trauma, and later in producing PTG, there are types of rumination that may be counterproductive, including regrets and wishing the trauma had not happened (Greenberg, 1995). We focus here on more constructive versions of rumination that involve finding meaning in the event and noticing changes in the self, both of which tend to be related to PTG.

The individual differences in cognitive processing discussed as pretrauma characteristics come into play during the aftermath of trauma during rumination. Much of this processing is devoted to dealing with important goals that have been blocked because of the trauma, beliefs about how the world functions, and the meaning that life has under new conditions posttrauma (Horowitz, 1986). Goals, beliefs, and identity have been described as comprised of elements organized in a hierarchical fashion (Emmons, 1989; Janoff-Bulman, 1992; Martin & Tesser, 1989; McCann & Pearlman, 1990).

The higher order aspects of goals, beliefs, and identity are linked to PTG because they provide a general framework within which lower order activities related to goals, life purpose, and self are meaningful. These higher order meanings create a sense of stability and predictability in life (Baumeister, 1991) that is shattered by trauma. It is important to reconsider these preexisting hierarchical structures of meaning in the wake of trauma. We have suggested (Calhoun, Tedeschi, & Lincourt, 1992) that cognitive structures that are not empirically disconfirmable may be better able to withstand such assaults, or may be created out of trauma. These nondisconfirmable structures tend to be metaphysical. An important element of the rumination process, for some individuals, is the degree to which the event produces rumination that is spiritual or existential in character. For these persons, the increased rumination in the existential domain may lay the foundation for changes in a philosophy of life that the individual subsequently views as a growth experience.

Let us consider, then, the kind of person who enters the rumination process posttrauma with the greatest likelihood of benefiting from it, and what the process may be like for them. In doing so, we consider the experience of persons who experience gradual changes and those who experience sudden transformations, both of whom report PTG, but each of whom describes a different pathway to this growth.

Almost all persons who experience traumatic events have in common an extreme emotional reaction, with some attempt, consciously or not, to control the emotions, or comfort themselves (Horowitz, 1986). Just as posttraumatic stress disorder has a crucial affective component, so does PTG. Persons experiencing trauma also encounter the need to disengage from beliefs, goals, and related activities that no longer make sense in the new circumstances. For PTG to take place, something has to replace what has been put aside through disengagement processes.

Rumination is involved in this disengagement process. It is not as simple as saying, "oh, I have to give this up" and moving on. Because the goals and beliefs involved are higher order ones from which so much of one's life has derived meaning, disengagement is usually a struggle. It is often not clear for some time whether a certain goal or activity that leads to a goal must be foregone. For example, persons experiencing paraplegia may believe for some period of time that they will be able to walk again. It may be years before the permanence of this situation becomes apparent to the individual affected. Persons who are bereaved but have not identified the deceased's body may cling to the idea that there has been some mistake and the loved one will return. The terminally ill seek alternative medical treatments in search of a miraculous recovery. As Carver and Scheier (in press) pointed out, one of the most important life skills is the ability to distinguish between situations where persistence is appropriate and those where disengagement is necessary. Similarly, people may have to disengage from assumptions they have made about their physical safety, the benevolence of the world, and so on, and find beliefs that better accommodate the trauma.

Another aspect of rumination is grief. Trauma almost always involves some kind of loss, of a loved one, a role, of "innocence." This grief work, although not necessarily universal, is quite common (Stroebe, van den Bout, & Schut, 1994; Wortman & Silver, 1989), and involves emotion-focused coping and solving the problem of how to live with the loss, and whether any replacement is possible. For example, a man whose wife died found himself attracted to another woman 4 months after his wife's death. He ruminated about what this attraction meant about his love for his wife, whether he could ever love in the same passionate way again, and whether he should encourage this new relationship. Ways of answering these questions seem to lead some persons to PTG. The rumination process sometimes may be deliberate and effortful in that there may be fairly specific questions about living to be answered. The answers, however, may come in unexpected ways, and may be surprising in themselves. These answers seem to represent the non-effortful, "automatic" nature of PTG.

There is some evidence that persons who experience non-effortful religious conversions or life transformations have been distressed or dissatisfied with their lives before the trauma leading to a greater willingness to give up (Pargament, 1996). If a person believes that happiness (a higher order goal) is linked with attainment of certain goals, and this attainment has been unsuccessful, they are more likely to engage in rumination and experience emotional distress (McIntosh, 1996). Trauma may finally make apparent that certain paths to goals just do not work, and when this is recognized, the rumination can end along with the frustration and accompanying distress. However, the void left by disengaging from a goal linked with happiness may need to be filled by some new goal, path, or belief, thereby continuing the ruminative process as these are redefined. This may be most important for some ordered thinkers. Chaotic thinkers may be better able to tolerate ambiguity.

Our expectations are that persons who undergo *sudden* life transformations in their PTG are more likely to be ordered thinkers who have been unhappy with their life, who experience trauma that finally releases them from their futile attempts to fine-tune their paths to important higher order goals or from certain beliefs that are counterproductive to happiness, and who are presented with alternative goals and beliefs. Certain seeds might have been sown early that now can sprout because the forest fire of trauma has cleared the way for new growth. For example, one individual who experienced a disabling injury described how he had realized for some time that he was alienated from his family, and suffering his injury made it more necessary to do something about it.

For persons experiencing *more gradual* PTG, the rumination process may occur after trauma and loss in an otherwise satisfying life. There may be a need to ruminate about the loss, but less need to change other aspects of life that have been satisfactory. Furthermore, these may be people who are better able to tolerate ambiguity, disorder, and unpredictability—the chaotic thinkers. With a more satisfactory life adaptation, there is less need, or room, to grow.

It seems to be the case that most people do not experience PTG immediately after the trauma, although the time frame may be quite short in some cases. Finkel (1975) reported that his participants described cognitive restructuring of trauma as usually occurring 2 weeks to 4 months after the event. Even these rapid "converters" stated that they needed to be "removed enough from the agony of the time" (p. 176) to gain a new perspective. Time can allow for shock and denial to be overcome, and for disengagement from goals and beliefs to be seen as necessary. This disengagement may be easier when alternative beliefs and goals are available (Bandura, 1982).

We see the process of rumination as taking a turn at the point of disengagement. Beforehand, there was an internal battle with wishes about how things could be the way they used to be, that dreams might be realized rather than dashed. Intrusive thoughts and strong emotions are common. As the need to disengage from old beliefs and goals becomes more apparent, a more deliberate process of rumination can supersede that automatic processing that is more the hallmark of the earlier phase. This more deliberate processing involves the active surrender, acceptance, and consideration of alternative beliefs and goals. Growth may be more likely for those who find it rapidly (Finkel, 1975) than for those who are still engaged in a search for meaning many years later (Silver, Boon, & Stones, 1983; Tait & Silver, 1989).

The more emotionally laden, automatic, and intrusive process of rumination in the early wake of trauma may be a necessary antecedent to the later reported growth in changed goals and beliefs, providing the "raw data" that can be used more deliberately (Greenberg, 1995). Rumination early in the wake of trauma would then be expected to correlate with greater

experienced growth. However, for individuals in whom automatic rumination levels are high early on, and in whom rumination persists over extended
periods of time, the level of distress will be higher later, and the level of
growth is likely to be lower (McIntosh, Silver, & Wortman, 1993). But it is
likely that PTG is most likely when there is first an automatic ruminative
process superseded later by a more deliberative one. This sequence represents a balance of affective and intellectual elements, where learning from
the trauma may have its greatest and most constructive impact.

Social Influences

Clearly these individual covert events occur in the context of individual
styles of behaving and personality characteristics that antecede the traumatic event, and they also occur in a milieu that influences the individual
by way of the behavior of significant others in the social support system
(Schaefer & Moos, chap. 5, this volume). As Bloom suggests (chap. 8, this
volume), the impact of commonly experienced events on large social units
may need to be considered. The mutual interplay of influence of individuals
on the group and the group on the individual may also have an impact on
the degree of growth experienced by the individual person. The social
context is especially important in either providing relief from the trauma or
perpetuating it. One of the most important sources of new goals and beliefs
may be veterans of similar traumas who model ways that life might be
satisfying, even improved in the new circumstances. Support groups operate
on this principle. What is offered by such sources may be considered in a
more conscious process of rumination, testing these ideas in one's own
unique situation.

Chronic and Acute Trauma

Persons experiencing such chronic trauma as concentration camps, continuing sexual abuse, and chronic illnesses have reported PTG. Yet, they
have been introduced suddenly to their distress at some point: when
rounded up to be forcibly moved to a concentration camp, when first abused,
or when first confronted with a diagnosis or symptoms of illness. These
persons experienced *both* sudden and chronic trauma. People in other
circumstances experience the trauma in a relatively brief time frame. But
the aftermath is like an extension of the trauma: the daily recognition that
the loved one is gone, trying to find a new career or job after being fired,
putting one's home back together after a natural disaster. There are a few

traumas where everything apparently returns to "normal" afterward, for example, being taken hostage or surviving a transportation accident without physical harm. But even these persons may make the trauma more chronic through rumination about it, although the event is "over." PTG may be a development from both the sudden and extended aspects of trauma. But, for PTG to develop, it may be necessary for some relief to occur from the direct confrontation with the trauma and the accompanying extreme distress. In our model of PTG we separate initial success at coping and true PTG in time, recognizing that continuing extreme levels of distress may be an impediment to growth in most persons. A sense of looking back, reflection from a safe distance, provides the best opportunity for growth, probably because cognitive processes can be more constructively devoted to the development of growth when they are not disrupted by so much distress.

Narrative and Identity Development

The individual's active construction of traumatic events can produce a significant revision of the life narrative (Kelly, 1955; McAdams, 1993; Neimeyer & Stewart, 1996; Weber & Harvey, 1994). For some persons, the trauma may produce the first conscious examination of the life story. Given that there was a great loss, and a memorable struggle with psychological distress, and that previously held higher order goals and beliefs may have undergone substantial changes, it is readily apparent that the trauma was a crucial event in the person's life history. Reflections on how the trauma was handled and what was learned can become important evidence to individuals for what kind of persons they are, and had been before the trauma. In this way, the critical event and its aftermath may come to occupy a significant place in that narrative, with the individual seeing the event as a point where a radical change occurred, and where life took a sharp turn. For persons experiencing PTG, the turn is viewed as a turn for the better, at least in certain ways, with a more meaningful and fulfilling life subsequent to the trauma.

Life narrative and identity seem to be closely related because the sense of who we are is shaped by the context of our lives. Telling the story of the traumatic event in the context of what had happened earlier in life can make the meaning of the event clear. For example, Neimeyer and Stewart (1996) described a psychotherapy client who had been savagely beaten while working as an electric company lineman. After his physical recovery he found himself continually angry, and he assaulted another person. Understanding his own assault experience in the context of an adolescence where he was beaten and picked on and where he had to "act crazy" to stop the beatings, helped to shed light on the unique meaning of the recent assault he received.

The meaning of trauma in the context of what has happened subsequent to it allows for a potential contrast to be noticed between what one was like before the trauma and what one is like after the incident. What is told about life before the trauma and afterward, therefore, can be much more revealing of the self. Without such contrast, the character of self is less evident. Furthermore, in response to trauma, a truer sense of self may be revealed. In the most difficult of circumstances, how did the person do? In PTG, a strength may become apparent that could not have been noticed before, because previous to the trauma there had not been a real test of it. The trauma may bring into focus the differential responses of various aspects of the self not clearly considered before (Showers & Ryff, 1996). As identity is elaborated in this way, people can see they may rely on different aspects of themselves to help them through subsequent difficulties. Such elaboration also provides a more general plan for the rest of life, with new goals that make what is to come meaningful. McAdams (1989) referred to the "generativity script" that involves a plan that leaves a useful legacy. The entire life, including the crucial trauma, can be viewed as a creation and carrying out of this plan. Of course, all this reconstruction may be less than accurate (Klein & Kunda, 1993; Taylor & Brown, 1988), but accuracy may be less important than what is remembered and the meaning it has for the individual (Uematsu, 1996).

Wisdom

The individual who has experienced significant levels of PTG can be identified by many of the same descriptors as the individual who has achieved wisdom. Wisdom is apparently achieved through affective experience rather than by an exclusively intellectual process (Tedeschi & Calhoun, 1995), and this learning leads to an enhanced ability to utilize dialectical thinking in understanding life's vicissitudes. Paradoxes are appreciated among persons who have developed PTG: in loss there is gain; to manage one must wait for healing and pursue healing; the trauma must be left in the past, and made meaningful by the use of it to shed light on the future; one must recognize the need to receive help, but that the healing ultimately occurs within; both peace and distress can coexist. Only an integrative perspective taken by the wise can encompass these paradoxes of trauma and growth.

The recent work on wisdom by Sternberg, Baltes, and others (e.g., Baltes, Staudinger, Maercker, & Smith, 1995; Sternberg, 1990) should be considered together with the work on PTG. Baltes describes wisdom as expert level performance in the fundamental pragmatics of life: "insights into the quintessential aspects of the human condition and human life" (Baltes et al., 1995, p. 155). This appears to be the existential, metaphysical, or spiritual domain we see as being addressed in PTG. Furthermore, one of the metalevel criteria that Baltes cites as important to the fundamental pragmatics of life is the recognition and management of uncertainty. This, too, seems to parallel the experience of persons who report PTG: Managing the chaos into which one is thrown in the aftermath of trauma produces a recognition that in the uncertainties of life, one is able to be strong. Therefore, trauma may be a key catalyst for the development of wisdom in some people, or "wisdom-facilitative life experiences" (Baltes et al., 1995, p. 156), and the processes of developing PTG may shed light on the development of wisdom as well.

In recent attempts to assess wisdom, Baltes has relied upon a technique that presents participants with both life-planning and existential life management dilemmas. The latter are essentially crisis situations around life-and-death issues such as suicide. It would be interesting to look at the relationship between performance on existential life management, history of trauma, and scores on PTG measures, especially the spiritual change and appreciation of life factors of the PTGI. Wisdom may be most closely related to these dimensions of PTG.

REVISING THE PERSPECTIVE ON STRESS AND TRAUMA RESEARCH

The general idea that science tends to operate within the parameters of sets of shared assumptions is widely recognized (Kuhn, 1970). Although there may be a need for a general paradigm shift in the study of health and stress (O'Leary & Ickovicks, 1995), our proposal is more modest.

There is no dispute that for many persons, perhaps a significant majority, the occurrence of traumatic events places them at risk for significant physical and psychological dysfunction. Even when the events do not produce identifiable pathologies, major life stressors can cause significant distress and impair functioning significantly. However, a necessary modification to the study of trauma and its effects is a revision of perspective, so that the area is viewed differently. It is not appropriate to discontinue the study of the negative and often disastrous impact of major life stressors, but simply to expand the perspective so that the possibility of PTG is routinely acknowledged and becomes an integral part of the study of how people cope with highly negative sets of circumstances. A shift in perspective is needed, so that psychological growth is recognized as a routine possibility when individuals struggle with highly disrupting life events. It is not a question of dismantling one paradigm and substituting another for it, but simply widening the focus of the lens so that both negative *and* positive consequences are investigated. Clinicians and scholars who work in the area of traumatic stress need to revise their assumptions, so that they systematically attend to the possibility of PTG, even for the majority of persons who are more distressed than before the trauma's occurrence.

POSTTRAUMATIC GROWTH
IN CLINICAL WORK

It is especially important in clinical work to be sensitive to the possibilities for growth that survivors of trauma often explore. We previously (Calhoun & Tedeschi, 1991; Tedeschi & Calhoun, 1995) offered a brief outline of how clinicians can encourage PTG. Given that we expand greatly on this in a companion volume to this book that is planned by this publisher, we reduce the discussion of the clinical approach to PTG to its essential elements. First, the clinician has to be open to the possibility of growth, highlighting the movement of the trauma survivor in this direction as this movement becomes evident. Second, the clinician must be willing to go on existential quests with clients, as clients struggle to discover meaning in these events. The clinician must be open to discussing both spiritual and religious issues with clients. Third, the clinician must recognize and support the individuals' views of their trauma and growth, and understand that different persons experiencing PTG may have very different perspectives. Consider, for example, a man who became paraplegic in an automobile accident: "This was the one thing that happened in my life that I needed to have happen; it was probably the best thing that ever happened to me ... I would want it to happen the same way. I would not want it not to happen." (Tedeschi & Calhoun, 1995, p. 1). Contrast that with what Rabbi Harold Kushner says about the death of his son: "I am a more sensitive person, a more effective pastor, a more sympathetic counselor because of Aaron's life and death than I would ever have been without it. And I would give up all those gains in a second if I could have my son back ... But I cannot choose." (Viorst, 1986,

p. 295). Different traumas, different aftermaths. There is growth in both cases, but a good clinician can support the different perspectives taken by survivors. Finally, it is important for clinicians who recognize and support the possibilities for PTG not to perceive those who do not report these outcomes as having failed to manage trauma constructively. Survivorship is enough of an accomplishment in the face of traumas that many experience. The gift of PTG is hardly universal, comes with great distress, needs time for healing, and requires a perspective-taking of which some may be incapable. However, the sensitive clinician can continue to hold out hope for survivors' futures, offering the growth perspective without minimizing the negative effects of the trauma. We hope that our next volume will make it clear how this can be done.

REFERENCES

Baltes, P. B., Staudinger, U. M., Maercker, A., & Smith, J. (1995). People nominated as wise: A comparative study of wisdom-related knowledge. *Psychology and Aging, 10*, 155–166.

Baumeister, R. F. (1991). *Meanings of life.* New York: Guilford.

Bandura, A. (1982). The psychology of chance encounters and life paths. *American Psychologist, 37*, 747–755.

Calhoun, L. G., & Tedeschi, R. G. (1991). Perceiving benefits in traumatic events: Some issues for practicing psychologists. *The Journal of Training & Practice in Professional Psychology, 5*, 45–52.

Calhoun, L. G., Tedeschi, R. G., & Lincourt, A. (1992, August). *Life crises and religious beliefs: Changed beliefs or assimilated events?* Paper presented at the meeting of the American Psychological Association, Washington, DC.

Carver, C. S., & Scheier, M. F. (in press). *On the self-regulation of behavior.* New York: Cambridge University Press.

Edmonds, S., & Hooker, K. (1992). Perceived changes in life meaning following bereavement. *Omega, 25*, 307–318.

Emmons, R. A. (1989). The personal striving approach to personality. In L. A. Pervin (Ed.), *Goal concepts in personality and social psychology* (pp. 87–126). Hillsdale, NJ: Lawrence Erlbaum Associates.

Epstein, S. (1990). The self-concept, the traumatic neurosis, and the structure of personality. In D. Ozer, J. M. Healy, Jr., & A. J. Stewart (Eds.), *Perspectives on personality* (Vol. 3). Greenwich, CT: JAI Press.

Farran, C. J., Herth, K. A., & Popovich, J. M. (1995). *Hope and hopelessness: Critical clinical constructs.* Thousand Oaks, CA: Sage.

Finke, R. A., & Bettle, J. (1996). *Chaotic cognition.* Mahwah, NJ: Lawrence Erlbaum Associates.

Finkel, N. J. (1975). Strens, traumas and trauma resolution. *American Journal of Community Psychology, 3*, 173–178.

Greenberg, M. A. (1995). Cognitive processing of traumas: The role of intrusive thoughts and reappraisals. *Journal of Applied Social Psychology, 25*, 1262–1296.

Guba, E., & Lincoln, Y. (1989). *Fourth generation evaluation*. Thousand Oaks, CA: Sage.

Horowitz, M. J. (1986). *Stress response syndromes* (2nd ed.). Northvale, NJ: Jason Aronson.

Janoff-Bulman, R. (1992). *Shattered assumptions*. New York: The Free Press.

Joseph, S., Williams, R., & Yule, W. (1993). Changes in outlook following disaster: The preliminary development of a measure to assess positive and negative responses. *Journal of Traumatic Stress, 6*, 271–279.

Kelly, G. A. (1955). *The psychology of personal constructs* (Vol. 1). New York: Norton.

Klein, W. M., & Kunda, Z. (1993). Maintaining self-serving social comparisons: Biased reconstruction of one's past behaviors. *Personality and Social Psychology Bulletin, 19*, 732–739.

Kuhn, T. (1970). *The structure of scientific revolutions* (2nd. ed.). Chicago: University of Chicago Press.

Martin, L. L., & Tesser, A. (1989). Toward a motivational and structural theory of ruminative thought. In J. S. Uleman & J. A. Bargh (Eds.), *Unintended thought* (pp. 306–326). New York: Guilford.

Martin, L. L., Tesser, A., & McIntosh, W. D. (1993). Wanting but not having: The effects of unattained goals on thoughts and feelings. In D. M. Wegner & J. W. Pennebaker (Eds.), *Handbook of mental control* (pp. 552–572). Englewood Cliffs, NJ: Prentice-Hall.

McAdams, D. P. (1989). The development of a narrative identity, In D. M. Buss & N. Cantor (Eds.), *Personality psychology: Recent trends and emerging directions* (pp. 160–174). New York: Springer-Verlag.

McAdams, D. P. (1993). *The stories we live by: Personal myths and the making of the self*. New York: Morrow.

McCann, I. L., & Pearlman, L. A. (1990). *Psychological trauma and the adult survivor: Theory, therapy, and transformation*. New York: Brunner/Mazel.

McIntosh, D. N., Silver, R., & Wortman, C. (1993). Religion's role in adjustment to a negative life event: Coping with the death of a child. *Journal of Personality and Social Psychology, 65*, 812–821.

McIntosh, W. D. (1996). When does goal nonattainment lead to negative emotional reaction, and when doesn't it?: The role of linking and rumination. In L. L. Martin & A. Tesser (Eds.), *Striving and feeling: Interactions among goals, affect, and self-regulation* (pp. 53–77). Mahwah, NJ: Lawrence Erlbaum Associates.

McMillen, C., Zuravin, S., & Rideout, G. (1995). Perceiving benefits from child sexual abuse. *Journal of Consulting and Clinical Psychology, 63*, 1037–1043.

Miller, W. R., & C'deBaca. J. (1994) Quantum change: Toward a psychology of transformation. In T. F. Heatherton & J. L. Weinberger (Eds.), *Can personality change?* (pp. 253–280). Washington, DC: American Psychological Association.

Morgan, H. J., & Janoff-Bulman, R. (1994). Positive and negative self-complexity: Patterns of adjustment following traumatic versus non-traumatic life experiences. *Journal of Social and Clinical Psychology, 13*, 63–85.

Neimeyer, R. A., & Stewart, A. E. (1996). Trauma, healing, and the narrative emplotment of loss. *Families in Society: The Journal of Contemporary Human Services, Special Issue: Constructivism in Social Work Practice*, 360–374.

O'Leary, V. E., & Ickovics, J. R. (1995). Resilience and thriving in response to challenge: An opportunity for a paradigm shift in women's health. *Women's Health: Research on Gender, Behavior, and Policy, 1*, 121–142.

Pargament, K. I. (1996). Religious methods of coping: Resources for the conservation and transformation of significance. In E. P. Shafranske (Ed.), *Religion and the clinical practice of psychology* (pp. 215–240). Washington, DC: American Psychological Association.

Park, C. L., Cohen, L., & Murch, R. (1996). Assessment and prediction of stress-related growth. *Journal of Personality, 64,* 71–105.

Rothbaum, F., Weisz, J. R., & Snyder, S. S. (1982). Changing the world and changing the self: A two-process model of perceived control. *Journal of Personality and Social Psychology, 42,* 5–37.

Scheier, M. F., & Carver, C. S. (1985). Optimism, coping, and health: Assessment and implications of generalized outcome expectancies. *Health Psychology, 4,* 219–247.

Shafranske, E. P., & Malony, H. N. (1996). Religion and the clinical practice of psychology: A case for inclusion. In E. P. Shafranske (Ed.), *Religion and the clinical practice of psychology* (pp. 561–586). Washington, DC: American Psychological Association.

Showers, C. J., & Ryff, C. D. (1996). Self-differentiation and well-being in a life transition. *Personality and Social Psychology Bulletin, 22,* 448–460.

Silver, R. C., Boon, C., & Stones, M. H. (1983). Searching for meaning in misfortune: Making sense of incest. *Journal of Social Issues, 39,* 81–102.

Sternberg, R. J. (1985). Implicit theories of intelligence, creativity, and wisdom. *Journal of Personality and Social Psychology, 49,* 607–627.

Sternberg, R. J. (Ed.). (1990). *Wisdom: Its nature, origins, and development.* Cambridge, England: Cambridge University Press.

Strickland, B. R. (1989). Internal–external control expectancies: From contingency to creativity. *American Psychologist, 44,* 1–12.

Stroebe, M., van den Bout, J., & Schut, H. (1994). Myths and misconceptions about bereavement: The opening of a debate. *Omega, 29,* 187–203.

Tait, R., & Silver, R. C. (1989). Coming to terms with major negative life events. In J. S. Uleman & J. A. Bargh (Eds.), *Unintended thought* (pp. 351–382). New York: Guilford.

Taylor, S. E., & Brown, J. D. (1988). Illusion and well-being: A social psychological perspective on mental health. *Psychological Bulletin, 103,* 193–210.

Tedeschi, R. G., & Calhoun, L. G. (1995). *Trauma and transformation.* Thousand Oaks, CA: Sage.

Tedeschi, R. G., & Calhoun, L. G. (1996). The PTG inventory: Measuring the positive legacy of trauma. *Journal of Traumatic Stress, 9,* 455–471.

Tennen, H., & Affleck, G. (1990). Blaming others for threatening events. *Psychological Bulletin, 108,* 209–232.

Uematsu, M. A. (1996). Giving voice to the account: The healing power of writing about loss. *Journal of Personal and Interpersonal Loss, 1,* 17–28.

Viorst, J. (1986). *Necessary losses.* New York: Ballantine.

Weber, A. L., & Harvey, J. H. (1994). Accounts in coping with relationship loss. In A. L. Weber & J. H. Harvey (Eds.), *A perspective on close relationships* (pp. 285–306). Boston: Allyn & Bacon.

Wortman, C. B., & Silver, R. C. (1989). The myths of coping with loss. *Journal of Consulting and Clinical Psychology, 57,* 349–357.

Yalom, I. D., & Lieberman, M. A. (1991). Bereavement and heightened existential awareness. *Psychiatry, 54,* 334–345.

Author Index

Subject Index